PC

New Frontiers in Women's Studies

New Frontiers in Women's Studies:
Knowledge, Identity and Nationalism

Edited by
Mary Maynard and June Purvis

Taylor & Francis
Publishers since 1798

UK   Taylor & Francis Ltd, 1 Gunpowder Sq., London EC4A 3DE
USA   Taylor & Francis Inc., 1900 Frost Road, Suite 101, Bristol, PA
       19007

First published 1996

A Catalogue Record for this book is available from the British Library

ISBN 0 7484 0287 X
ISBN 0 7484 0288 8 (pbk)   **04175335**

Library of Congress Cataloging-in-Publication Data are available on request

Typeset in Times by Best-set Typesetter Ltd., Hong Kong

Printed in Great Britain by SRP Ltd, Exeter

Contents

Contents

Acknowledgements

We would like to acknowledge, with very grateful thanks, the editorial assistance provided by Heloise Brown, of the Centre for Women's Studies at the University of York, in the preparation of this book. Without her careful bibliographic, writing and word-processing skills it is unlikely to have been produced.

We are also grateful to David Trend, editor of *Socialist Review*, for permission to reprint Jasbir Puar's article, 'Resituating Discourses of "Whiteness" and "Asianness" in Northern England: Second Generation Sikh Women and Constructions of Identity', which appeared in numbers 1 and 2, 1995.

Introduction

New Frontiers in Women's Studies

Mary Maynard and June Purvis

Most of the chapters in this book were originally presented as papers at the Women's Studies Network (UK) Association conference, which we organized at the University of Portsmouth in July 1994. One edited conference volume, *(Hetero)sexual Politics*, was published in 1995, its content reflecting the keen interest that currently exists in issues relating to sexuality (Maynard and Purvis, 1995). The focus of the book to which this is an introduction, however, is more closely related to the central conference theme, 'Women's Studies in an International Context'. The title was chosen in an endeavour to broaden both the scope of the material covered, together with the backgrounds of those participating in what is the major annual and national Women's Studies conference in Britain. The intention behind this was to offer a challenge to the white, Western and ethnocentric bias which often characterizes Women's Studies' work. The conference presented an opportunity for women from a wide range of ethnic and cultural groups to discuss their research and extend the boundaries of what is normally accepted on a Women's Studies' agenda. The latter is what is being alluded to in the term 'new frontiers', which forms part of the title of this volume.

The 'new frontiers' with which this book is concerned are of two kinds, which are reflected in its structure. The first, addressed in the section 'On the Move: New Agendas for Women's Studies', relates to what counts as knowledge in Women's Studies, how that knowledge is portrayed and the parameters within which scholars and researchers operate. It focuses, in particular, on how the boundaries of a hegemonic white and Western Women's Studies might be challenged and on the struggles faced by women who are attempting this in different parts of the world.

The second kind of 'new frontier' which the book addresses is metaphorical and is designed to call attention to women's experiences of migration and nationalistic struggles, together with the consequences of these for their sense of self, worth and identity. For 'Women in Movement: Identity, Migration and Nationalism', as this section is called, any previous certainties about identity or self, in relation to specific 'others' or belonging to particular communities, are likely to become fractured or blurred in the face of changing geographical, cultural and political locations. As several of our contributors point out, despite the frequence of women's movement in this sense of the term, it is an under-researched area in Women's Studies. Focusing on this issue, then, as an area of substantive and empirical significance for feminists, is also to contribute to an extension of Women's Studies' knowledge and its frameworks. In this way, the two 'new frontiers' to which we refer are linked together. The first, by pushing forward the limits of Women's Studies, is suggestive of new areas for research; the second, in putting additional issues on the Women's Studies' agenda, contributes to its conceptual and theoretical development.

At this point, it is worth reflecting briefly on the changes that have taken place in Women's Studies since feminists introduced it into higher education in the West during the 1970s. The aim at that time was to challenge the ways in which women had been excluded, made invisible and barred from both the creation and the distribution of knowledge (Klein, 1991). Further, Women's Studies was not intended simply to produce just *any* knowledge about women, as Klein has noted. Instead, it was understood that 'what was needed was ... knowledge ... that gave us power to empower ourselves and that gave us strength, based on women's *diversity*' (Klein, 1991 p. 75). In other words, Women's Studies was conceived as a political activity with the express purpose of contesting the masculinist nature of what had previously passed as academic knowledge and understanding. The critical energy involved in the intellectual challenge to gender-blind and gender-biased scholarship, together with the close links between scholarly and political agendas for women, fed into the growth, diversification and effectiveness of what came to be known as Women's Studies.

Subsequently, the Western Women's Studies project has involved three interrelated processes: those of recuperation, reconstruction and reflexivity (de Groot and Maynard, 1993). Recuperation itself involved two corollaries. On the one hand, it raised questions as to why and how women had 'disappeared' from academic concerns. On the other, it stimulated creative endeavours to design concepts and theories, practical research projects and explanatory frameworks which might redress the situation. Assumptions were questioned, empirical evidence obtained and disseminated and women-centred initiatives developed. Reconstruction entailed re-evaluating and re-designing the terms and topics which had structured the practices of existing academic disciplines. Terms such as 'work', 'leisure', 'class' and 'family' came to have different meanings and new areas: for example, those of sexuality, violence towards women, motherhood and childbirth were introduced as legitimate areas for discussion. Indeed, from the mid-1970s, many disciplines from literary studies to industrial relations, from history to social policy, from sociology to development studies experienced the impact of both recuperative and reconstructive schemes of various kinds. Emphasis also came to be given to the richness deriving from interdisciplinary work and the benefits to be obtained from such disciplinary collaboration.

The activities of recuperation and reconstruction have also generated reflexivity – that is self-awareness and self-criticism – among practitioners in the Women's Studies' field. This has led to serious conceptual and theoretical debates about such issues as the nature of patriarchy or male power; the relationship between gender power and inequality and other forms of domination and exploitation; and the interaction of cultural and material elements in the formation of women's experiences. It has also raised questions about diversities between women and in particular the white, Western, privileged and heterosexual biases in Women's Studies, with Black women, women of colour and Third World women, especially, making important criticisms of their exclusion from mainstream feminist concerns.

It is within this context that *New Frontiers in Women's Studies: Knowledge, Identity and Nationalism* needs to be located. Its first section is specifically concerned with the generation of forms of Women's Studies' knowledge and understanding which might be more all-encompassing and inclusive. In examining this, contributors focus, in particular, on issues of race, racism and ethnicity and explore the kinds of Women's Studies which are currently emerging in countries with different cultures and expectations from those where it initially developed. Overall, the section draws attention to the need for Women's Studies to extend its horizons and continually to question its assumptions and basic concerns. It demonstrates that women continue to be marginalized and misinterpreted, both in contemporary and historical work, by the very subject that was created to remedy such marginalization.

For example, in their chapters Mary Maynard and Joanna de Groot each focus on the need for Women's Studies to develop a more global approach to its subject matter and both are concerned about racism and ethnocentrism. Maynard, who tends to be more pessimistic about the state of Women's Studies than de Groot, argues that to acknowledge the importance of race and ethnicity in the structuring of all women's lives is not necessarily the same as confronting racism. She suggests that a concern for race and racism continues to remain at the level of rhetoric alone in many Women's Studies' projects and she addresses some of the issues responsible for fostering such tokenism, before suggesting some ways forward.

Similarly, de Groot, utilizing her expertise as an historian with a keen interdisciplinary eye, draws on debates among Middle Eastern women in order to demonstrate the specificities of women's experiences and the importance of exploring the dynamics between colonialism/anti-colonialism and imperialism/anti-imperialism. Her consideration of the role of nationalisms in constructing both identity and a gendered politics anticipates some of the arguments put forward in the second section of this volume, where contributors focus on identity, migration and nationalism *per se*. While contributing to this debate, de Groot's chapter is also noteworthy for the way in which she discusses the process of 'otherizing'. One important aspect of this is her argument that imperialism, ethnocentrism and racism are significant not only for how they help to construct Black and Third World women as 'other', but also for their impact on the making and maintenance of gender and gender identities in Western societies themselves.

Bunie M. Matlanyane Sexwale is also concerned with racism in Women's Studies and the parameters it includes. Following on from Maynard's point that gender and development is an important, but neglected, area in Women's Studies, she focuses on one aspect of this which has received little treatment in the literature: training about gender issues for practitioners involved in Third World development work. Although rarely discussed from a Women's Studies point of view, 'gender training', as it is known in the West, is both big business and influential. Women's Studies and gender training are linked because the latter emerged as a result of feminist critiques of the gender blindness which plagued the development industry. Yet, despite its clearly political agenda and concern to combat patriarchy, Sexwale argues that gender training has become depoliticized and reformist. In her chapter, she explores some of the reasons for this, pointing to the roles of racism, technicism and femocracy.

The remaining chapters in this section also explore the parameters of Women's Studies scholarship in differing contexts. Delia Davin's contribution, for instance, focuses on China where, although there is growing interest in Women's Studies and women's issues generally, as indicated by the 1995 UN conference held in Beijing, most of those creating and disseminating knowledge have worked for and supported the State. Davin explains how most producers of social criticism were on the Left, leading to their silencing under communist rule when criticism of society was regarded as both anti-socialist and unpatriotic. As she says: 'it was all too easy to be accused of divisive or bourgeois feminism, of lacking class feeling or of promoting bourgeois romanticism' when trying to discuss social and women's issues (p. 64). The rejection of the ideology of the Cultural Revolution following Mao's death, however, has led to the emergence of a new literature re-evaluating previous policies, although Davin emphasizes that writers and activists are still under heavy official pressure, as the events in Tiananmen Square in June 1989 demonstrate. Still, by past standards the writers of the 1980s had unprecedented freedom to look at social issues. In particular, women, despite forming a small proportion of writers in China, have been particularly active in writing about issues relating to them. As Davin explains, they have been especially influential in writing about love, marriage and the private sphere: areas regarded as inappropriate during the Cultural Revolution. Her analysis of issues such as divorce, abortion, the family and single women in Chinese women's fiction in the 1980s is important for what it tells us about the significance of these in women's lives and the difficulties they have had in publicly addressing them. Although not usually explicitly feminist, such work explored the gender-based suffering of women in Chinese society, as well as exposing and condemning discrimination against them. It thus constitutes an example of women's struggle for their voices to be heard under specific and inauspicious circumstances.

Pursuing the theme of which women are allowed to speak and to whom we listen, June Purvis, in her chapter, questions the representations of our feminist past to be found in some feminist accounts of history. Drawing on her extensive archival work on the suffragettes, Emmeline and Christabel Pankhurst, Purvis argues that the dominant narrative about these leaders of the Women's Social and Political Union has ignored both their women-centred approach to politics and misrepresented their views. This is because liberalism has been the dominant interpretive framework in history writing generally, with socialist feminism the prevailing perspective shaping and influencing the growth of feminist history since the 1970s. Purvis argues persuasively for another reading of these two Pankhurst women, one which acknowledges their political flair, their qualities as tacticians, their oratory and their analyses of male power. While it is important for current feminists to know about their past, it is equally important to question the politics behind how this is constructed and represented.

The two remaining chapters in the first section extend discussion of the parameters of Women's Studies and how these are related to specific histories and sociopolitical situations. Drawing on their experiences in two post-communist European countries, Jitka Malečková and Svetlana Kupryashkina reflect on the possibilities of developing Women's Studies courses and research in the Czech Republic and Ukraine repectively. It is clear that in both countries the situation is changing rapidly. However, both Malečková and Kupryashkina are somewhat pessimistic about prospects for the immediate future. It is interesting to compare their assessments of the treatment of women's issues with that offered by Davin for China.

For Malečková, as for Kupryashkina, part of the difficulty of establishing Women's Studies in their part of the world lies in the ways that the communist regimes claimed that the women's question had been solved. This, it was said, had been achieved by improving the position of women generally and creating equality between the sexes. Official language eschewed any acknowledgement of gender differences and opposition to the regimes occurred from gender-neutral, rather than gender-specific, positions. In what is now the Czech Republic, as Malečková demonstrates, books about women were either ideological in nature or studies were conducted in gender-blind ways. Currently, although some women are working hard to establish research centres and publish relevant material, the reaction of men and women, in both the public and academic domains, is negative towards the very terms 'feminism', 'women's movement' and 'Women's Studies'.

Similarly, Kupryashkina describes how the long history of women organizing together in Ukraine was erased by Soviet historiography. Further, as in the Czech Republic, the systematic abuse of terms such as 'feminist' by Soviet propaganda, together with the cynical use of women for Party purposes, has generated a deep distrust of women, women leaders and feminism in general. Despite this, however, there have been some important Women's Studies developments in Ukraine. More freedom in foreign travel, access to literature and the ending of censorship mean that academic women, in particular, have increasing opportunities to debate women's issues.

In the second section of the book, 'Women in Movement: Identity, Migration and Nationalism', contributors expand on some of the issues relating to nationhood, colonialism and subjectivity already indicated as important for Women's Studies in previous chapters. The concept of 'diaspora' is crucial to this section. This refers to the global dispersal of a group of people either as a result of migration or of the forces of nationalism. The idea of diaspora is important, since it questions the ties that are normally presumed to exist between community, culture and place. Breda Gray, for instance, in her chapter, refers to work which defines diasporic identities as reaching outside of both the geographic territory and the temporality that is constitutive of the nation-state (p. 175). She suggests that Ireland is a 'dispersed nation' because of the numerous waves of migration which it has had to endure (p. 164). This, then, has consequences for how Irish people negotiate both their national and migrant identities.

However, those who have studied and theorized issues to do with the nation, migration and identity have tended to do so in non-gendered ways, either ignoring women or assuming their experiences to be the same as men's. The chapters presented in this second section of the book therefore, are concerned with notions of home, community, the sense of self and the sense of belonging as they relate, in particular, to 'women who move'. As such they make an important contribution to the development of feminist knowledge in this area, as well as challenging the racist, stereotypical definitions of such women which are to be found in everyday life and in academic literature.

Jasbir Puar, in her chapter on these issues, draws on her research with second-generation Sikh women in northern England to show how Western dichotomies of white/black, East/West and oppressor/oppressed construct Asianness as a distinct category, which operates only in relation to whiteness. She argues that such a construct derives from colonialist notions, is inherently racist and contains a clear gender dimension. Further, it assumes that identity is a fixed, static and bounded state. Puar adopts the term 'oppositionally active whiteness' to demonstrate how the women whom she interviewed resist identification with both South Asian and white society. Rather, in a process which involves 'bargaining with racism', they refuse to be consumed by, and fully integrated into, Western ways of life, while doing so from a critical evaluation and appreciation of their own culture.

Following this, Magdalene Ang-Lygate focuses on issues relating to 'otherizing' and identity for ex-colonial diasporic women. Drawing on her ethnographic study of Chinese and Filipina women who originate from Pacific and South East Asian countries and now live in Glasgow, she points to how the ways in which we try to see and understand each other are constrained by deficiencies in vocabulary. There are difficulties with linguistic terminology, such as 'Black' women or 'Third World' women, because they stereotype, homogenize and are used in opposition to 'white' and 'First World' women who are then constructed as the norm. Ang-Lygate describes how, in her own research, she qualifies ethnic descriptors with reference to place of origin or to country of settlement. She argues, however, that the problem of language remains one of the major concerns for post-colonial and Women's Studies scholarship. Research focusing on women's experiences of diaspora can help to challenge traditional meanings and create new understandings of the construction of social identities.

In her chapter, Breda Gray also continues with the diasporic theme. Having traced the history of Irish women's migration this century, she goes on to consider how dominant stereotypes of Irishness, themselves heavily influenced by colonialism and racism, affect Irish women's identities in England. Although many Irish women migrants identify with their Irish nationality, they have also been constructed in limited, passive roles and made invisible by that identity. Further, while some post-colonial theorists emphasize the necessary hybridity and diversity of diaspora identities, Gray suggests that their ability to destabilize fixed and ethnocentric meanings are limited, precisely because of the powerful effects of colonialism in the form of anti-Irish racism.

The chapters by Puar, Ang-Lygate and Gray each refer to the significance of nation, nation-state and colonialism in the creation of women's diasporic identities. Jan Jindy Pettman explores the former issues further in her discussion of women as the symbol of the nation and of the construction of women as mothers of the nation, often portrayed as responsible for its physical, cultural and social reproduction. She analyses the ways in which discourses of nation and of nationalism are gendered, together with the uses made of women in constructing national boundaries and markers of difference. Pettman argues that, despite the existence of different forms of nationalisms, there are remarkable similarities in the ways they construct women. This is an area where discourses around women's bodies are especially prominent, resulting in their vulnerability to body policing and to sexual violence.

Similarly, Suruchi Thapar-Björkert's chapter also focuses on the relationship between gender, colonialism and nationalism, this time in India and in the historical context of the anti-colonial struggle for independence. As with Pettman, Thapar-Björkert emphasizes how women were important, both symbolically and materially, to nationalist politics, especially the significance and responsibilities of the 'mother' in this regard. She discusses the various ways in which women were represented in nationalist literature, showing how these enabled women to play a political role by opening up different avenues for, and meanings of, activism in both the private and public domains. Like the previous contributors to this section, she also draws on original empirical work to support her arguments. Interviews with women who were active in various aspects of the nationalist movement indicate that the role they played within it was crucially affected by dynamics of gender.

Finally, Hanna Behrend considers how the lives of East German women have been profoundly affected by the extremely rapid changes that have taken place since the fall of the communist regime in October 1989. However, from Behrend's point of view, this has not had the positive consequences for women that were initially envisaged. In her contribution, she charts the processes through which the West German nation-state has taken away many of the social and legal benefits that East German women previously held. Further, in order to cope with the backlash against them, women's groups tend to have refocused their attention away from formally organized politics to various kinds of self-help groups. Behrend argues that, as a result of the tremendous upheaval inflicted by one nation on another in Germany, former East German women have undergone a profound process of discovery about themselves and the world. They may not have moved physically but the social, economic and political changes have been extensive. This has had consequences for their sense of identity, their consciousness of themselves and their feelings of dignity and worth.

The chapters collected in this book indicate that, as we approach the twenty-first century, Women's Studies' practitioners still have much work to do. Currently, the world is characterized by a growth in racism and in ethnic cleansing, economic recessions, the political consequences of decolonization, the collapse of the former Soviet bloc, together with new forms of globalization. As Rattansi and Westwood (1994, p. 2) explain, these 'have combined to undermine the certainties of material comfort, space and time, territory and history, which underpinned for white, especially male Westerners a sense of what must have appeared to be unshakeable security and superiority'.

Much of this book explores the variety of consequences of these processes both for women and for the practice of Women's Studies. It does this in terms of contributing to debates about the kinds of frameworks we would like to see Women's Studies develop and the content these should encompass. Our overall argument is that race, racism, nationalism, migration and identity currently have a particular resonance for women. They therefore form important aspects of the new frontiers in Women's Studies' knowledge which we wish to see it pursue.

References

DE GROOT, JOANNA and MAYNARD, MARY (1993) 'Doing Things Differently? A Context for Women's Studies in the Next Decade', in DE GROOT, JOANNA and MAYNARD, MARY (Eds) *Women's Studies in the 1990s. Doing Things Differently?*, London, Macmillan.

KLEIN, RENATE D. (1991) 'Passion and politics in Women's Studies in the 1990s', in AARON, JANE and WALBY, SYLVIA (Eds) *Out of the Margins: Women's Studies in the Nineties*, London, Falmer.

MAYNARD, MARY and PURVIS, JUNE (Eds) (1995) *(Hetero)sexual Politics*, London, Taylor & Francis.

RATTANSI, ALI and WESTWOOD, SALLIE (1994) 'Modern Racisms, Racialized Identities', in RATTANSI, ALI and WESTWOOD, SALLIE (Eds) *Racism, Modernity and Identity*, Cambridge, Polity.

Section I

*On the Move: New Agendas for
Women's Studies*

Chapter 1

Challenging the Boundaries: Towards an Anti-racist Women's Studies

Mary Maynard

Introduction

Much has been written criticizing the cosy assumptions that all women could be defined in terms of the things they experienced and shared in common, which characterized the early stages of Women's Studies publishing and teaching (Bhavnani, 1993; Collins, 1990; Frye, 1983; hooks, 1982, 1984, 1989, 1991; Lorde, 1984, Ramazanoglu, 1989). The one-dimensional notions of oppression being employed at that time took for granted that such oppression had the same meanings and occurred through similar processes and mechanisms for all women. Of course, there were different kinds of feminist theories explaining the nature of gender oppression and offering different political programmes for challenging this. Each, however, appeared to assume that its framework had worldwide relevance and applicability. As Audre Lorde summed up, '[b]y and large . . . white women focus upon their oppression as women, and ignore differences of race, sexual preference, class and age. There is a pretence to a homogeneity of experience covered by the word *sisterhood* that does not in fact exist' (Lorde, 1984, p. 114).

This chapter focuses on issues of race and racism in Women's Studies. It questions how far white feminists in the West have really heard and taken to the heart of our agenda the criticisms raised about both our subject matter and how this is approached. The first section, 'Challenging White Women's Studies', considers some of these criticisms, arguing that in the main there has been a fairly tokenistic response. The second section, 'Issues of Race and Racism in Women's Studies', focuses on several issues which might be regarded as currently hindering the development of an anti-racist approach. These relate to the unproblematized use of the concept of difference, a focus on multiculturalism rather than racism, a tendency towards cultural relativism and the effects of cultural imperialism. The third section, 'Facing the Challenge', suggests some ways in which the process of developing an anti-racist perspective for Women's Studies might be taken forward. The chapter finishes with a few brief concluding remarks.

Challenging White Women's Studies

Challenges to the idea of a universal sisterhood, to be found in Women's Studies and feminism more generally, came from a variety of sources, although many originated from Black women in the US and Britain.[1] Black women pointed to the ways in which Women's Studies spoke only of a white, Western, largely middle-class world and the extent to which they were invisible in much of the literature. Women's Studies, they argued, had suppressed the ideas of Black women, so that few of these managed to find their way into mainstream debate (Amos and Parmar, 1984; Collins, 1990; hooks, 1982, 1984). Women from the (so-called) Third World also pointed to the differentiation and variation in women's economic and social experiences in a wide range of societies other than those of 'advanced' industrial countries. This work underscored the plurality of meanings in women's lives of phenomena such as family, work, nation and citizenship. It also pointed to the consequences for women of being involved in national and liberation struggles, thus illuminating and extending the critique which Black Western women had mounted.

Some of the specific criticisms that were made of Women's Studies can be set out as follows. One charge, for instance, was that Women's Studies was racist. Racism is usually taken to refer to those beliefs, statements and acts which assume that certain ethnic groups are intrinsically inferior and which are used as a basis for denying rights or equality (Anthias and Yuval-Davis, 1992; Essed, 1991). Moreover, as Anthias and Yuval-Davis have implied, intention cannot be a criterion in adjudicating racism. They write:

> Our view is that all those exclusionary practices that are formulated on the categorization of individuals into groups whereby ethnic or 'racial' origin are criteria of access or selection are endemically racist. Further, our view is that racist practices are also those whose outcome, if not intention, is to work on different categories of the population in this way. (Anthias and Yuval-Davis, 1992, p. 16)

The focus on white women's experiences, to the virtual exclusion of Black and Third World women's lives, in early Women's Studies work constitutes a form of racism, as does the tendency to develop concepts, theories and explanations which are both limited and partial. Such 'erasure' is racist since it is only possible because of the existence of underlying power relations based on racial privilege (Bhavnani, 1993). These normalize the concerns of certain white women and turn them into what is routinely expected, prioritized and, therefore, unquestioned about Women's Studies scholarship. Thus it is in the silences, the absences and the omissions – in what is *not* said as much as what is – that the racism of Women's Studies is to be found.

Another charge which has been levied by Black and Third World women, one associated with that of racism, is that Women's Studies tends to be ethnocentric. This can take two forms. Ethnocentrism occurs when one's indigenous culture is unproblematically taken for granted as the main focus for study and when other cultures are judged and evaluated according to criteria which are specific to one's own. So, for example, not only has Women's Studies tended to ignore the circumstances of non-white women who live in their midst, it has also disregarded those who live in different parts of the world. Certainly, there is a strong gender dimension and a forceful feminist presence in work undertaken as part of development studies. But, sadly, this material would appear to be treated as marginal in most Women's Studies texts and courses. Despite many excellent books addressing the situation of women in different parts of the 'developing' world, this is still not treated as 'mainstream' literature. Development issues, when considered at all, are sidelined into optional courses in academic programmes. A decade ago, in an article that has recently been reprinted, June Jordan (1995, p. 27) remarked that 'most of the women of the world persist far from the heart of the usual Women's Studies syllabus'. Ten years later Chandra Mohanty (1991, p. 54) writes about the 'overwhelming silence about the experiences of women in these countries'. Even when the latter are included, there is the danger that they will be presented in stereotypical ways, with emphasis given to what, from a white Western perspective, appears particularly exotic or culturally bizarre. This, in part, explains early concerns about the process of veiling, arranged marriages and purdah. Further, as Mohanty has pointed out, Western feminist work on women in the 'Third World' has a tendency to imply that the latter passively experience a singular, monolithic and homogenous oppression. This in turn leads to the construction of an 'average Third World woman'.

> This average Third World woman leads an essentially truncated life based on her feminine gender (read: sexually constrained) and her being 'Third World' (read: ignorant, poor, uneducated, tradition-bound, domestic, family-oriented, victimized, etc.). This, I suggest, is in contrast to the (implicit) self-representation of Western women as educated, as modern, as having control over their own bodies and sexualities, and the freedom to make their own decisions. (Mohanty, 1991, p. 56)

This kind of ethnocentrism, as de Groot indicates in her chapter for this book, 'otherizes' women in different parts of the world, treating their lives as 'data' or 'evidence' upon which Western commentators can impose their own analysis and commentary.

Women's Studies has also been criticized in the past for adopting an additive approach to studying the interconnections of race and gender (Brittan and Maynard, 1984). The additive model implies that race merely increases the degree of inequality and oppression which non-white women experience as women. But, just as it has been argued that gender cannot be simply added on to class analysis, so too it is mistaken merely to add race on to existing analyses of gender. This is because race does not just make the experience of women's subordination greater. It qualitatively changes the nature of that subordination. Black women are not simply subjected to more disadvantages than white women. Rather, their oppression, because of racism, is of a qualitatively different kind. Positing the relationship between race and gender in terms of adding them to each other also overlooks any social structural connections which they might have. Further, it detracts from an understanding of how different configurations of race and gender (and we might add here other forms of diversity, such as age, sexual orientation and class) develop and what the overall implications of this might be.

The additive model also tends to treat race only as a source of oppression, constructing those affected by it as victims and ignoring how the adoption of a racial or ethnic identity can be a source of celebration, support, resistance and pride. It also classifies people into dichotomized categories, such as either Black or white, oppressor or oppressed. This makes race appear to be a fixed category, rather than one which is socially constructed and whose meaning changes over time (Anderson and Collins, 1995b). Such an approach also overlooks how an individual or group may be privileged by one factor, say race, at the same time as being disempowered by another, say gender. A further problem with the adding-in model is the implication that race is an issue only for those groups whose racialization is either clearly visible or explicitly acknowledged. But race is not the kind of minority experience that this assumes. As Haleh Afshar and I have pointed out elsewhere, not only do the majority of the world's peoples live in situations where ascriptions about race are defining features in their lives, it is also the case that to be labelled 'white' is also to be allotted a racial category, albeit one which is privileged, relatively unanalysed, taken for granted and itself a 'minority' status (Afshar and Maynard, 1994).

Now this presents, in a fairly schematic form, some of the issues relating to race with which Western Women's Studies has been grappling over the past decade. Indeed, it would be true to say that a certain amount of progress has been made. Race is now discussed as a significant component of feminist analysis and other disciplines have begun borrowing from the insights it has developed. More work by Black feminists has appeared in print (Bhavnani and Phoenix, 1994; Collins, 1990; Essed, 1991; James and Busia, 1993). There is some evidence that the scope of feminist scholarship is being re-thought in terms of shifting both its focus and its emphasis (de Groot, Chapter 2, this volume). However, there certainly is no room for complacency about any of these developments. In many ways a concern for race and for racism remains at the level of rhetoric alone in a great number of Women's Studies projects. To profess an interest in racial matters is the trendy, 'politically correct' and 'done' thing to do. How far this has, in reality, affected the general agenda of what is still, in the main, white Women's Studies scholarship is more difficult to ascertain. In the following section I address some of the issues which appear to be responsible for hindering progress and for the tokenism which ensues.

Issues of Race and Racism in Women's Studies

The Concept of Difference

One major problem with how Women's Studies and feminism more generally have discussed issues about race is that it tends to be done by using the concept of 'difference'. There are two main connotations of difference, drawing on feminist concerns with experience and post-modern perspectives, although what makes each appealing is surprisingly similar (Maynard, 1994). The concept of difference has been regarded as important by feminists because of its potential for emphasizing the diversity of women's lives. Its focus on heterogeneity and its implicit critique of universal statements and grandiose theoretical frameworks have made it a very useful tool in challenging the essentialism and ideas about a shared sisterhood which characterized the early Women's Studies literature. A focus on difference, which variously includes factors relating to class, region, sexuality, religion, disability and age, as well as race and ethnicity, draws attention to the unquestioned dualism and oppositionalism in the Black-versus-white and male-versus-female approaches. It subverts the unity and meaning of terms such as 'race', 'Black', 'oppression', 'patriarchy' and 'woman', with the implication that these kinds of categories are too internally differentiated to be useful.

This, in turn, has led to a concern for subjectivity and the fragmentation of identity. bell hooks (1991), for example, has argued for the need to reformulate outmoded notions of identity, which are often narrow and constricting in the ways in which they relate ideas of 'Blackness' only to colonial and imperialist paradigms. Similar arguments have been made about the deterministic and stereotyped definitions of womanhood and femininity, with commentators suggesting that an emphasis on difference allows for multiple identities. The implication, therefore, is that it can also open up new possibilities for emancipatory selves (Flax, 1987; Skeggs, 1991). One constructive consequence of all of this is that 'Blackness' and 'womanhood' come to be associated with positive connotations and are not just seen in terms of oppression (Brah, 1991). Difference, then, has the potential to transcend passive labels, such as 'Black woman' or 'white woman', suggesting alternative subject formations.

There are, however, dangers with the way in which the concept of difference tends to be used in the Women's Studies literature. One, for example, relates to the tendency to slide towards the much critiqued position of liberal pluralism. Here the social world is seen simply as an amalgam of differing groups or individuals. In such pluralism, differences tend to be treated as existing all on one plane, in the same way and on the same level. All forms of diversity are indiscriminately lumped together as examples of difference, implying that they are similar kinds of phenomena with similar explanations. This kind of parallelism, as I commented in an earlier article on the subject, was heavily critiqued by Hazel Carby at the beginning of the 1980s (Carby, 1982; Maynard, 1994). So many forms of difference are created that it becomes impossible to analyse them in terms of relations of inequality and power. 'Race', for instance, becomes just another form of difference, to be mentioned in the same sentence or breath as all the others. This discourages commentators from confronting the question why particular races come to be socially constructed in particular kinds of ways. It prevents us from exploring both what is specific to the processes of racialization and how they might be interlinked to other forms of differentiation.

Another difficulty in treating race and ethnicity as one among many forms of difference is the implicit evaluation to which this can give rise. It runs the risk of overemphasizing what is distinct or perceived to be unusual about particular groups. It can imply the existence of a supposed cultural norm that applies to some women, but not to others, so that it is the women who are not white who are the different ones (Spelman, 1988). Whiteness here is not itself seen as a racialized identity. White people are not racialized in the way that Black people are and 'race' is presented as a problem for the latter and not for the former. Such a stance leads to the proliferation of discrete studies of a wide variety of experiences, but it makes no effective challenge to the categories or frameworks within which they are discussed. Significantly, it can lead to an analysis which is assumptively benign, where issues to do with power continue to be underplayed. Acknowledging that 'race' gives rise to forms of difference, for example, is not the same as paying attention to *racism* (both institutional discrimination and individual prejudice) as it exists in the social world or feminist work. Thus feminist concerns about 'race' need to be founded not so much in an understanding of difference, as it is currently articulated, as in getting to grips with issues of hierarchy and power. The force of racism, as Rothenberg (1990) points out, is in the assigning of *value* to difference, which is then used to justify denigration and aggression. It does not reside in difference *per se*.

A further problem with using the concept of difference is that it tends to emphasize what divides women, at the expense of those experiences that they might possibly share or have in common. Yet cultural differences are not absolute, as is sometimes implied, and similarities between cultures are as important as their differences. While we live in an increasingly culturally fragmented world, there is also the paradox that it is at the same time becoming more global. In pointing to this contradiction, the Turkish feminist, Fatmagül Berktay (1993, p. 110), writes about 'a world which is One – shared by all of us who are marginalised and oppressed, whatever our differences'. She is critical of what she regards as the bland political pluralism arising out of an uncritical acceptance of women's experiences in different contexts. As a result of this, 'nobody really listens to, and takes, anyone else seriously' (Berktay, 1993, p. 111). Berktay argues that if women are to be able to transform existing power relations, they have to communicate and forge alliances. While it is clear that the previous single theory approach of feminism will not do, a return to empiricism based on local experiences and ultimate differences does not provide the answer either.

The Multicultural Approach

Another problem with how Women's Studies has been approaching issues of race and racism is the unproblematic use of a multicultural perspective. The term 'multiculturalism' is becoming yet another intellectual fad in Women's Studies, particularly in the United States and in parts of continental Europe, not least because of post-modernist influences on feminist theory. For this reason it is also linked to the concept of difference which has already been discussed. One way in which the multicultural approach has developed is in terms of the metaphor of voices (Anderson and Collins, 1995a). This has arisen from challenging the silences concerning many groups' experiences and encouraging the latter to speak about their own condition. The legitimacy of this has been encapsulated in such phrases as 'finding a voice' or 'listening to the voices of' previously silenced groups. As with the idea of difference, the emphasis is on recognizing the existence of a plurality of views and experiences – on cultural diversity. Experience in this context is regarded as a matter of competing discourses, where the voice or discourse is treated as if it, in itself, constitutes lived experience (Anderson and Collins, 1995a).

Now the significance of our own understanding of our experiences has been one of the hallmarks of feminism and is an important part of coming to understand the interrelations of race and gender. On its own, however, it is not enough. It also needs to be linked to an interpretive and synthesizing process which connects experience to analysis. This is in order to render intelligible those repetitions in social life which may be invisible or perceived by individuals in purely isolated and personal terms. Further, there is a political history to the emergence of the multiculturalist movement in the United States and in Britain concerning which many feminists seem unaware. This latter needs to be understood before turning to more specific criticisms.

Multiculturalism emerged in the 1960s in response to the realisation that previous liberal approaches to racism had not worked (Anthias and Yuval-Davis, 1992). The latter assumed that racism was caused by the strangeness of 'outsiders' to an 'insider' community. It predicted that the gradual acculturation and eventual assimilation of these 'strangers' and their children would cause racism to disappear. In contrast, multiculturalism presents society as comprising 'a hegemonic homogeneous majority', alongside which exist small ethnic minority groups (Anthias and Yuval-Davis, 1992, p. 158). These have their own different communities and cultures which need to be understood and accepted in order that harmonious race relations exist.

Multiculturalism, which in Britain was particularly prominent in the field of education and curricula development and is still very much part of the official discourse on race, has been subjected to much criticism. In particular, it came to be regarded as a means of dividing the Black community within itself and as a distraction from focusing on the discrimination and structural disadvantages of Black peoples. Most importantly, it was unable to focus on relations of differential power. Essed, for example, has drawn attention to the norm of tolerance which she regards as characterizing multiculturalism. This 'presupposes that one group has the power to tolerate, and others have to wait and see whether they are going to be rejected or tolerated' (Essed, 1991, p. 210). She regards such cultural tolerance as a form of cultural control, remarking that it is the most pervasive but most hidden part of what constitutes multiculturalism.

Over the years, much has been written about multiculturalism and there is no space to review all the arguments here (Centre for Contemporary Cultural Studies, 1982; Cohen and Bains, 1988; Cohen and Cohen, 1986). It is worrying, however, that part of the Women's Studies approach to studying race appears to employ the multicultural perspective, or at least the language of multiculturalism, in apparent ignorance of the key assumptions on which it is based. Multiculturalism tolerates other cultures as long as they do not fundamentally question prevailing relations of power and privilege. So it would not appear to be an approach towards analysing racial issues with which Women's Studies should be associated.

Other criticisms of multiculturalism centre on its preoccupation with culture. As Anderson and Collins (1995a) point out, analysing race and gender requires more than appreciating the cultural diversity of, and hearing a variety of voices from, an array of human groups. It means recognizing and analysing the hierarchies and systems of domination that permeate societies, giving some groups the ability systematically to dominate and control others. On the one hand, it is important to challenge the idea that diversity has significance only at the level of culture, for it has many other important social and material manifestations. On the other, it is also necessary to point out how an analysis of culture *per se* looks only at the group itself and not necessarily at the broader conditions within which the group lives. While a sensitivity to different cultural forms is to be encouraged, multiculturalism misses the broader point of understanding how racism, sexism and other discriminatory practices shape these. To study race in terms only of Black British, African-American or Asian-American culture implies that such groups are to be blamed for their own subordination and ignores how this is created in structured and systematic ways (Anderson and Collins, 1995a). It also suggests that only supposedly 'minority' groups possess the quaintness of culture, thereby normalizing the culture of the majority.

The Dangers of Cultural Relativism

A third difficulty with the way in which the race dimension has been treated in Women's Studies is the tendency towards cultural relativism. Cultural relativists insist on the uniqueness of different cultures, which they regard as providing a self-contained framework for understanding experience. Because each culture is governed by its own rules, its own symbols and meanings and its own frameworks for understanding, there can be no transcultural standards by which specific cultures might be judged and no ways in which their relative worth might be assessed. Such a stance has characterized some forms of anthropology, although it has generally been disparaged by most social science disciplines. For the cultural relativist, different cultural forms are neither better nor worse than each other. They are simply to be understood in their own terms (Sweder and LeVine, 1984).

In her very provocative article on the topic, Berktay (1993) points towards the similarities between cultural relativist arguments and the views being advanced, both explicitly and implicitly, by some feminists. She suggests that current post-modernist thought has taken off from where anthropology's so-called romantic rebellion and its relativization of the world ended. Post-modernism has proved attractive to feminists for a variety of reasons, not least because of its critique of meta-narratives and meta-theories. However, the picture of fragmentation and diversity to which this gives rise sometimes encourages us to seek 'theoretical refuge' in a form of cultural relativism (Berktay, 1993, p. 118). Such a stance is also fostered by white Western feminists' worries about making value judgements about 'other' cultures from a position of voyeuristic privilege. This is a very real concern, given what we know about monolithic and imperialist forms of knowledge and the assumptions of those in the West that they can understand peoples in the Third World better than they can themselves. But, Berktay argues, feminists' anxieties in this area mean that they run the risk of uncritically supporting practices for women in other cultures that they would not support in their own. She cites examples of studies of women in Muslim societies, where 'romanticisation of the "other"' has led researchers to accept and rationalize male domination (Berktay, 1993, p. 121). She further claims that worries about how to deal with 'otherness' have led many feminists to distance themselves from women's movements in the Third World. One consequence of this has been that, in turn, Third World women have distanced themselves from Western feminism on the grounds that the problems faced by women in the Third World are much more serious, material and fundamental than the issues preoccupying women in the West.

Berktay's arguments are contentious. However, she usefully draws our attention to the difficulties that exist when thinking about 'others'. Writing from 'the "other" side', as a feminist for whom the West is 'other', she distinguishes between criticizing Eurocentric perspectives and a cultural relativism which is uncritically content to describe existing local traditions or customs. In this she follows Ramazanoglu (1989, p. 144) who has argued for the:

> need to distinguish . . . between *cultural relativism*, which leaves each culture as acceptable on its own terms, and offers women no common ground between them, and *respect for each other's cultures*, which leaves us able to understand, evaluate, compare, and choose, but without a need to condone indiscriminately.

These arguments about cultural relativism raise the question whether women from one culture should be studying those from another at all? Is it ever possible to move beyond the process of 'otherizing'? Clearly, it is important for those who are members of particular ethnic groups to take a significant part in the creation of knowledge about themselves. However, as bell hooks cautions, while it is crucial that white women listen to what those from a diverse range of groups have to say, it is also vital that the latter are not necessarily expected to take primary responsibility for providing information, thus being placed, yet again, in the position of servicing whites (1989). hooks argues that, while she would expect any white researcher to be very clear about why they were studying a culture that was not their own, learning about other groups can help to rid oneself of racism.

The significant point here is to acknowledge the power relations that underpin the development of particular forms of knowledge. What is required, as discussed in further detail in the following section, is more open discussion of the politics of location and speaking. The small numbers of non-white women who are currently members of faculty in those countries where Women's Studies is most flourishing, and the pressures they are under, make it imperative that those white women who do have academic positions offer more than guilty and apologetic statements about race and racism (Marshall, 1994; Skeggs, 1995; Wekker, 1995). Here there is an important distinction to be made between advocation and appropriation. Whereas the former should involve putting forward and publicizing the experiences of others, the latter means doing so in an alienating and objectifying way. Appropriation also connotes the reworking and redefinition of other women's material. It is thus a means of silencing. This should be contrasted with advocation, which is one strategy for providing the means for the silenced to speak out. bell hooks (1989, p. 48) sums up the issue in the following way:

> problems arise not when white women choose to write about the experiences of non-white people, but when such material is presented as 'authoritative' . . . I do not wish for a situation where only Black women are encouraged to write about issues related to Black female experience. I do, however, wish to help make a world wherein scholarship and work by Black women is valued so that we will be motivated to do such work, so that our voices will be heard.

The Role of Cultural Imperialism

The fourth problem for a Women's Studies concerned about race and racism is that of cultural imperialism. This takes two particular forms. First, as Mary Eagleton (1994) has remarked in a slightly different context, our concept of world territory is still quite parochial. Western Women's Studies' global awareness appears very limited in terms of the geographical spaces it circumscribes. To a certain extent this has been changing, given the current concern for Europe and attempts to extend how the latter is defined to include eastern, central and southern countries. Welcome though this is, however, it can be no substitute for looking and thinking beyond the boundaries of 'Europe'. This is important if we are not to continue to be constrained by culturally restrictive meanings and definitions.

The second and related point is to do with what Chandra Mohanty (1991, p. 52) refers to as the 'global hegemony of Western feminism'. By this she means the ways in which certain groups of feminists, using specific brands of feminism, have been able to ask questions, provide analyses and speak for women in other parts of the world and all from a particular geographical and cultural perspective. Mohanty regards this as a form of colonization, arguing that Women's Studies scholarly practices inscribe relations of power. Unless such power relations are explicitly acknowledged, the knowledge to be gained from studying other cultures will inevitably be distorted.

The global hegemony of Western feminism has certain features which require addressing individually. One of these relates to the linguistic imperialism of the English language. The fact that English is the main medium for discussion in Women's Studies means that the most important debates, with a few notable exceptions, are frequently taken to be those that occur in English. These may then be translated into other languages. By contrast, the flow of ideas the other way – from other languages into English – is not so commonplace. Even when this does occur there are problems concerning the politics of translation (Spivak, 1992). As Satow (1987) has pointed out, one word in a non-English language may require whole sentences of explication in English itself. At the workshop on which Satow's observations were based, women from non-European countries expressed anger at having to spend time translating their experiences in this way. A further difficulty involves the continual use of Western concepts, when these have been developed from a particular intellectual tradition. Satow, for instance, cites examples of concepts used in Nepalese culture which have different meanings and connotations from those understood in the West. Thus in Nepal, the concept of beauty in a woman involves the idea of strength. Yet to translate this understanding for the benefit of a Western readership would necessitate considerable explanation. Similarly, the concept of menopause does not exist for many Nepalese women. For them it is the loss of bleeding, but it does not necessarily signal a rite of passage at all.

Part of the problem here is that a lot of feminist discourse is based on Western ideas about individualism, free will and self-determination. It cannot be assumed, however, that these are a priority for all women. Many are negotiating for rights and responsibilities from within strong familial social contexts and have communal and kinship-based perspectives and strategies. This means for Muslim women, for example, that feminist battles have to be fought on terms such as those of equal worth or equal reciprocity. It needs to be understood that the language of Western feminism does not necessarily translate worldwide.

Another factor relating to the influence of Western Women's Studies is the domination of American publishing houses, which then have the power to determine what appears in print and by whom it is written (Eagleton, 1994). Eagleton has pointed to how, for feminist literary criticism, the most recognized writers are white and heterosexual, with only a small number being chosen to represent lesbians, Black women or women from the Third World. Further, the relative wealth of American higher educational institutions, together with the infrastructure of journals, Women's Studies programmes, grants and scholarships, means that the US has a particular gravitational pull for feminist academics. Since academics in the US, like those in Britain and Australia, are under a lot of pressure to publish, this only increases the amount of Women's Studies material which is produced from sources geographically located in the West. As Mohanty (1991, p. 54) says:

> Western feminist scholarship cannot avoid the challenge of situating itself and examining its role in such a global economic and political framework. To do any less would be to ignore the complex interconnections between first and third world economies and the profound effect of this on the lives of women in all countries.

In sum, then, Mohanty exhorts us to take account of the effects that the cultural imperialism of the first world have on Third World women.

Facing the Challenge

So far in this chapter I have discussed some of the criticisms that have been levied at Women's Studies concerning racism and the ways in which race issues have been treated. I then considered some of the further difficulties that have arisen. In this section I suggest some of the steps that need to be taken on the way to developing an anti-racist Women's Studies. What follows is by no means exhaustive but is intended to serve as one contribution to what is surely an ongoing debate.

The first point to make is to reiterate Mohanty's call for Women's Studies to situate itself within a global political and economic framework. Increasing economic and technological globalization has been accompanied by major realignments in the structuring of the political world order (Anderson and Collins, 1995c; Wekker, 1995). This has also led to unprecedented migration and political fragmentation, whereby nationalist movements and forms of neo-racism are also on the increase. It is crucial that Women's Studies does not accept the 'inward turning cultural gaze' that such changes promote (Wekker, 1995, p. 2). Further, it is imperative that in endeavouring to create a Women's Studies which is more inclusive, we do not simultaneously construct a new exclusivity, by ghettoizing the experiences of Black and Third World women into some kind of opaque 'otherness'. In a world of unequal power relationships this is, indeed, a serious danger and it is to the issue of unequal power that Women's Studies should give particular heed.

Post-modern perspectives, currently in ascendance in feminist work, have difficulty in addressing the nature of social structures, together with the inequalities and hierarchies which are related to them and to which they give rise (Callinicos, 1989; Harvey, 1989; Norris, 1992). Yet power – the ability to order, influence and control – is a critical concept for the anti-racist Women's Studies agenda. The concept of power can draw attention to the *material* as well as to the cultural structures of inequality among women, both within particular collectivities and worldwide. Unless the power relations deriving from race, gender, nationality and class are *explicitly* recognized, the knowledge gained from studying other cultures will, necessarily, be distorted (Berktay, 1993). If the power ensuing from *racism* is displaced into a benign concern for race as merely one form of many differences, as seems currently to be the case in a great deal of feminist work, we will fail to address a crucial and crushing feature of many women's everyday lives (Essed, 1991).

Of course, it is possible for *individuals* to exist in relationships of power, as feminist arguments concerning the personal being political have demonstrated; and personalized forms of racism should never be overlooked. Yet to focus on racism as an individual problem alone is certainly to miss the point. For it is its structured, routinized and institutional nature which also needs to be analysed and challenged. Racism is systemic, which means that it is part of societal structures. It is not just present in the minds and deeds of individual bigots. The implications, then, for Women's Studies are that a concern for racism and for other ways in which racialized power is expressed, must constitute a central concern in our work. This needs to happen both in terms of the subjects which are chosen for study and the questions asked, as well as in a reflexive monitoring of the assumptions embedded in any analyses offered.

Another point, and one connected to the issue of power discussed above, is the need for Women's Studies to pay far more attention to debates on women and development than happens at present. Data produced by the United Nations indicate why this should be the case. For example, women do two-thirds of the world's work, earn one-tenth of the world's income and own less than one hundredth of the world's property. A quarter of the world's women suffer domestic violence, more than a million newborn girls are murdered every year and there are 600 million illiterate women in the world, twice as many as men (UN figures quoted by Brittan, 1995).

The last two decades have seen women brought into the centre of the debate on development. It is now accepted that investment in women is one of the major ways to challenge poverty and that investment in women's education is the key both to their own health, that of their children and to curbing population growth, although action lags well behind this knowledge. Further,

23

campaigns such as those in favour of debt cancellation or against the structural adjustment programmes of the World Bank and the International Monetary Fund are vitally important to women because the latter are the main victims of increasing poverty worldwide (Brittan, 1995). Structural adjustment policies, for instance, are aimed at increasing monetarist, market-based economies at national and international levels, with corresponding cuts in public expenditure, higher unemployment and the removal of import controls. These have had an adverse impact on women, both as consumers of welfare and public sector services and as their providers and employees (Afshar and Dennis, 1992). It is important that material and economic issues such as these, which have such negative consequences for so many women, are placed at the heart of Women's Studies' concerns. In other words, the parameters of our subject need to be extended so that a focus on development becomes part of the mainstream Women's Studies agenda.

A further issue which an anti-racist Women's Studies needs to keep in mind is that the meaning of race itself changes over time. Despite the fact that it has long been recognized that races do not exist in any scientifically demonstrable way, in many societies people have often acted – and continue to act – as if race is a fixed, objective category. Yet societies construct race and racial meanings. These constantly change as different groups challenge prevailing racial definitions which give some groups power at the expense of others (Anderson and Collins, 1995b). Thus race is a social-historical-political concept, 'an unstable and "decentred" complex of social meanings constantly being transformed by political struggle' (Omi and Winant, 1986, p. 68). This point is well illustrated by Anderson and Collins in their discussion of the changing definitions of race in the US Census (Anderson and Collins, 1995b). As they indicate, in 1860 only three 'races' existed. By 1890 this had increased to eight. At the turn of the century the list had shrunk to five and this has been continually revised throughout the subsequent decades.

Since race cannot be treated as a constant, it is also necessary to think in terms of *racisms*. For racism is not a unitary phenomenon. Rather, it is multi-faceted and can take differing forms. Racisms are constructed and acted on in the context of both the specific sociopolitical histories of dominant and subordinate groups and in the history of their relationships with each other. Further, different geographical and historical situations, as well as socioeconomic status, may affect a group's ability to transcend racism. Thus anti-Black, anti-Muslim, anti-Irish, anti-Jewish and anti-Romany racisms, for example, cannot be assumed to be the same (Wekker, 1995). This draws attention to the fact that racism is not exclusively a white-on-black phenomenon. Racisms are also gendered, so that dominant groups will construct differing perceptions of women and men in subordinate groups. These women and men may then experience different forms of racism.

In drawing attention to the necessity of adopting an historical perspective in relation to understanding race and racisms, it is important to emphasize, as does de Groot in Chapter 2 for this book, that an awareness of any colonial or imperialist context to their development should also be maintained. Further, this is not just important in terms of considering their impact on Black and Third World women or, indeed, on other women who are both victims and survivors of racism. Rather, as de Groot powerfully argues, racism, colonialism and imperialism are important elements in the making and maintenance of gender relations in Western societies themselves. As Brah (1993, p. 21) has suggested for Europe, it is important not to 'perpetuate the erroneous view that European racisms directed against people outside Europe were not an internal dynamic of the historical constitution of "Europe"' itself. Thus, for white Western women, our construction of ourselves as women, mothers, workers and partners has previously been and continues to be shaped by reference to 'exotic, alien inferiorised "others"' (de Groot, Chapter 2).

It is therefore necessary to question the construction of whiteness as it relates to gender ((charles), 1992; Ware, 1992). This will involve analysing how the various systems of racial privilege become invisible to those who benefit from it. Drawing attention to how white people are taught not to recognize white privilege in the same way that men deny male privilege, McIntosh (1995, p. 76) writes: 'As a white person, I realised I had been taught about racism as something that puts others at a disadvantage, but had been taught not to see one of its corollary aspects, white privilege, which puts me at an advantage.' One crucial feature of an anti-racist Women's Studies, then, must be to put its original subjects – white Western women – under analytical scrutiny. In part, this is to be done by challenging the boundaries of what we currently mean by Women's Studies in the West and establishing a global and more inclusive context for our work.

Concluding Remarks

This chapter has tried to unravel some of the difficult issues involved in working towards an anti-racist perspective in Women's Studies work. It may have raised many questions and resolved few. Difficult problems of language and terminology (see note 1 below) have barely been addressed. There is an apparent call for an inclusive, all-encompassing framework that is probably far from being completed and one which will be difficult to achieve. Nevertheless, it is important to think globally, to be reflexive about our assumptions and the contexts in which they are made, even if our own particular work is more specific and localized in content. While it is impossible to do everything at once and selection and partiality would seem inevitable, it is important for Women's Studies to confront the potential racism that such partiality may hide. Failure to stand up against racism, refusing to admit one's own racism and that of the disciplines in which we work, acknowledging only extreme forms of racism and dismissing Black people who indicate when racism occurs are all strategies of denial employed by white people (Essed, 1991). White Women's

Mary Maynard

Studies practitioners need to be aware of such pitfalls. We certainly cannot claim to be absolved or to be immune from their implications.

Note

I am grateful to Haleh Afshar, Waqar Ahmad and Bob Coles for comments on an earlier draft of this chapter.

1 The use of terms such as 'Black' and 'Third World' are inherently problematic. They serve to homogenize very diverse groups and raise questions as to whose definitions are being used and to what purpose. In this chapter I use such terminology to identify the challenge mounted by diverse groups to the unproblematized hegemony of white Western women's perspectives and accounts. This is done, however, with much political and intellectual unease and an awareness of the dangers invoked in employing such language.

References

AFSHAR, HALEH and DENNIS, CAROLYNE (1992) 'Women, recession and adjustment in the Third World: Some introductory remarks' in AFSHAR, HALEH and DENNIS, CAROLYNE (Eds) *Women and Adjustment Policies in the Third World*, London, Macmillan.

AFSHAR, HALEH and MAYNARD, MARY (1994) 'The Dynamics of "Race" and Gender', in AFSHAR, HALEH and MAYNARD, MARY (Eds) *The Dynamics of 'Race' and Gender: Some Feminist Interventions*, London, Taylor & Francis.

AMOS, VALERIE and PARMAR, PRATIBHA (1984) 'Challenging imperial feminism', *Feminist Review*, 17, pp. 3–20.

ANDERSON, MARGARET L. and COLLINS, PATRICIA HILL (1995a) 'Preface', in ANDERSON, MARGARET and COLLINS, PATRICIA HILL (Eds) *Race, Class and Gender. An Anthology*, Belmont Ca., Wadsworth.

ANDERSON, MARGARET L. and COLLINS, PATRICIA HILL (1995b) 'Conceptualizing Race, Class and Gender', in ANDERSON, MARGARET L. and COLLINS, PATRICIA HILL (Eds) *Race, Class and Gender. An Anthology*, Belmont Ca., Wadsworth.

ANDERSON, MARGARET L. and COLLINS, PATRICIA HILL (1995c) 'Rethinking Institutions', in ANDERSON, MARGARET L. and COLLINS, PATRICIA HILL (Eds) *Race, Class and Gender. An Anthology*, Belmont Ca., Wadsworth.

ANTHIAS, FLOYA and YUVAL-DAVIS, NIRA (1992) *Racialized Boundaries*, London, Routledge.

BERKTAY, FATMAGÜL (1993) 'Looking from the "other" side: Is cultural relativism a way out?', in DE GROOT, JOANNA and MAYNARD, MARY (Eds) *Women's Studies in the 1990s. Doing Things Differently?*, London, Macmillan.

BHAVNANI, KUM-KUM (1993) 'Talking racism and the editing of Women's Studies', in RICHARDSON, DIANE and ROBINSON, VICTORIA (Eds) *Introducing Women's Studies*, London, Macmillan.

BHAVNANI, KUM-KUM and PHOENIX, ANN (Eds) (1994) *Shifting Identities. Shifting Racisms*, London, Sage.

BRAH, AVTAR (1991) 'Questions of difference and international feminism', in AARON, JANE and WALBY, SYLVIA (Eds) *Out of the Margins*, London, Falmer.

BRAH, AVTAR (1993) 'Re-framing Europe: Engendered racisms, ethnicities and nationalisms in contemporary Western Europe', *Feminist Review*, 45, pp. 9–29.

BRITTAN, ARTHUR and MAYNARD, MARY (1984) *Sexism, Racism and Oppression*, Oxford, Blackwell.

BRITTAN, VICTORIA (1995) 'Riding the tigress', *The Guardian*, Monday 28 August.

CALLINICOS, ALEX (1989) *Against Postmodernism: A Marxist Critique*, Cambridge, Polity.

CARBY, HAZEL (1982) 'White woman listen! Black feminism and the boundaries of sisterhood', in CENTRE FOR CONTEMPORARY CULTURAL STUDIES (Eds) *The Empire Strikes Back*, London, Hutchinson.

CENTRE FOR CONTEMPORARY CULTURAL STUDIES (Eds) (1982) *The Empire Strikes Back*, London, Hutchinson.

(CHARLES), HELEN (1992) 'Whiteness – the relevance of politically colouring the "Non"', in HINDS, HILARY, PHOENIX, ANN and STACEY, JACKIE (Eds) *Working Out*, London, Falmer.

COHEN, L. and COHEN, A. (1986) *Multi-Cultural Education*, London, Harper & Row.

COHEN, P. and BAINS, H. S. (1988) *Multi-Racist Britain*, London, Macmillan.

COLLINS, PATRICIA HILL (1990) *Black Feminist Thought*, London, Unwin Hyman.

EAGLETON, MARY (1994) 'Whose who and where's where in constructing feminist literary criticism?', paper presented to the staff/graduate seminar at the Centre for Women's Studies, University of York, 7 December.

ESSED, PHILOMENA (1991) *Understanding Everyday Racism*, London, Sage.

FLAX, JANE (1987) 'Postmodernism and gender relations in feminist theory', *Signs*, 12 (4).

FRYE, MARILYN (1983) *The Politics of Reality: Essays in Feminist Theory*, New York, The Crossing Press.

HARVEY, DAVID (1989) *The Condition of Postmodernity*, Oxford, Basil Blackwell.

HOOKS, BELL (1982) *Ain't I A Woman?*, London, Pluto.

HOOKS, BELL (1984) *Feminist Theory: From Margin to Centre*, Boston, South End Press.

HOOKS, BELL (1989) *Talking Back*, London, Sheba.

HOOKS, BELL (1991) *Yearning*, London, Turnaround.

JAMES, STANLIE M. and BUSIA, ABENA P. A. (Eds) (1993) *Theorizing Black Feminisms*, London, Routledge.

JORDAN, JUNE (1995) 'Report from the Bahamas', in ANDERSON, MARGARET L. and COLLINS, PATRICIA HILL (Eds) *Race, Class and Gender. An Anthology*, Belmont Ca, Wadsworth.

LORDE, AUDRE (1984) *Sister Outsider: Essays and Speeches*, New York, The Crossing Press.

MARSHALL, ANNECKA (1994) 'Sensuous sapphires: A study of the social construction of Black female sexuality', in MAYNARD, MARY and PURVIS, JUNE (Eds) *Researching Women's Lives from a Feminist Perspective*, London, Taylor & Francis.

MAYNARD, MARY (1994) '"Race", gender and the concept of "difference" in feminist thought', in AFSHAR, HALEH and MAYNARD, MARY (Eds) *The Dynamics of 'Race' and Gender: Some Feminist Interventions*, London, Taylor & Francis.

MCINTOSH, PEGGY (1995) 'White privilege and male privilege: A personal account of coming to see correspondence through work in Women's Studies', in ANDERSON, MARGARET L. and COLLINS, PATRICIA HILL (Eds) *Race, Class and Gender. An Anthology*, Belmont Ca, Wadsworth.

MOHANTY, CHANDRA TALPADE (1991) 'Under Western eyes: Feminist scholarship and colonial discourses', in MOHANTY, CHANDRA, TALPADE, RUSSO, ANN and TORRES, LOURDES (Eds) *Third World Women and the Politics of Feminism*, Bloomington and Indianapolis, Indiana University Press.

NORRIS, CHRISTOPHER (1992) *Uncritical Theory*, London, Lawrence & Wishart.

OMI, MICHAEL and WINANT, HOWARD (1986) *Racial Formation in the United States: From the 1960s to the 1980s*, New York, Routledge & Kegan Paul.

RAMAZANOGLU, CAROLINE (1989) *Feminism and the Contradictions of Oppression*, London, Routledge.

ROTHENBERG, PAULA (1990) 'The construction, deconstruction and reconstruction of difference', *Hypatia*, 5 (1).

SATOW, MIKA (1987) 'Translating realities' in EQUALITY OF THE SEXES COMMITTEE (Eds) *Workshop on Women and Research*, London, British Sociological Association.

SKEGGS, BEVERLEY (1991) 'A spanking good time', *Magazine of Cultural Studies*, 3.

SKEGGS, BEVERLEY (1995) 'Women's Studies in Britian in the 1990s: Entitlement cultures and institutional constraints', *Women's Studies International Forum*, 18 (4), pp. 475–86.

SPELMAN, ELIZABETH (1988) *Inessential Woman*, London, The Women's Press.

SPIVAK, GAYATRI CHAKRAVORTY (1992) 'The politics of translation', in BARRETT, MICHELE and PHILLIPS, ANNE (Eds) *Destabilizing Theory*, Cambridge, Polity.

SWEDER, RICHARD A. and LEVINE, ROBERT A. (Eds) (1984) *Culture Theory*, Cambridge, Cambridge University Press.

WARE, VROM (1992) *Beyond the Pale: White Women, Racism and History*, London, Verso.

WEKKER, GLORIA (1995) '"After the last sky, where do the birds fly"?', in LUTZ, HELMA, PHOENIX, ANN and YUVAL-DAVIS, NIRA (Eds) *Crossfires*, London, Pluto.

Chapter 2

Anti-colonial Subjects? Post-colonial Subjects? Nationalisms, Ethnocentrisms and Feminist Scholarship

Joanna de Groot

Over the last decade, the debates within feminist scholarship which arose from critiques of its ethnocentrism and/or racist aspects and of the history of colonial and post-colonial power relations among women generally and within Western feminism in particular have reached a new maturity. Reception of the early work of Nawal el Saadawi and Fatima Mernissi, and of African-American feminist/womanists (Amos and Parmar, 1984; Davis, 1982; el Saadawi, 1980; hooks, 1984; Hull, Bell Scott and Smith, 1982; Mernissi, 1975; Walker, 1984) stimulated wide-ranging explorations of various strategies for deepening those critiques, tracking their implications and meeting the challenges contained within them in practical ways. A growing quantity of work in history, anthropology, literary and cultural analysis and development studies was used and developed the initial impetus. This produced approaches ranging from the textual work of Gayatri Spivak and Lata Mani to the empirically based analyses of Hazel Carby, Leila Ahmed and Shula Marks and the conceptual and methodological discussions of Chandra Mohanty, bell hooks and Deniz Kandiyoti[1] (Ahmed, 1992; Carby, 1987; hooks, 1984, 1989; Kandiyoti, 1987, 1988, 1991a, 1992, 1993; Mani, 1989, 1991; Marks, 1987; Mohanty, 1988, Mohanty, Russo and Torres, 1991; Spivak, 1987).

This chapter is a contribution to this discussion. It reflects my great debt to such work, my interest in debates on gender, race and identity and my involvement in historical and feminist scholarship and in the study of the Middle East. I emphasize the issue of debt since I think that Western feminists need to go beyond conventional acknowledgements of existing scholarship and place themselves in a responsive relationship to the critiques of women from outside its traditions and practices. I focus my discussion on potentially useful concepts and methods for non-ethnocentric women's studies as a result of my experience as a teacher and scholar in the field. My choice of Middle Eastern material as the testing area for my arguments reflects my particular study of that area. My intention is to draw on the history of debates among Middle Eastern women on questions of gender and feminism and the roles, experiences and identities of women to illuminate some important strategies for non-ethnocentric practice in feminist scholarship and Women's Studies.

First I focus on the main issues now facing those who want to develop such a practice. Existing critiques of Western feminist scholarship have the effect of requiring a *repositioning* of that scholarship, its practitioners and its subject matter (Western women) in terms of theories, concepts and methods as well as of content. On the one hand feminist scholars need to incorporate analyses (historical and contemporary) of the power and privilege of various groups of Western women in the wider world. These range from histories of the missionary and philanthropic interventions of such women in societies under European colonial control, or of the class and race power of white women in systems of slavery and racial hierarchy in the Americas or South Africa, to studies of racial/ethnic divisions and inequalities between women in contemporary Europe and North America. Such incorporation needs to go beyond apologetic references or guilty self-criticism to explore the complexities, variations and contradictions in histories and analyses of the gender, race, class and colonial dimensions of women's lives and of the elements of power and inequality in relations among different women.

This requires both empirical and analytical effort in order to address both the social/historical specificities and the conceptual challenges involved in pursuing a fully globalized and multicultural feminist scholarship. In historical terms Fox-Genovese's work on women and American plantation slavery, or the contributions to Strobel and Chaudhuri's volume on white women and empire are examples of such efforts, paralleled by the theoretical and contemporary work of Spelman, Maynard, Russo, Molyneux or Ware[2] (Brittan and Maynard, 1984; Fox-Genovese, 1988; Maynard, 1994; Molyneux, 1982; Spelman, 1988; Strobel and Chaudhuri, 1992; Ware, 1992).

What is significant about this work is that either explicitly or implicitly it *shifts the focus and emphasis* of feminist scholarship, as well as the available knowledge and interpretations of women's activities and experiences in the world. Rather than just adding new material to the existing canon of questions and analyses, this type of scholarship invites us to *rethink* that canon by placing the present and past of non-white, non-Western women at the centre of our teaching, research or learning about 'women'.

Until recently, the lives and work of such women tended to appear as additional items on the agenda of Women's Studies and feminist scholarship, or as the problematic, anti-paradigmatic 'Other' of their core themes, concerns and concepts ('motherhood/sexuality is like this for women, but "they" do it differently'). The challenge now emerging is to place, for example, Indian, African or Latin American women *centrally* as *focal/starting points* for investigations, conceptualizations and analyses of women, as *no less typical/normal* 'women' than their white, Western counterparts, as historic and contemporary *majorities* of females in the world. To do so, as Jaggar and Rothenberg recognized in their reworked student reader *Feminist Frameworks*, is to look for different bases, structures and frameworks for the study and analysis of women (Jaggar and Rothenberg, 1978, pp. xi–xviii). Although such a project is still in its early stages, the prospect of moving from critiques of existing

Women's Studies to a *reconfiguration* of that tradition is hopeful and exciting as well as difficult and demanding. Although founded in the identity politics of silenced and marginalized groups of women, as were 'second-wave' white Western feminist interventions in the academy begun twenty-five years ago, this project is also as intellectually necessary as it is politically relevant.

One key element in the reconfiguring and reconceptualization of scholarship on women is their contribution from outside the dominant cultures of Europe and North America. Feminist scholars within these cultures have had access to ideas, information and interpretations from such women but have tended to deal with the offered material on a restricted and restrictive basis. Initially it became 'data'/'evidence'/subject-matter for discussion in Western texts and courses, positioning the women who provided material as 'native informants' from whom white Western scholars and students could take it and then provide their own analytical commentary.

This can and does improve awareness of the global diversity of women's circumstances and activities. It leads to useful comparative discussion, but it also sustains hierarchical relationships between the 'empirical' role assigned to Third World women and their intellectual work and the 'theoretical/interpretive' role of first world feminist scholarship. Any genuinely multicultural work in Women's Studies needs to critique and challenge this hierarchy and treat Black[3]/Third World women as *cultural*, *thinking agents* who speak, construct, conceptualize and comment on themselves and their world in diverse ways. As such they should be heard and addressed as *participants* in debates and investigations concerning women, rather than as resources for others to appropriate and exploit. Cultural analysts like Spivak and Mohanty, like anthropologists such as Abu-Lughod and Friedl have opened up critiques and practices which combine feminist commitment to giving women a voice with strategies to empower them to speak across cultural/social/ethnic divisions (Abu-Lughod, 1990a, 1990b, 1993; Afkhami and Friedl, 1994; Friedl, 1989; Mohanty, Russo and Torres, 1991; Spivak, 1992, 1987). Such strategies draw on the history of struggles for empowerment – cultural as much as material or political – in which subordinated groups claim agency and equality and serve to remove 'other' (notably Third World/Black) women from the position of passive, exotic objects of others' research. Recognition of the creative, critical cognitive work and range of concerns and debates with which such women are engaged is a vital component in any globally developed Women's Studies.

The inclusion and validation of Black and Third World women as practitioners of research, analysis and debate on women, as Mohanty argues, is not just a matter of cultural and intellectual recognition and respect, but also a grasp of the *material* structures of global inequality among women. Histories of colonial subordination, Black slavery, global systems of economic and political power or racial/ethnic discrimination form part of women's consciousness as well as of their experience. As such they have influenced the ideas and interests of women in many societies as actors, as commentators and as critics of those societies, of the global structures of which they are part and of feminist approaches to understanding or changing them. Indian widows, African-American slave women and Egyptian female nationalists in the ninteenth century, like Latina, African, Middle Eastern or African women today, created descriptions, interpretations and arguments about their own situation and the relations of power and inequality which contributed to their production. Such work addresses both material and cultural dimensions of the subordination and resistance which women experience and create. As it feeds into Women's Studies' work it contributes to *integrated* investigations and analyses of women as both acting and acted upon and of links between women's experiences and their understanding and cultural expression of those experiences. Among the key tasks for Women's Studies at present is exploration of creative solutions to the complex question of the interaction of material and cultural dynamics in women's lives and of the ways in which 'experience' is recorded *and* interpreted *and* constructed as women speak about it (de Groot and Maynard, 1993a). Best practices in feminist scholarship open up possibilities for avoiding unreal polarities between 'material' and 'cultural' aspects of life, or between 'experience' and knowledge/understanding/expression of experience, without buying into entirely textualized, language-based approaches. The discussion here pursues this objective, arguing that work by and about women in a global and multicultural context is one of the most significant contributions to our practice.

In identifying the broad prerequisites for an effectively non-ethnocentric Women's Studies, feminist scholars need to go beyond guilt and apology to consider the specific and complex relations among women in the world in particular times and places. The study of variety and inequalities among women and full recognition for the voices and experiences of non-white, non-Western women transforms our sense of categories such as 'woman', 'gender' or 'patriarchy' not just by testing them in a global multicultural setting but also by re-evaluating them in European and North American contexts. Historical and contemporary accounts of 'femininity' and gender relations need to be shaped by an understanding of the interactions of global and colonial power, and constructions of racial and cultural difference and inequality with gender and class relations and cultures *within* Western societies.

The issue here is not only the impact on Black and Third World women of imperialism, ethnocentrism or racism (including white Western women's involvement in these phenomena), but also the significant role of racial, colonial or ethnocentric elements in the making and maintenance of gender in Western societies themselves. The historic encounters of Europeans and white Americans with people in Asia, the Americas, Africa or the Middle East created situations in which peoples could be dominated materially, culturally and politically. They also created the material and cultural means whereby structures and relations of power and inequality in Western societies, including those associated with gender, acquired a racialized and colonial dimension. There is a range of studies exploring the associations between masculinity and imperial/racial dominance, the use of distinctions between 'acceptable' sexual or maternal conduct for women and unacceptable 'foreign' or lower-class variants and the links between Western feminist campaigns for rights and opportunities and their ideas of national/racial hierarchy (Davis, 1982; de Groot, 1989; Hall, 1992; Melman, 1992). Such studies reveal how Westerners' constructions of themselves as women, men, reformers, workers, mothers or feminists were in part shaped by reference to exotic, alien, inferiorized 'others', a legacy which still resonates today. Thus we need to complete the circle of argument on ethnocentrism in Western feminist scholarship by fully placing its original subject-matter – white Western women – in the multicultural context established by the inclusion of other women's experiences and discourses within Women's Studies.

However, my concern here is to give priority to those discourses in order to reflect on how women whose analyses are based on experience outside Western societies have constructed arguments on the relations between women and gender issues and colonialism, post-colonial state formation, ethnicity and cultural identities. I have chosen a specific tradition, that of discussion among Middle Eastern women on these matters, rather than a comparative approach for several reasons. It enables us to challenge and open-up the misleading and monolithic category 'Third World'/'non-Western' women by appreciating the specificities of women's histories in a particular area of the world. That area has had its own distinctive history of dynamics between colonialism/anti-colonialism and questions of culture, religion and gender relations which, in the view of many women from the region, create a set of common concerns linking them in their diversity. The long history of female activism and debate in the area has stimulated rich scholarship and discussion among Egyptian, Iranian, North African and Turkish women which forms a most valuable contribution to Women's Studies. The long history of European involvements in the Middle East has created an important and developed dynamic between the gendering of European views of exoticized, 'oriental' others and the exoticizing and 'orientalizing' of European constructs of gender in their own cultures.

My aim is to integrate debates and perceptions of Middle Eastern women about their own histories and identities within the field of Women's Studies and to position them in their historical contexts during the later nineteenth and twentieth centuries. These debates and perceptions illustrate the productive cultural and intellectual work of Middle Eastern women and also throw a different and distinctive light on Western women's assumptions about their own histories and identities. In bringing this work to the attention of Western readers concerned with Women's Studies, I hope to contribute to some of the processes which I have identified as important for the globalized, multicultural development of the field.

The context of Middle Eastern women's development over the nineteenth and twentieth centuries has been deeply influenced by experiences of a new quantity and quality of material, political and cultural interventions by

French, British or Russian military, commercial, diplomatic and cultural agents, paralleled after the Second World War by a comparable American impact. Three points can usefully be made about what is in fact a diverse, complex set of histories.

First, these experiences varied considerably over time and space. The intense involvement of Europeans in Egypt led both to significant economic incorporation into the world system from the 1850s and to direct European political control between the 1880s and the 1920s, whereas in Iran, although European involvement began at a similar period, the range and intensity of connections was more restricted and Russo-British pressure not sharply felt until the end of the nineteenth century (Haroun, 1979; Issawi 1966, 1971; Keddie, 1981).

Second, European power, whether colonial as in Algeria or Egypt, or commerical and diplomatic as in the Ottoman Empire or Iran, was not exercised over passive Middle Eastern victims. Rather, it involved a range of interactions with local rulers, commercial groups, landlords, peasants, intellectuals and bureaucrats.

Third, the political and material dynamics of European intervention were accompanied by cultural encounters which shaped powerful European views of the Middle East expressed in academic scholarship, popular imagery and prestigious artistic productions. This complex of images, theories, information and ideas is often generally termed 'orientalism' – a set of assumptions, stereotypes and interpretations concerning people and communities in the Middle East which also influenced Europeans' views of themselves and in which women and gender issues figured to a significant degree (Graham-Brown, 1988; de Groot, 1989; Said, 1978).

In a setting where many women's lives were being altered by new forms and practices of government, production and property relations, stimulated by involvement in the world system and initiatives by local élites and regimes to intensify and modernize their material and political power, women also embarked on new forms of political and cultural activity. More particularly, questions and discussions around the roles and rights of women began to emerge among groups of women with some access to formal education and/or the diversity of cultural and intellectual currents developing in the urban centres of the Eastern Mediterranean, Iran and North Africa.

Such women came largely from élite backgrounds or from families engaged in the growing professional and commercial sectors of their societies. By the end of the nineteenth century, women in Egypt, Turkish areas of the Ottoman Empire and Syria/Lebanon were writing and producing magazines and pamphlets, undertaking professional health and educational work and linking their activities to increasingly audible arguments about women's contributions to and claims on their communities/politics (Ahmed, 1984, 1992; Badran, 1989; Badran and Cooke, 1990; Baron, 1993; Cole, 1981; Kandiyoti, 1991b; Marsot, 1978; Shaarawi, 1986).

In the first decades of the twentieth century, political upheavals in Egypt, Iran and the Ottoman Empire – the Iranian constitutional movement 1905–1911, the Young Turk era 1908–1919, Egyptian nationalist upheavals 1919–1924 – occasioned more explicit organization and political activism among women. In the cities of Iran, educational and literary initiatives by élite women, which in Turkey or Egypt had preceded political activism, emerged simultaneously with it. This raises interesting questions about the contrasting pre-histories of women's political interventions in Iran as compared with those in Egypt or Turkey (Sanasarian, 1982, Chapters 1–3; Afary, 1989; Abadan-Unat, 1981; Kandiyoti, 1988, 1989, 1991a; Ahmed, 1984, 1992, pt 3; Baron, 1991, 1993, 1994; Badran, 1989, 1991, 1993; Shaarawi, 1986). More generally we may note that in the Middle East, as in the Indian subcontinent or Japan, the emergence of feminist initiatives dates from a period coinciding with the development of so-called 'first wave feminism' in Europe and North America.

The political activities and arguments initiated by Middle Eastern women between the 1890s and the 1920s reflected and refracted political concerns in their societies during that period. Much political energy at the time was focused on challenging external interventions by foreign powers and commercial interests and around associated indigenous projects of State construction or adaptation. One element in this dynamic was the creation of (male-dominated) movements to 'modernize' systems of government, production and education and to seek the political and material autonomy deemed necessary for such projects. Another element was the articulation of claims for autonomy formulated in terms both of 'rights', 'progress' and 'liberty' and also of 'imagined communities' of national/cultural identity and authenticity. It is significant that terms like 'fatherland', 'constitution' and 'nation', or ethnicized labels like 'Young Turk' or 'Iranian awakening' were attached to various attempts to reform or replace existing regimes and to confront foreign presences in the Middle East. Equally significantly, male nationalists, reformers and anti-colonialists constructed a *gendered* politics in which social reform, 'national' identity (past or present) and cultural authenticity were linked to formulations of the rights and roles of women, not as individuals or as a distinctive group but as signifiers and representatives of community, modernity, ethnicity or progress. Nationalist ideologues like the Turk Ziya Gokalp, the Egyptian Qasim Amin or the Iranian Mirza Aga Khan Kermani articulated views on women's seclusion or education as symbolic of progress or the 'true' culture of their 'nation', just as they produced gendered views of the loss of 'national' autonomy or threats to indigenous culture (Baron, 1991; Cole, 1981; de Groot, 1993; Kandiyoti, 1988, 1989).

Women also engaged with questions of national culture, political autonomy, communal stability and progress, as they created demands and arguments about their own situations. They might pose such demands in relation to a culturally authentic 'national' past (Pharaonic in Egypt, Central Asian in Turkey, pre-Islamic in Iran) in order to negotiate potential clashes between nationalist projects and women's interests. They developed a clear concern to position women-centred politics or analyses in relation to their experience, identity and understanding as *Muslims*, seeing Islamic traditions and practices both as part of a shared national or communal heritage and as objects of Western criticism and colonial intervention. Women participated in lively debate about the links between such traditions and practices and national/ ethnic identity and about the appropriateness of reform or criticism within existing Islamic thought or practice. Thus while male thinkers and activists might treat women as symbols or objects within their discourses, women were in fact *actively engaged* in arguing out and acting on varied views of their relationships to men, to the 'national' community and culture and to Western influences and interventions. In both intellectual and political initiatives they demonstrated their varied and contested senses of themselves as 'mothers', 'Muslims', 'patriots', or 'women' and the complex negotiations they undertook with nationalist politics, Western feminism and religious traditions. Located within specific, sometimes restricted milieux and both empowered and constrained by their connections with other political and intellectual movements, these early generations of Egyptian, Turkish or Iranian female activists set important precedents for their successors (Badran, 1993; Baron, 1994; Sanasarian, 1982).

The legacy of educated women's aspirations to new forms of fulfilment, of male politicians' appropriation of women within their various projects and of links between constructions of women's rights and roles and nationalist and anti-colonial politics helped to shape the interactions of women, State and society between the 1920s and the 1970s. The processes of State-building, whether in Iran, Egypt and Turkey in the 1920s and 1930s or by the post-colonial regimes in the eastern Mediterranean and North Africa in the 1950s and 1960s, featured all these phenomena. The gendered spin given to official programmes of modernization, State formation and 'development', incorporated, objectified and brought under government control (or even repression) some of the agendas set by earlier generations of women and nationalists.

In Kemalist Turkey a republican, secularizing and authoritarian regime successfully established a lasting shift in the material position and cultural construction of women, which might be contrasted with the more limited and contested interventions of the Pahlavi dynasty in Iran. In Egypt, during both the Wafdist and Nasser periods, there were elements both of government intervention in the condition of women and of the use of gendered rhetoric and symbolism within nationalist, reforming and popular politics (Islamic and secular) (Abadan-Unat, 1981; Abrahamian, 1982; Badran, 1991, pp. 206–21; Fischer 1981; Haddad, 1984; Kandiyoti, 1991a, pp. 37–42; Keddie, 1981; Sanasarian, 1982). Questions of rights to education or to political participation and cultural definitions of women as wives and mothers, as custodians of communal/national values and cultural identities or as potential disrupters of order figured significantly in political practice and argument in all these cases. Although in fact all kinds of localisms and ethnic diversities shaped much of women's experience in these areas, discourses of nationalism, religion and anti-colonialism, with their gendered rhetoric, played a growing role as varied official and oppositional political groupings sought popular bases. This paralleled the growth of 'national' structures of government and economic life and the continuing importance of post-colonial global pressures, both material and political.

If politics, including gender politics, in the Middle East in the period 1920–1970 focused on agendas of national development and State-building in which women spoke and were addressed as objects and participants in those processes, the period since 1970 is one in which such agendas faltered, fractured or were questioned, facilitating the emergence of cultural nationalism. On the one hand the regimes and political classes who developed the earlier projects found themselves externally constrained by Great Power political pressures in the region, by the dynamics of the global economy, particularly by the distinctive role of oil in Middle Eastern links to the world system. On the other hand the regimes/political classes themselves, however 'popular' their initial mandate, came to rely on an increasingly narrow base of clients, supporters and functionaries, while being challenged by the many serious inequalities and conflicts of interest within the societies they ruled. Their solutions to these problems tended to feature forms of repression and militarization, legitimized by reference to anti-colonial discourses and to the need for solidarity, as well as to the emotive Palestinian/Israeli question which compelled continuing Arab and Muslim concern. Paradoxically, these regimes also resorted to accommodations with Great Power political interests and with global economic pressures. This context of material uncertainty, political restriction, external pressure and internal division makes it easier to understand the disintegration and criticism of the former dominant anti-colonial/post-colonial agendas, whether liberal, leftist, nationalist or populist.

The decline of conviction about or commitment to national projects with a material and secular emphasis which had failed to fulfil their promises offered opportunities for more cultural and religious forms of political discourse to exercise greater influence. The 'cultural nationalism' of the 1970s and the 1980s mobilized anti-colonial traditions already embedded in political culture, addressed the various discontents of post-colonial modernity and, by focusing on religion as *the* badge of cultural authenticity, challenged Western denigration of Islam while ironically endorsing orientalist views of its centrality. The turn to Islamism[4] seen in Iran, in the Arab countries and to some extent in Turkey during the 1980s, expressed this shift, as well as other political and material realities ranging from the grievances of various disadvantaged urban groups to the occupation of one of the few available spaces for protest in civil societies deprived of political rights (Arjomand, 1984; Dessouki, 1982; Esposito, 1983; Haddad, 1982; Ibrahim, 1982; Knauss, 1987; Sharabi, 1988; Warburg and Kupferschmidt, 1983; Zubaida, 1988).

While this development has many diversities and complexities worth discussion, it is the powerful gender element within it which is relevant here. In the kinds of Islamized, nationalistic, anti-Western identity politics we are describing, women play a number of crucial roles. For some women such politics offer a means to pursue ends they deem important: it may allow them to express their sense of identity when challenged by the personal, material and social upheavals associated with urban immigration. It may be a way to claim dignity and recognition in the family or community. It may be a strategy to gain allies and challenge critics in the pursuit of rights and opportunities. There is evidence and argument to sustain any of these interpretations and to consider other positions, including that of women who critique or refuse Islamist politics (Afshar, 1993; Ahmed, 1992, chs 10–12; al Guindy, 1981; Paidar, forthcoming; Tohidi, 1991, 1994, pp. 135–41).

Whatever the involvement of women, it is also significant for Middle Eastern feminists and others that Islamist movements place great emphasis on female conduct, gender discourse and sexual imagery in the construction of their ideas and practices. The linkage of cultural authenticity with particular female roles, the sexualized anti-Western political language, the policing of women's behaviour (dress, mobility, employment, legal rights) in the name of communal morality are striking features of the FIS in Algeria, the Islamic Republic in Iran and Muslim movements in Lebanon, Egypt and the Palestinian territories (Ahmed, 1992; Cherifati-Merabtine, 1994; Kandiyoti, 1991b, 1992; Mernissi, 1987a, 1988, 1993a, 1993b; Moghadam, 1991, 1994a, 1994b; Paidar, forthcoming; Tohidi, 1991, 1994).

The purpose of this compressed but deliberate narrative is to establish a number of key points. First, our knowledge of much that has been presented here is derived from scholarly and other work by Middle Eastern women investigating, analysing and commenting on their past and present. Second, the work of these scholars, like that of a whole range of other writers and activists, illustrates the intellectual and political agency of women in the region, too frequently portrayed only as victims/objects. Third, the forms taken by questions of 'identity' (political, material, cultural) for women in the Middle East represent the outcomes of complex, shifting interactions and negotiations between a number of histories and specificities impacting on their lives. This creates both the distinctive features particular to the experience of Egyptian communist, Iranian Islamist, or Moroccan feminist women and a basis for comparison among diverse groups of women in the Middle East and elsewhere. Last, we are made aware of the extended and lively history of women's debate and analysis in the Middle East, ranging from debates among Egyptian feminists in the 1910s and 1920s to the changing strategies of Iranian or Moroccan or Palestinian women in the 1980s and 1990s. This debate and analysis has also engaged creatively and critically with Western traditional theory, politics and scholarship by and about women over the last century, making its own contribution to discussions on gender as role, relationship or identity.

The early positioning of Middle Eastern women in relation to 'nation' and 'community' by women activists in the region at the start of this century owed much to the colonial or quasi-colonial experiences and relationships which were so visible and contentious for women of their particular background at that time. The views of these women about their identity and interests exhibited a complex tension between analyses which posed women's demands within projects of reform and modernization and those which were part of an historical-cultural quest for 'authentic community'. Their interests in education, marriage and sociopolitical action (philanthropic or demonstrative) sought both to use the legitimizing power of tradition and to critique or clarify that tradition in ways reminiscent of women's engagement with other religious traditions (English Evangelical, French Catholic, American Quaker). Contesting the rights and status of women in Islamic tradition, exploring the opportunities and restrictions flowing from the links between women's politics and anti-colonial nationalism, recognizing the tensions between women's commitments to motherhood and family with their aspirations in other spheres, they created a significant legacy (Badran and Cooke, 1990; Baron, 1994; Edib, 1926).

In the era of post-colonial State-construction and development projects, Middle Eastern women recast some of this legacy in the language of social science, nation-building and modernization. State legislation and social policy, analyses of the material conditions of women's household and workplace activities and support and empowerment for larger groups of women were the characteristic preoccupations of women activists in the 1960s and 1970s. The expansion of access to higher education, whether within the region or in the West, allowed a much increased number of women to explore and investigate at a sophisticated level and to encounter the work of 'second-wave' Western feminists. This encounter added to the repertoire of ideas and approaches available to Middle Eastern women and also stimulated a critical response to ethnocentric, inappropriate or unhelpful aspects of Western feminist scholarship. The work of Nawal el Saadawi in Egypt and Fatima Mernissi in Morocco, which has becom available to Western readers, illustrates this critical engagement and the preference of women thinkers like them to focus on material political power and their ideological underpinnings rather than, say, the cultural concerns of radical feminism (el Saadawi, 1980; Mernissi, 1975).

However, the very fact of interaction between Middle Eastern women and Western feminist thought and politics stimulated critiques which developed during the 1980s, challenging the apparent certainty of categories like 'difference', 'patriarchy' and indeed 'woman/women' with which feminists worked. The debates on these questions involved important contributions from Middle Eastern feminist scholars, focusing on questions of cultural relativism, feminist scholarly practice and what Gayatri Spivak has called 'tactical humanism'. The Algerian, Marnia Lazreg, and the Turk, Fatmagül Berktay, both attempted to clarify the problematic nature of relativism as a strategy which can validate indifference to and collusion with oppressions identified not by chauvinist Westerners but by Middle Eastern women. The Palestinian-American, Abu-Lughod, has analysed the role of ethnographer as feminist in relation to the cultural differences and inequalities between observer and observed as an outsider/native relationship (Abu-Lughod, 1990a, 1990b, 1993; Berktay, 1993; Lazreg, 1988).

The rise of Islamism gave a particular edge to Middle Eastern women's debate, both on the gender dimensions of religio-cultural identity and anti-Western politics and on the agency and choices of women with respect to Islamist movements. In particular, writers like Ahmed, Kandiyoti and Abu-Lughod have drawn attention to the multiple considerations shaping the identities and strategies of particular women whose relationship to and definition of 'their' Islam may express complex negotiations of gender, generational conflict, social disadvantage and ethnic nationalism. Abu-Lughod's exposition of 'critical ethnography' and Kandiyoti's conceptualization of strategic 'bargaining with patriarchy' and of the intersection of Islamic belief/practice with other structures of power, culture and inequality represent sophisticated interventions in a rich, highly politically invested debate (Ahmed, 1992, pp. 208–48; Kandiyoti, 1987, 1988, 1992; Abu Lughod, 1990a, 1990b, 1993). This conceptual work complements an enlarged and enriched empirically based scholarship on Middle Eastern women, past and present.

Rather than impose a somewhat artificial closure by asserting my own particular views, I use the rest of my discussion to evoke the diverse and difficult debates among Middle Eastern feminist scholars by use of some powerful and accessible examples. The first of these, the work of the Moroccan Fatima Mernissi between the 1970s and the 1980s, expresses some of the important political and intellectual shifts which have affected some scholars. It also offers a distinctive synthesis of the personal and psychological treatment of gender and sexuality with a sharp sense of their larger material and political dimensions (employment, legal systems, religious tradition, civic/constitutional rights).

In her early work *Beyond the Veil*, Mernissi's accounts of women in Morocco and in more recent texts like *Women and Islam* and *Islam and Democracy* address the relationships between women and male-dominated religious or political systems from a cultural, personalized perspective, as well as in relation to education, work and family life (Mernissi, 1975, 1987b, 1982a, 1982b, 1982c, 1988, 1991, 1993a). Until the early 1980s, she pursued this analysis with reference to social scientific evidence and ideas and to post-colonial concerns with modernization, progress and social justice. Her more recent work offers a more directly woman-centred ideological-critical engagement with Islamism and its cultural and political power. Mernissi's explicit project is to challenge the dominant constructions of 'Islam' and to recuperate a more humanistic and democratic construction. This work shows both the power and the problems of operating within an established, often hostile, convention as a radical critic, a route chosen not just by Mernissi but by a number of women thinkers and activists in the region. Their choice expresses the immediacy and gravity of the politico-cultural issues around Islamism in the Middle East in the 1990s and draws on indigenous feminist traditions reaching back over a century, as well as on the 'cultural' turn in feminism globally.

If Mernissi's work conveys profound dissatisfaction with the material, cultural and political constraints of her own culture, while offering an alternative somehow grounded in its own 'best' traditions, that of the Egyptian, Leila Ahmed, now based in the USA, is more clearly addressed to Western orientalism and ethnocentrism. She too has embarked on the 'recuperative' revisioning of women in relation to Islam, but most recently produced an extended critique of that Western orientalist tradition, using a thematic account of selected aspects of Middle Eastern women's history over a thousand years (Ahmed, 1982, 1986, 1992). She focuses on European misconceptions of 'women's oppression' in the region and their manipulative appropriation of the realities of sexism and gender inequality there as part of their colonial and post-colonial projects. The latter part of her text is a more detailed discussion of the history of Middle Eastern feminism, which raises critical doubts about the benefits to be gained when feminists in the region drew on what she argues were often irrelevant and sometimes oppressive Western feminist ideas.

Ahmed poses something of a duality between 'indigenous' and 'interationalist' feminist endeavours, mainly in Egypt, although in the course of her analysis she indicates the difficulties of sustaining that duality. In many ways, this well reflects the tensions and nuances in the intellectual and political choices faced by Middle Eastern feminists at the start of this century. It also conveys some of the anger and defensiveness involved in sustaining relationships within current feminist networks, influenced as they are by the divisive effects of colonialism and ethnocentrism. The polemical force in Ahmed's work comes from the energy with which she seeks to present Middle Eastern women's disadvantages in their own societies, as well as the limited, uninformed and ideologically grounded assumptions made by Western commentators. Whatever scholarly points might be made about the text, it gives access to a significant and evolving set of concerns which engage the attention and energy of Middle Eastern women.

My last illustrative case is the work of Deniz Kandiyoti, an academic from Turkey, now practising in the UK. Her work on women's social development in the Middle East has led her into explorations of the cultural and political structures which impact on their material life in households, workplaces and communities. This, in turn, has led her to develop theoretical commentaries and critical evaluations of the methods, concepts and findings in the literature on Middle Eastern women. Like Ahmed, Kandiyoti has a critique of Western feminist scholarship, but emphasizes not so much the problem of its ethnocentric presuppositions as its need to refine its concepts and methodologies. In recent work, Kandiyoti uses the concept of 'strategy', both to convey complex social and historical specificities with which women deal in any society and to discuss the most fruitful approaches or frameworks for informed feminist analysis and understanding of such specificities.

Other recent texts survey the history of scholarship on women in the Middle East. They examine the value of comparative study for delineating both the convergence and divergence of Middle Eastern and other experiences and analyse the political context of debates on Middle Eastern women. Kandiyoti's view of Islamic structures and traditions questions the benefits of giving them uncritical or undue emphasis, while recognizing their place in recent histories of State formation, of social change and continuities and of political movements and ideas (Kandiyoti, 1987, 1988, 1989, 1991a, 1991b, 1992, 1993, forthcoming). This work illustrates, draws on and engages with the now highly evolved and diverse traditions of political and scholarly work by Middle Eastern women.

Each of these scholars, drawing as they do on both experience and scholarship, on both indigenous Middle Eastern and Western ideas and insights, merits much fuller textual and contextual analysis than has been possible here. However, my intention in presenting them is to provide not so much a textual exegesis as an indication of the history and resources within Middle Eastern women's experiences, politics and thought to be valued *not* as data for some meta-analysis, but as analysis which should be addressed as such. The question of 'identity' – often a dangerously static or one-dimensional category unless carefully approached – has been both the occasion/stimulus and the conceptual tool for feminist scholarship in the Middle East, as elsewhere. The particular uses made by Middle Eastern feminist thinkers and writers of both the occasions and the intellectual work which have addressed the issue of identity offer a valuable and distinctive contribution to our global discussions on this awkward matter.

Notes

1 These are selected examples, albeit in my view distinguished ones, of a very large *oeuvre* addressing issues which concern me in this piece from non-Western perspectives.
2 These are deliberately chosen to illustrate work by white European and North American feminists which addresses these issues.
3 I use the term 'Black' to refer to those women who identify themselves as being at the receiving end of discrimination and unequal relationships based on or legitimized by reference to race/ethnicity/colour.
4 I use this term to distance the discussion from the assumptions implied in terms like 'fundamentalist' or 'revivalist'.

References

ABADAN-UNAT, N. with KANDIYOTI, D. and KIRAY, M. B. (Ed.) (1981) *Women in Turkish Society*, Leiden, E.J. Brill.

ABRAHAMIAN, E. (1982) *Iran between Two Revolutions*, Princeton, N.J., Princeton University Press.

ABU-LUGHOD, L. (1990a) 'Can there be a feminist ethnography?', *Women and Performance*, 5 (1), pp. 7–27.

ABU-LUGHOD, L. (1990b) 'The romance of resistance: tracing transformations of power through Bedouin women', *American Ethnologist*, 18, pp. 41–55.

ABU-LUGHOD, L. (1993) *Writing Women's Worlds: Bedouin Stories*, Berkeley, London, University of California Press.

AFARY, J. (1989) 'On the origins of feminism in early twentieth century Iran', *Journal of Women's History*, 1 (2), pp. 65–87.

AFKHAMI, M. and FRIEDL, E. (Eds) (1994) *In the Eye of the Storm*: Women in Post-revolutionary Iran, London, I.B. Tauris.

AFSHAR, HALEH (Ed.) (1993) *Women in the Middle East*, London, Macmillan.

AHMED, L. (1982) 'Feminism and feminist movements in the Middle East', in AL-HIBVI, A. (Ed.) *Women and Islam*, Oxford, Pergamon Press.

AHMED, L. (1984) 'Early feminist movements in Turkey and Egypt', in HUSSEIN, F. (Ed.) *Muslim Women*, London, Croom Helm.

AHMED, L. (1986) 'Women and the advent of Islam', *Signs*, 11 (4), pp. 665–91.

AHMED, L. (1992) *Gender, Women and Islam: Historical Roots of a Modern Debate*, Yale, Yale University Press.

AMOS, V. and PARMAR, P. (1984) 'Challenging imperial feminism', *Feminist Review*, 17, pp. 3–21.

ARJOMAND, S. A. (1984) *From Nationalism to Revolutionary Islam*, New York, University of New York Press.

BADRAN, M. (1989) 'The origins of feminism in Egypt', in ANGERMAN, A., BINNEMA, G., KEUNEN, A., POELS, V. and ZIRKZEE, J. (Eds) *Current Issues in Women's History*, London, Routledge.

BADRAN, M. (1991) 'Competing agenda: feminists, Islam and the State in nineteenth and twentieth century Egypt', in KANDIYOTI, D. (Ed.) *Women, Islam and the State*, London, Macmillan.

BADRAN, M. (1993) 'Independent women: more than a century of feminism in modern Egypt', in TUCKER, J. (Ed.) *Arab Women: Old boundaries, New Frontiers*, Bloomington, Indiana, Indiana University Press.

BADRAN, M. and COOKE, M. (Eds) (1990) *Opening the Gates: a Century of Arab Feminist Writing*, London, Virago.

BARON, B. (1991) 'Mothers, morality and nationalism in pre-1919 Egypt', in KHALIDI, R. et al. (Eds) *The Origins of Arab Nationalism*, New York, Columbia University Press.

BARON, B. (1993) 'The construction of national honour in Egypt', *Gender and History*, 5 (2), pp. 244–55.

BARON, B. (1994) *The Women's Awakening in Egypt: Culture, Society and the Press*, New Haven, Connecticut, Yale University Press.

BERKTAY, F. (1993) 'Is cultural relativism a way out?', in DE GROOT, J. and MAYNARD, M. (Eds) *Women's Studies in the 1990s: Doing Things Differently*, London, Macmillan.

BRITTAN, A. and MAYNARD, M. (1984) *Sexism, Racism and Oppression*, Oxford, Basil Blackwell.

CARBY, H. V. (1987) *Reconstructing Womanhood: the Emergence of the Afro-American Woman Novelist*, Oxford, Oxford University Press.

CHERIFATI-MERABTINE, D. (1994) 'Algeria at a crossroads: national liberation, Islamisation and women', in MOGHADAM, V. (Ed.) *Gender and National Identity*, London, Zed Press.

COLE, J. (1981) 'Feminism, class and Islam in turn-of-the-century Egypt', *International Journal of Middle East Studies*, 13 (4), pp. 387–407.

DAVIS, A. (1982) *Women, Race and Class*, London, The Women's Press.

DESSOUKI, A. (1982) *Islamic Resurgence in the Arab World*, London, Praeger.

EDIB, H. (1926) *Memoirs*, London, John Murray.

EDIB, H. (1928) *The Turkish Ordeal*, London, John Murray.

EL SAADAWI, N. (1980) *The Hidden Face of Eve*, London, Zed Press.

ESPOSITO, J. (Ed.) (1983) *Voices of Resurgent Islam*, Oxford, Oxford University Press.

FISCHER, M. (1981) *Iran: from Religious Dispute to Revolution*, Cambridge, Mass, Harvard University Press.

FOX-GENOVESE, E. (1988) *Within the Plantation Household: Black and White Women of the Old South*, Chapel Hill, NC, University of North Carolina Press.

FRIEDL, ERICA (1989) *Women of Den Koh: Lives in an Iranian Village*, London, Smithsonian Institution Press.

GRAHAM-BROWN, S. (1988) *Images of Women: the Portrayal of Women in Photography of the Middle East, 1860–1950*, London, Quarket.

DE GROOT, JOANNA (1989) ' "Sex" and "race": the construction of image and language in the nineteenth century', in MENDUS, S. and RANDALL, J. (Eds) *Sexuality and Subordination*, London, Methuen.

DE GROOT, JOANNA (1993) 'The dialectics of gender: women, men and political discourses in Iran c.1890–1930', *Gender and History*, 5 (2), pp. 256–68.

DE GROOT, J. and MAYNARD, M. (1993a) 'Prospects for the 1990s', in DE GROOT, J. and MAYNARD, M. (Eds) *Women's Studies in the 1990s: Doing Things Differently*, London, Macmillan.

AL GUINDY, F. (1981) 'Veiling *infitah* with Muslim ethnic: Egypt's contemporary Islamic movement', *Social Problems*, 28 (4), pp. 465–85.

HADDAD, Y. (1982) *Contemporary Islam and the Challenge of History*, New York, State University of New York Press.

HADDAD, Y. (1984) 'Women and revolution in twentieth century Arab thoughts', *The Muslim World*, 74 (3–4), pp. 137–60.

HALL, C. (1992) *White, Male and Middle Class: Explorations in Feminism and History*, Oxford, Polity Press.

HAROUN, A. A. (1979) *Cotton in the Egyptian Economy*, Leuven, Geografisch Instituut, Katholieke Universiteit.

HOOKS, B. (1984) *Feminist Theory: From Margin to Centre*, Boston, Ma., South End Press.

HOOKS, B. (1989) *Talking Back: Thinking Feminist, Thinking Black*, London, Sheba Feminist Publishers.

HULL, G., BELL SCOTT, P. and SMITH, B. (Eds) (1982) *All the Women are White, All the Men are Black, But Some of Us are Brave*, Black Women's Studies, Old Westbury, NY, Feminist Press.

IBRAHIM, S. (1982) *The New Arab Social Order*, Oxford, West View Press.

ISSAWI, C. (1966) *Economic History of the Middle East 1800–1914*, Chicago, University of Chicago Press.

ISSAWI, C. (1971) *Economic History of Iran 1800–1914*, Chicago, University of Chicago Press.

JAGGAR, A. and ROTHENBERG STRUHL, P. (Eds) (1978) *Feminist Frameworks: Alternative Theoretical Accounts of the Relations Between Women and Men*, London, McGraw Hill.

KANDIYOTI, D. (1987) 'Emancipated but unliberated? Reflections on the Turkish case', *Feminist Issues*, 13, pp. 35–50.

KANDIYOTI, D. (1988) 'Bargaining with patriarchy', *Gender and Society*, 2, pp. 274–90.

KANDIYOTI, D. (1989) 'Women and the Turkish State: political actors or symbolic pawns', in ANTHIAS, F. and YUVAL-DAVIES, N. (Eds) *Woman-Nation-State*, London, Macmillan.

KANDIYOTI, D. (1991a) 'Introduction' and 'The end of empire: Islam, nationalism and women in Turkey', in KANDIYOTI, D. (Ed.) *Women, Islam and the State*, London, Macmillan.

KANDIYOTI, D. (Ed.) (1991b) *Women, Islam and the State*, London, Macmillan.

KANDIYOTI, D. (1992) 'Islam and patriarchy', in KEDDIE, N. and BARON, B. (Eds) *Women in Middle Eastern History*, New Haven, Connecticut, Yale University Press.

KANDIYOTI, D. (1993) 'Strategies for feminist scholarship in the Middle East', unpublished paper.

KANDIYOTI, D. (forthcoming) 'Introduction', in KANDIYOTI, D. (Ed.), *Gendering the Middle East: Alternative Perspectives*, London, I.B. Taurus.

KEDDIE, N. (1981) *Rocks of Revolution*, New Haven, Connecticut, Yale University Press.

KNAUSS, P. (1987) *The Persistence of Patriarchy: Class Ideology and Gender in Twentieth Century Algeria*, London, Praeger.

LAZREG M. (1988) 'Feminism and difference: the perils of writing as a woman on women in Algeria', *Feminist Studies*, 14 (1), pp. 81–107.

MANI, L. (1989) 'Contentious traditions: the debate on "Sati" in Colonial India', in SANGARI, K. and VAID, S. (Eds) *Recasting Women: Eassays in Indian Colonial History*, New Delhi, Kali for Women.

MANI, L. (1991) 'Cultural theory, colonial texts: Reading eye-witness accounts of widow burning', in GROSSBERG, L., NELSON, G. and TREICHLER, P. (Eds) *Cultural Studies*, London, Routledge.

MARKS, S. (1987) *Not Either an Experimental Doll: the Separate Worlds of Three South-African Women*, London, Women's Press.

MARSOT, A. L. AL-SAYYID (1978) 'The revolutionary gentlewomen in Egypt', in BECK, L. and KEDDIE, N. (Eds) *Women in the Muslim World*, Cambridge, Mass., Harvard University Press.

MAYNARD, M. (1994) '"Race", gender and the concept of "Difference" in Feminist thought', in AFSHAR, H. and MAYNARD, M. (Eds) *The Dynamics of 'Race' and Gender*, London, Taylor & Francis.

MELMAN, B. (1992) *Women's Orients*, London, Macmillan.

MENDUS, S. and RENDALL, J. (Eds) (1989) *Sexuality and Subordination*, London, Methuen.

MERNISSI, F. (1975) *Beyond the Veil*, Bloomington, Indiana, Indiana University Press.

MERNISSI, F. (1982a) 'Virginity and Patriarchy', in ALHIBRI, A. (Ed.) *Women and Islam*, Oxford, Pergamon.

MERNISSI, F. (1982b) 'Zhor's world: a Moroccan domestic worker speaks out', *Feminist Issues*, 2, pp. 15–29.

MERNISSI, F. (1982c–83) 'Women and the impact of capitalist development in Morocco', *Feminist Issues*, 2 parts, 2, 3 (1), pp. 49–61.

MERNISSI, F. (1987a) 'Muslim women and fundamentalism', in MERNISSI, F. *Beyond the Veil*, 2nd revised edn, Bloomington, Indiana, Indiana University Press.

MERNISSI, F. (1987b) *Beyond the Veil*, 2nd revised edn, Bloomington, Indiana, Indiana University Press.

MERNISSI, F. (1988) *Doing Daily Battle: Interviews with Moroccan Women* (*Le Maroc raconté par ses femmes*), London, Women's Press.

MERNISSI, F. (1991) *Women and Islam: an Historical and Theological Enquiry*, (*Le Harem Politique*, (1987)) Oxford, Blackwell.

MERNISSI, F. (1993a) *Islam and Democracy*, London, Virago.

MERNISSI, F. (1993b) *The Forgotten Queens of Islam* (*Sultanes oubliées*), trans. Lakeland, M.J., Cambridge, Polity Press.

MOGHADAM, V. (1991) 'Islamist movements and women's responses', *Gender and History*, 3 (3), pp. 268–86.

MOGHADAM, V. (Ed.) (1994a) *Identity, Politics and Women*, Oxford, Westview Press.

MOGHADAM, V. (Ed.) (1994b) *Gender and National Identity*, London, Zed Press.

MOHANTY, C. (1988) 'Under Western eyes', *Feminist Review*, 30, pp. 61–88.

MOHANTY, C., RUSSO, A. and TORRES, L. (Eds) (1991) *Third World Women and the Politics of Feminism*, Bloomington, Indiana, Indiana University Press.

MOLYNEUX, M. (1982) *State Policies and the Position of Women Workers in the People's Democratic Republic of Yemen 1967–1977*, Geneva, International Labour Office.

PAIDAR, P. (forthcoming) *Women in the Political Discourse of Twentieth Century Iran*, Cambridge, Cambridge University Press.

SAID, E. (1978) *Orientalism*, London, Routledge.

Joanna de Groot

SANASARIAN, E. (1982) *The Women's Rights Movement in Iran*, London, Praeger.

SHAARAWI, H. (1986) *Harem Years: Memoirs of an Egyptian Feminist*, trans. and ed. Badran, M., London, Virago.

SHARABI, H. (1988) *Neopatriarchy: a Theory of Distorted Change in Arab Society*, Oxford, Oxford University Press.

SPELMAN, E. V. (1988) *Inessential Woman: Problems of Exclusion in Feminist Thought*, London, Women's Press.

SPIVAK, G. (1987) *In Other Worlds: Essays in Cultural Politics*, London, Routledge.

SPIVAK, G. (1992) 'Women's indifference', in PARKER, A., RUSSO, M., SOMMER, D. and YAEGER, P. (Eds) *Nationalisms and Sexualities*, London, Routledge.

STROBEL, M. and CHAUDHURI, N. (Eds) (1992) *Western Women and Imperialism*, Bloomington, Indiana, Indiana University Press.

TOHIDI, N. (1991) 'Gender and Islamic fundamentalism: feminist politics in Iran', in MOHANTY, C., RUSSO, A. and TORRES, L. (Eds) *Third World Women and the Politics of Feminism*, Bloomington, Indiana, Indiana University Press.

TOHIDI, N. (1994) 'Modernity, Islamisation and women in Iran', in MOGHADAM, V. (Ed.) *Gender and National Identity*, London, Zed Press.

WALKER, A. (1984) *In Search of Our Mother's Gardens: Womanist Prose*, London, Women's Press.

WARBURG, G. R. and KUPFERSCHMIDT, U. M. (Eds) (1983) *Islam, Nationalism and Radicalism in Egypt and the Sudan*, NY, Praeger.

WARE, V. (1992) *Beyond the Pale: White Women, Racism and History*, London, Verso.

ZUBAIDA, S. (1988) *Islam, the People and the State*, London, Routledge.

Further Reading

ABU-LUGHOD, L. (1986) *Veiled Sentiments: Honor and Poetry in a Bedouin Society*, Berkeley, London, University of California Press.

ABU-LUGHOD, L. (1988) 'Fieldwork of a dutiful daughter', in AL TORKI, S. and FAWZI EL-SOLH, C. (Eds), *Arab Women in the Field: Studying your Own Society*, Syracuse, New York, Syracuse University Press.

AFSHAR, H. and MAYNARD, M. (Eds) (1994) *The Dynamics of 'Race' and Gender*, London, Taylor & Francis.

AL-HIBVI, A. (Ed.) (1982) *Women and Islam*, Oxford, Pergamon Press.

AL TORKI, S. and FAWZI EL-SOLH, C. (Eds) (1988) *Arab Women in the Field: Studying your Own Society*, Syracuse, New York, Syracuse University Press.

ANGERMAN, A., BINNEMA, G., KEUNEN, A., POELS, V. and ZIRKZEE, J. (Eds) (1989) *Current Issues in Women's History*, London, Routledge.

ANTHIAS, F. and YUVAL-DAVIES, N. (Eds) (1989) *Woman-Nation-State*, London, Macmillan.

BARON, B. (1989) 'Unveiling in early twentieth century Egypt: practical and symbolic considerations', *Middle East Studies*, 25 (3), pp. 370–86.

BECK, L. and KEDDIE, N. (Eds) (1978) *Women in the Muslim World*, Cambridge, Mass, Harvard University Press.

BOTMAN, S. (1987) 'Women's participation in radical Egyptian politics 1939–1952', in KHAMSIN COLLECTIVE (Ed.) *Women in the Middle East*, London, Zed Press.

GATES, H. (Ed.) (1986) *'Race' Writing and Difference*, Chicago, Chicago University Press.

DE GROOT, J. and MAYNARD, M. (Eds) (1993b) *Women's Studies in the 1990s: Doing Things Differently*, London, Macmillan.

GROSSBERG, L., NELSON, G. and TREICHLER, P. (Eds) (1992) *Cultural Studies*, London, Routledge.

HOOKS, B. (1981) *Ain't I a Woman? Black Women and Feminism*, London, Pluto.

HUSSEIN, F. (Ed.) (1984) *Muslim Women*, London, Croom Helm.

KEDDIE, N. and BARON, B. (Eds) (1992) *Women in Middle Eastern History*, New Haven, Connecticut, Yale University Press.

KHALIDI, R. et al. (Eds) (1991) *The Origins of Arab Nationalism*, New York, Columbia University Press.

KHAMSIN COLLECTIVE (Ed.) (1987) *Women in the Middle East*, London, Zed Press.

KHATER, A. and NELSON, C. (1988) 'al-Harakah al-nissaiyah: the women's movement and political participation in modern Egypt', *Women's Studies International Forum*, 11 (5), pp. 465–83.

MANI, L. (1992) 'Travelling texts, changing contexts: the consolidation of Baptist missionary discourse in India', unpublished paper.

MARSOT, A. L. AL-SAYYID (1977) *Egypt's Liberal Experiment 1922–1936*, Berkeley, London, University of California Press.

MOLYNEUX, M. (1991) 'The law, the State and socialist policies with regard to women: the case of the People's Democratic Republic of Yemen', in KANDIYOTI, D. (Ed.) *Women, Islam and the State*, London, Macmillan.

NAJMABADI, A. (1991) 'Hazards of modernity and morality: women, State and ideology in contemporary Iran', in KANDIYOTI, D. (Ed.) *Women, Islam and the State*, London, Macmillan.

NELSON, C. and GROSSBERG, L. (Eds) (1988) *Marxism and the Interpretation of Culture*, Houndmills, Macmillan Education.

PARKER, A., RUSSO, M., SOMMER, D. and YAEGER, P. (Eds) (1992) *Nationalisms and Sexualities*, London, Routledge.

SANGARI, K. and VAID, S. (Eds) (1990) *Recasting Women: Essays in Indian Colonial History*, New Brunswick, NJ, Rutgers University Press.

SPIVAK, G. (1986) 'Three women's texts and a critique of imperialism', in GATES, H. (Ed.) *'Race' Writing and Difference*, Chicago, Chicago University Press.

Joanna de Groot

Spivak, G. (1988) 'Can the subaltern speak?', in Nelson, C. and Grossberg, L. (Eds) *Marxism and the Interpretation of Culture*, Basingstoke, Macmillan Education.

Tucker, J. (Ed.) (1993) *Arab Women: Old Boundaries, New Frontiers*, Bloomington, Indiana, Indiana University Press.

Chapter 3

What Happened to Feminist Politics in 'Gender Training'?

Bunie M. Matlanyane Sexwale

SOMETIMES, THE RACIAL CRY

Sometimes, as children we gaze in wonder
and comfort
knowing that speech patterns do not
preclude the stimulation of thought.

And then as speech and thought wrap arms around
each other
they make comfortable the
patterns of expression
    either way.

Sometimes, as adults I can't believe how perfectly pitched
discordant echoes of sound
be – come
into subdued ears that were
long ago lulled into a true
sense of security.

And sometimes we need
to scream the racial cry
so that bastards can remind themselves
of recently dulled history in the name of
western development.

Helen (charles) – 1994

Contradictory and conflicting historical processes hang in the background of, and at times wrestle over, WGD (Women, Gender and Development) education. On the one hand imperialism and neo-colonialism are manifested in the many forms of oppression, exploitation and domination that assail current relations between and within nations and people. Patriarchy is shaped by, defines and permeates these relations of domination and subordination. On the other hand feminism grapples with understanding, thinking through, strategizing and struggling against women's subordination, exploitation and oppression in different societies. For many, social transformation is the goal.

The institutionalization of feminist struggles of the 1960s and 1970s led to Women's Studies, commonly situated within institutions of higher learning. It also set in motion the process of femocratization: as pressure was brought to bear on non-governmental organizations, international, interstate and State institutions, a growing number of women, among them (used to be) feminists, were absorbed into bureaucracies of these institutions to 'fight the struggle from within', becoming femocrats. As they set off to work, Women in Development (WID) as an approach to 'integrate women into development' was popularized internationally. Ideally feminist activism, Women's Studies and femocrats should feed and complement each other, although in practice this is not always the case.

Particularly since the mid-1980s, Women's Studies and life experience have pointed to a continued overall deterioration of women's condition, situation and quality of life. Wars and famine persist. The world economy leaps from crisis to worse crisis. The International Monetary Fund and the World Bank imposed structural adjustment programmes on Latin America, the Caribbean, Africa, Asia and the Pacific (the LACAAP countries), programmes which have had devastating effects on the poor generally and women specifically. Gender violence escalates and women are brutalized in various ways. Male-biased development continues to make the world unsafe to live in, due to environmental degradation and the imposition of harmful hormonal substances to control women's bodies and sexuality. Women and men continue their struggles for better life but it has become clear that strategies hitherto adopted were fallacious.

The critique of WID programmes, with their strategy of 'Integration' (see for instance Lycklama, 1987), led to the exploration of the concept 'gender', hitherto in usage mainly in anthropological studies. Moving away from an analysis of women's oppression, which led largely to separatism in political organization as well as in efforts to put women on the agenda of development, gender as an analytical tool encourages an understanding of women's subordination, oppression, exploitation and resistance thereto, which recognizes women and men (and children) in relation to each other and to society. Furthermore, an holistic gender analysis situates this relation within political, economic, social, cultural and cognitive structures as manifested in institutions and processes over time and space. So an understanding of how societies, institutions and ideologies construct or define and are defined by gender relations, not simply as a process leading to varied but equal positions and roles, but as a process which results in relations of power where women are subordinated, may lead to the development and sharpening of more holistic strategies for transformation. If guided by revolutionary visions, this holistic conceptualization of gender may also lead to more efficient ways of organizing and struggling against patriarchal and other forms of domination. For such strategies to be realistic and achievable, it is crucial that they are informed by a gender analysis which recognizes commonalities and differences between and among (groups of) women and men, emanating from their specific locations within a multiplicity of contexts, relations and factors – North/South, national, race, class, religion, space, sexuality, disability, age and so on – which contribute to our identities.

As femocrats and others identified the systemic gender bias which plagues the development industry at all its stages, it was not difficult to recall the once most common activity of feminist movement: consciousness raising. The need for raising gender consciousness was translated in this context into training. Having become much formalized by now, WGD training, named 'gender training' by Western schools of thought, is far from being homogeneous. It can be distinguished from academic Women's Studies and Gender Studies in that it is aimed primarily at development practitioners, lasts anything from a few hours to several weeks and takes place at the workplace or at institutes, universities and other venues of retreat. The content, methods and procedures are directed towards raising gender awareness or, as the jargon goes, to 'gender sensitize' participants. This kind of training usually falls within the domain of femocrats. They may deliver the training themselves, or, as is increasingly the case, commission others to do so. Arguably they also wield power mainly by controlling and allocating the finances for this activity to those seeking sponsorships and to those financially working within projects and programmes under the auspices of these femocrats and their institutions.

This is the context within which I understand training on WGD to have emerged as one of the many strategies to combat patriarchy and as a clearly political agenda, which occurred through visioning and revisioning feminism and relocating venues of education for critical political consciousness. Why then is mainstream 'gender training' so predominantly depoliticized? Why has it become so technicist? Why is it geared so much to reform rather than to transformation?

The questions I raise here arise as much from lived experience as from interaction with those involved in training and learning in aspects of Women, Gender and Development internationally. A 'gender trainers' workshop held in Amsterdam in 1993 provided a wonderful opportunity as it brought together more than forty trainers from all over the world. Networks and friendships were initiated or strengthened. Through glimpses of impressive work presented, discussions held, interaction with fellow participants and sheer observation, both by what was and what was not addressed, it evoked and confirmed many political, ethical and methodological questions over which I continue to ponder.

The workshop is mentioned here not because of its uniqueness. On the contrary, it is actually a good example of common practice, treating 'gender training' and relations among trainers and between them and participants as if the whole terrain was outside the sphere of challenging subordination. Our behaviour towards each other emulates hierarchical and patriarchal ways of organizing and relating, while we easily shy away from challenging both our-selves and others. It seems much more comfortable, *at face value*, to go along with the generalized, simplistic notion of global sisterhood based on the belief that *all women are oppressed*. In the long run, however, as the Amsterdam and other experiences demonstrate, this often goes with a great deal of pain for those whose political consciousness and practice centre around challenging these politics of domination wherever and however they surface. If we are to learn, to advance and to grow and if we are to practise what we preach, we ought to remove the veil cast over these issues.

A mobilization slogan borrowed by the feminist movement from the Western student movement of the 1960s, 'the personal is political', has been used in Women's Studies to validate the study of women's subjective experi-ence and gained academic credibility (McNeil, 1992). It seems to me that a further very necessary step is a serious perusal of (inter)personal politics within the Women's Studies profession generally. Though here I concentrate on 'gender training', a branch of Women's Studies, the perusal is as imperative for all branches and areas of feminist study and praxis. I question the educa-tors and the process itself. Let me take a leaf from the above-mentioned workshop.

About the only common factor between the women and the two African men participating was our involvement with training whose subject was under-stood as *gender*. Age, class, race, ethnicity, nationality, gender, space, aca-demic background and discipline, profession and sexual orientation were among the many factors, in various dialectical combinations, which defined difference between and among the group. Participating in a workshop to-gether with people means entering into a relationship with them. Once this happens the multiplicity of identities also spells out power and its dynamics. In itself power is not a negative factor: what is crucial is how it is exercised. Some dynamics remain vivid in my mind. First, some of the women worked for funding organizations and pursued this interest in several hegemonic and patronizing ways during the conference. Although their actions might have been well intended, it turned out that they were largely experienced and interpreted quite negatively by many of the LACAAP women.

Second, on the very first day we were informed by the organizers that the working groups would be divided according to continents. At the onset, some in the 'North America and Europe' group raised an objection to the name. It was argued that although the women in that group are based in North America and Europe, their work was international, therefore they called themselves 'the global' group. The obvious political insensitivity and supremacist but false assumptions of this label were left unchallenged, but were certainly discussed in the corridors from then on.

Why were these women so uncomfortable with being associated with these geographic regions? Is it really true, as was implied, that only North American and Western European trainers work globally? Some of the Latinas, for instance, were currently based in the United States but were comfortable to have been placed in the 'Latin America and the Caribbean' group. I, for one, am not confined to one continent, considering my job, consultancies and activism, but I was happy to be classified under my home continent, Africa. Was the historic North/South power dynamic at play? Was it racism? Was it resistance against imposed identities, labelling? But if so, why would the objection be raised only in relation to one group rather than generally? Was the power of naming being exercised? I collaborated in this imperialist and neo-colonialist tendency by my silence, albeit with as much pain as I knew when I was once a wife who endured marital rape and all sorts of abuse, knowingly, but only because I had not yet found a strategy to say 'no' effectively. Then patriarchy had silenced me, as I later discovered it had done to many of us. What silenced me (us) in Amsterdam? Have we become afraid to face head on the subtle racism and other forms of domination rampant in these relations? Have we become weary of being labelled spoilers, that mechanism used so often to silence us while the dominant forces continue without losing any sleep over these matters?

Third, reflecting common North/South relations, the North took this opportunity to attempt – not always successfully – to use women of the South as sources of data for their current or forthcoming missions and consultancies. There is something about this which makes it difficult to swallow and pretend it is mutual exchange 'between sisters', when not even a feeble attempt at consciously forging political sisterhood is evident. Of the white Northerner women who approached me in their attempt to suck information out of me (and I later learned many others were also approached), none acknowledged difference and relative power and our disparate locations on the convergence of various forms of domination and subordination. Whiteness as an identity which comes with masses of access, privilege and power was not part of our repertoire. Neither was any exploration of how we could collaborate; no, we were informants as usual. Could any of them offer to give up their consultancies and pass them on to the Southerners, now that they might have found out that there are also capable Black and other 'non-white' indigens out there struggling for (political, economic and professional) survival in a competitive world where the playing field favours the North, the white and the haves? Information as power! I have recently encountered some dynamics with varying detail but similar implications at the Portsmouth Women's Studies conference. This struggle is indeed international and it continues.

It must not be imagined either that all was a bed of roses within groups at the Amsterdam workshop. Certainly, with the African group, because of the very silence placed on political and controversial issues, rapport remained a reality only in dreams. This group mirrored and acted out the publicly silenced political differences, diversity and divisions which characterized the conference overall. Issues such as who and what decides the agenda on activities and 'initiatives': are they donor driven and Western determined? Who represents whom, who speaks for whom? The time old black/white and North/South relationships underlined the difference of opinion and political perception which compelled us South Africans (one black, one white) to abstain from the post-conference programme of action adopted by the rest of the group.

Fellow Africans could not understand why we were not eager to support the proposal to organize a regional gender trainers' workshop modelled on the current one, as suggested by the organizers at the start of the workshop, especially as the donors had already indicated their eagerness to fund the effort. Colleagues were more concerned with writing a proposal before leaving Amsterdam and with our allocating ourselves as country or sub-regional representatives for the regional workshop. We, on the other hand, needed time to consult in Southern Africa and link up with ongoing local initiatives. It was not correct for us to be self-appointed representatives. We found it more important to openly discuss the issues which remained hushed up. Which people had been invited to this conference and why? What kind of organizational and institutional base did the participants come from? What was the ethos? Why did some things proceed in the way they did and how could we approach the organizers about this? What is 'gender training' and therefore who would be potential members of such a network? What would be its political culture in the making? Merely being African was not enough. There were important prerequisite political questions that needed addressing. We had not even begun to name, acknowledge and deal with the differences among us. Commonality of interest was assumed. A special meeting arranged as a result of our queries was instead devoted to charming a donor: a delaying or silencing tactic? The issues were never addressed. Subsequently, we were lobbied endlessly, but not on the basis of the group's refusal to give attention to our concerns. We were asked to endorse the final proposal 'because it would be a shame for us Africans to be seen as divided as often happens in international forums'.

The irony was that the very issues of race, power, access and representation of South Africa at international forums such as this one, and our differing interpretation of empowerment and affirmative action, had initially been the source of some tension between us South Africans. Perhaps that explains why the two of us were among those thirsty for information and an explanation of the invitation criteria. Thanks to mutual dissatisfaction with the group process and to shared (at least in this regard) political motivation, this was ultimately aired between us, an important step as the questions attract no easy answers. Although naming is therapeutic, it was equally painful for both of us. I respect my compatriot for admitting that she was hesitant in the Africa group because she was conscious not only of being white, but also of being a white South African among a group of all-Black Africans. I had begun to wonder why the questioning and querying was left to me, while she played only an uncaucused and therefore sometimes irritating supporting role.

The dynamics between us and the relevance of the debate need to be put in context beyond the Amsterdam workshop. It is common practice in progressive politics in South Africa, thanks to the rhetoric of non-racialism, to treat gender relations without linking them dialectically to 'race'. The most recent relevant example is an article reporting on a 'gender training' workshop conducted by the Centre for Adult Continuing Education (CACE) (Benjamin and Walters, 1994). Although this article was written to demonstrate the 'centrality of "power" and "resistance" for gender trainers', it also conjures up similar questions which are not necessarily the concern of the authors, but which I, nonetheless, find central to discussions on power relations in 'gender training' and the politics thereof and also to an analysis of the scenes described in this article.

Scene one describes an abortive attempt of a naïve trainer to define 'gender' at a 'gender training' workshop for academics, a failure which spells the demise of the workshop. It is interesting that the authors found this the only important moment to name the race of those involved in this educational exercise. And only two are named: the trainer, the 'young Black woman' who cannot tell 'what social theory informs her theoretical position', and one of the participants, the Black man who is the first to raise this question. What is the significance of the challenging participant being identified as Black? We are not told. What about the youth, blackness and womanness of the trainer? No analytical light is thrown in this direction, even though the central thesis of the article is to educate us on 'power', and 'resistance'. I wonder whether other factors qualifying her identity beyond these three might have been equally or more significant. For instance her academic and professional background and experience which would have gone some way towards preparing her for her task – or, in this case, her ordeal.

The fourth scene is a planning meeting (for 'gender training') between four people identified only by name and gender: three women and a man who is further identified by the educational title 'Dr'. The meeting is tense with power games, which incidentally are not addressed, while the individuals manoeuvre to avoid conflict. It is a pity not more detail is given on individual background and identity which would help us pinpoint the baggage that each of the trainers is bringing in. Nor are we informed of the institutional background or the reasons why they are lumped together in a painfully malfunctioning foursome – an experience all too familiar to me. Instead, the authors simplistically analyse this as the different ways in which individuals exercise power and resistance and as a manifestation of accommodation within gender relations. Whatever social theory informs the conception of 'power' and of 'gender relations' in a case like this and as analysed by these authors is a far cry from holism and from the feminist politic which emphasizes acknowledgement of difference and which advocates the challenging of hierarchies.

In a South Africa with such historically deep-rooted divisions, multiple and confused identities, naming, validation and acknowledgement are imperative. It is important to diagnose the problem and acknowledge the manifestations of exercised power and its dynamism. As trainers, we cannot be taken to have attitudes and attributes that are taken as given and therefore static. Not only are we 'not outside the gender relations we are seeking to change', as the article correctly points out, but we also have the responsibility to take initiatives to learn and grow, to commit ourselves to transformatory change. Such commitment to combat patriarchal and other forms of oppression should not only be embedded in what we teach and facilitate others to learn, but is also equally important in our relationships, in the way we consistently and constructively challenge each other and ourselves. This can be made possible by looking at power *also* in its more complex, institutionalized and collective and historical dynamics and at (individual and group) identities as they are dynamically and socially constructed and defined over time and space, in the process compounding power relations. For if we hope to change the world, all its levels need to be taken into account, complex as they may be. This is as true for South Africa as it is for anywhere else in the world.

The challenge that remains is to work out how to go beyond naming and acknowledging difference, towards working together within transparent relations. I feel white and Western women (and men) still have to identify and acknowledge their whiteness as well as personal racism (within the context of institutionalized racism) to themselves and those to whom they relate. In my experience it is too easy for them to literally rush to mention class when one tries to tackle white privilege. Yes class, among many other factors, is important and certainly with the fast-growing Black middle class who in a sense have no role models, as this has for centuries been an overwhelmingly white phenomenon (with a culture certainly not in the interest of progress to mimic), we indeed have to discuss and problematize class within Black communities and among Black and white women. However, we also have to take note that historically in South and Southern Africa, class has tended to blend with race in the construction of gender as a result of deliberate colonial and apartheid policies; and of the conjuncture of these with patriarchal culture and subcultures of all race, national and ethnic groups. Although imposed, apartheid State categories of 'race' which range in hierarchical order of power and privilege and, absurd as they may be deemed, permeate social (including gender) relations. The advent of an election cannot make this reality magically disappear. This is not to underplay the fact that, as a Black woman, I will continue to work on my historically created prejudice, which is not the same as institutionalized racism.

It was not until the last day of the week-long encounter at the Amsterdam workshop that some LACAAP participants were brave enough to field some salient concerns which had accumulated but been swept under the carpet since day one. This was despite the fact that some of these concerns had for days been pasted on the board where participants had been daily invited to broadcast their feelings and impressions. What was to be an evaluation session turned into an emotional encounter as tears of frustration, pain, relief and solidarity rolled down some cheeks and stuck in some throats. In the event this could only be a process of *airing* rather than the much-needed *working out* of contentious and controversial issues. Let's hope the lessons will be remembered.

One of the most disturbing aspects of dominant 'gender training' is the utter refusal and lack of responsibility in adhering to any ethics and a complete disregard of the ethical questions which have been debated, negotiated and by now broadly established within Women's Studies. With the exception of work by, or made popular by, those turned into gurus, people's work is often used without any acknowledgement. Plenty of in-house published training manuals and policy documents excerpt and rephrase chunks without any reference to the original. Some of these reflect no critical thinking, only recycling, even merely substituting newly fashionable terms (such as gender, gender-planning, practical and strategic gender needs) for those perceived to be outmoded (women, WID). Although it does not make it any the less unethical, most people in this field will easily recognize work that has become a popular standard text when it is unacknowledged. What usually happens is that, for many reasons, Black and LACAAP women often share ideas and methods created from their experience and knowledge, which have either not been written at all or which remain unpublished. These are routinely appropriated, never to be acknowledged. I have participated in many so-called sharing or brainstorming encounters with many (white, white-identified and other) colleagues and found no exchange of ideas, but systematic grilling and sucking followed almost invariably by appropriation. Sharing is always beneficial and we all grow from it. But I have witnessed my own thoughts, arguments and related creative work, over which I sweated for many a sleepless night, being repeated in my presence without even a wink in my direction. Instead of being taken in the spirit of constructive criticism, my queries have been met with dishonesty, ridicule, even threats where power permitted ('you cannot work in a team!' instead of 'you do not let me get away with appropriating your work'). Is it so difficult to admit we are all learning from each other? Recently, I have even been told that my personal lecture notes, designs and thoughts are institutional property. Are Western institutions regressing to slavery or have I just simply been blind, naïve and too trusting of humanity!?

For years, Black (and some white) women have been writing texts of protest against the non-validation of Black women's writing in publishing and the academy, where white supremacist, Eurocentric beliefs about knowledge and its production dominate. It is appalling to discover that the field of 'gender training' is also dominated by practices that invisibilize and make us out as less than human.

Shakespeare once observed that 'some are born great, some achieve greatness, and some have greatness thrust upon them'. It is rare to find anyone getting away with calling themselves political scientists if they are politicians, political activists or any other functionary within the area of politics. So for other disciplines. If they do, they are immediately called to order, denounced or punished. WID or GAD (Gender and Development) are the only specializations I know where many people become experts and/or 'gender trainers' only by having the title bestowed upon them by their employers or by themselves, without necessarily undergoing any relevant (formal or informal) extensive studies and/or research. Many have isolated themselves from feminist or any other activism which could enrich and ground their growing knowledge. Unfortunately, this contributes to the lack of credibility and validation of the struggle for women's emancipation, Women's Studies and 'gender training' specifically. Understandably but not excusably, some people have to, hopefully at least initially, mostly bluff their way out as often the appointment does not go with affording space and time for relevant study. Least of all is there ever a programme of deliberate political education. At best, such trainers concentrate on learning the technical side of training, without equipping themselves with feminist theories, debates and methodology which, in these circles, are often contemptuously referred to as academic and, therefore, irrelevant to themselves and their work. I wonder where those described in the CACE scenes would fit.

Consciousness-raising served a purpose but eventually reached a cul de sac in the women's movement. Trainers need to move on from consciousness raising or 'gender-sensitizing' to facilitating the mapping-out of short- and long-term strategies for transformation, beginning from the self to the organizational, contextual and the global: holism. With such a methodology, frustrations (such as those detailed in the CACE article) are reduced to a minimum. A few frameworks which have been developed in the North (including Moser, 1989; the 'USAID', also known as 'the Harvard model' championed by Overholt *et al.*, 1985, and their adaptations) are now being globalized and applied without respect to context. They are popularized and sometimes made imperative by funding agencies and the development industry, a move which undoubtedly thwarts creativity and discourages development. They are seldom subjected to theoretical and political interrogation but, rather commonly, they are evoked and sanctified. This freezing of a political issue of male domination, of people's life and struggle, into techniques, can only serve short-sighted reformism and deliver to patriarchy not even a dent.

At a poetry reading, Maya Angelo, talking about self-love, quoted an African saying that warns us to 'be suspicious of a naked man who offers a shirt'. This is pertinent to the discussion about trainers and our institutional bases. In the context within which we operate, WGD training has become another neo-colonial manifestation. Most of these courses are specifically developed for women (and when we are lucky, some men) of the LACAAP countries, whether they take place in the countries themselves or in Europe. Some also attract some European development consultants and others similarly engaged. A few are planned for Northern organizations servicing the South. In itself it is a noble idea to offer such opportunities. However, it bothers me that in these very institutions within which the training service emanates, race and gender relations leave much to be desired. Whatever happened to the old saying that charity beings at home? Why do Western institutions believe that the South has to be 'civilized' and forget at the same time to sweep their own verandas? The result of this institutional shortcoming is that critically conscious trainers who facilitate an holistic and challenging approach to the understanding of patriarchal relations and the social, economic, political and cultural contexts of development, face increasing time pressure as we compete against gender technicians. The patriarchal bias of the powers that be combines with pressures emanating from the current economic crisis to leave very little room for negotiation with unsympathetic (to transformation) institutions. Quantity is prioritized to the disregard of the quality offered to participants. Hence, preference is given to 'trainers' who treat 'gender' technically and do not threaten anyone by posing political, ideological and attitudinal questions.

The mushrooming of what I term 'gender technicians' is a worrying development. These are 'gender trainers' concentrating on acquiring (and appropriating) training tools – methods, techniques and so on – with little if any encouragement and effort to search for an understanding of the complexities and nuances of patriarchal domination and its intimate relationship with other forms of domination. Commitment to feminist politics, gender politics or the politics of transformation is another strikingly wanting aspect.

It should be of concern that a lot of this 'gender training' is a far cry from the ideals of education being a tool and process of liberation, 'the practice of freedom' advocated by Paulo Freire in his seminal *pedagogy of the oppressed*. It is not all 'gender training' that is geared to developing a critical consciousness: some of it clearly serves to preserve the *status quo*. It is not always sympathetic to ideals of a transformation of society from *all* forms of domination, oppression and exploitation, without which the goal of emancipation cannot be achieved. Situated within the relations of the development industry, relations within 'gender training' tend to reproduce rather than challenge domination. This is despite the fact that Women's Studies, the general category under which WGD training should fall, purportedly emanates from the feminist movement. Yet this should not come as a surprise since the women's movement cannot claim homogeneity: many streams flow into this massive river. It is logical (albeit a pity?), therefore, that the form, content, methodology and relations within this fast-growing river vary widely. But it is a big failure on the part of feminist activists, particularly those in Women's Studies and Development Studies, that the field is dominated by mainstream *status quo* adherents, women and some men, who aim narrowly, if at all, at cosmetic reform. Now is the time to face the challenge.

Note

Appreciative acknowledgement to Mary Maynard and the editors of *Agenda* for forcing me out of the joys, pains and depression of the election fever into completing the first draft of this article. What therapy! Mary, thanks again for your patience.

References

BENJAMIN, L. and WALTERS, S. (1994) '"Power" and "resistance" for gender training', *Agenda*, 22.

LYCKLAMA A NIJEHOLT, G. (1987) 'The fallacy of integration: The UN strategy of integating women revisited', *Netherlands Review of Development Studies*, 1 (87).

McNEIL, M. (1992) 'Pedagogical praxis and problems: Reflections on teaching about gender relations', in HINDS, H., PHOENIX, A. and STACEY, J. (Eds) *Working Out: New Directions in Women's Studies*, London, Falmer Press, pp. 18–28.

MOSER, C. O. N. (1989) 'Gender planning in the Third World: Meeting practical and strategic gender needs', *World Development*, 17 (11), pp. 1799–825.

OVERHOLT C., ANDERSON, M. B., CLOUD, K. and AUSTIN, J. E. (Eds) (1985) *Gender Roles in Development Projects: A Case Book*, West Hartford, Connecticut, Kumarian Press.

Further Reading

(charles), HELEN (1992) '"Whiteness" – the relevance of politically colouring the "non"', in HINDS, H., PHOENIX, A. and STACEY, J. (Eds) *Working Out: New directions for Women's Studies*, Falmer Press, London, pp. 29–35.

FREIRE, P. (1970, repr. 1985) *Pedagogy of the Oppressed*, Harmondsworth, Penguin.

FREIRE, P. (1969) *Education for Critical Conscience*, Santiago, Institute for Agricultural Reform, Continuum Publishing Co.

HINDS, H., PHOENIX, A. and STACEY, J. (Eds) (1992) *Working Out: New Directions for Women's Studies*, London, Falmer Press.

HOOKS, BELL (1989) *Talking Back, Thinking Feminist, Thinking Black*, London, Sheba Feminist Press.

Chapter 4

The Political and the Personal: Women's Writing in China in the 1980s

Delia Davin

The end of the 1970s and the decade of the 1980s in China saw a flowering of the literature of social criticism. Prominent in this writing was fiction by women concerned with issues such as love, courtship and marriage, abortion, divorce, negative attitudes to single and divorced women and the conflict between the demands of family and work. In this chapter I show how these voices can give us an understanding of the problems women in China faced at that time, or at least of how women intellectuals saw their problems. First, however, I explain something of the background to the literature of social criticism in China.

Chinese Intellectuals and the Literature of Social Criticism

For most of China's long history, culture-bearers and knowledge-bearers have worked for and supported the State, or at least aspired to do so. The same is true of China's modern intellectuals. The government of imperial China was staffed by the Confucian literati, the main educated group, whose whole training inclined them towards the maintenance of the *status quo*. There was some tradition of dissent; if a scholar felt that the State had violated some Confucian norm he had a duty, in theory at least, to remonstrate with the government but did so at his own risk. Neither law nor custom guaranteed his personal security (Goldman, 1981, p. 3). From the late nineteenth century Chinese intellectuals have felt and been weighed down by a sense of responsibility for China (Goldman, 1981; Goldman, Cheek and Hamrin, 1987; Link, 1992). They associated China's weakness as a nation, its many defeats and humiliations, the infringements of its sovereignty and the concessions it was forced to make with the weakness of its social and political institutions. A major project for Chinese intellectuals and writers since this time has been to answer the question, 'Whither China?'; to diagnose the disease from which Chinese society is suffering and to propose a cure.

This project produced a wealth of literature exposing and criticizing the bleak side of Chinese society throughout the first half of the twentieth century, most notably in the aftermath of the May Fourth Movement in the 1920s when an eclectic cultural movement sought to transform and modernize China (Schwarcz, 1986). Writers attacked targets such as inequality, social injustice and the oppression of the individual, especially the female, under the Chinese family system. They exposed the tragedies caused by poverty, ignorance and corruption. Issues of special relevance to women, such as the treatment of daughters and wives, footbinding, arranged marriages and the right of women to study received considerable attention in this era from both male and female writers. Improvements in women's education, health and status were seen as essential to 'modernization' and, in keeping with the social-Darwinist notions influential at the time, 'essential to the survival of the Chinese race'. A concern with such matters was therefore not exclusive to feminism, but very much part of the nationalist project (Dikötter, 1995).

Many writers of the literature of social criticism were on the left, yet it was a tradition that encountered great difficulties under communist rule (Goldman, 1967, 1981). It became muted as the literary establishment of the People's Republic strove to establish the identity of China's interests with those of the Party and the State. If it could get this accepted, then it could insist that criticism of the new society established by the Party was both anti-socialist and unpatriotic. There was still room for literature that criticized the feudal past or problems inherited from the past, which might include issues like arranged marriage or child-brides, but it was all too easy to be accused of divisive or bourgeois feminism, of lacking class feeling or of promoting bourgeois romanticism in dealing with such subjects. Writers such as Ding Ling and Zong Pu were early accused of such crimes (Benton and Hunter, 1996; Goldman, 1967; Jenner, 1983).

Love, marriage and the private sphere tended increasingly to be regarded as inappropriate or even incorrect if promoted as central themes for socialist literature. They could be used as secondary themes, but usually in order to show the triumph of public duty or the new communist morality over private feeling. By the time of the Cultural Revolution (1966–1976), the personal had always to be dealt with in relation to the political and to be shown as subordinate. Thus one could describe courtship if one showed the hero or heroine putting the demands of the collectivization campaign before those of the relationship (see, for example, Hao Ran, *Bright Sunny Skies* and other novels by the same author). Similarly, the sorrow of separation from loved ones might be an acceptable subject if the protagonist were shown accepting it cheerfully in order to take up a revolutionary task at the other end of the country.

With the rejection of the ideology of the Cultural Revolution following Mao's death in 1976, a new literature emerged that offered a re-evaluation of the policies of the Cultural Revolution. Gradually, as writers began to extend their criticism of the society of the People's Republic backwards to the period before the Cultural Revolution and forwards to the present and to touch on still forbidden areas like the Chinese Gulag, they began once more to incur official wrath. In the 1983–1984 campaign against 'spiritual pollution', in the 1987 campaign against bourgeois liberalism and after the massacre that suppressed the student demonstrations of June 1989, writers were under particularly heavy pressure. Nonetheless, by the standards of the past, the writers of the 1980s had unprecedented freedom to look critically at all social issues, including women's issues. Women writers have been to the fore in doing this.

Women were severely under-represented among those officially recognized as writers in the 1980s. They made up only one in ten of the members of the Writers' Association. However, they were prominent among those reclaiming personal matters as a proper subject for creative writing and some of the women writers I discuss here were among the most popular and successful in their time.

Although the readers of this literature were probably urban people with some secondary education, they were not only intellectuals. Neither reading matter nor audience was as highly segmented in China at the beginning of the 1980s as it had become by the end of the decade. The sort of middlebrow fiction I discuss here treated themes of concern to most urban people in a serious but easily accessible way. Short stories, novellas and reportage reached their audiences first through the many fiction magazines that were eagerly snatched up as they reached the stalls. Longer pieces were serialized and many later also became available in book form. Such fiction now has a much reduced market as it has to compete with an increasingly varied television output, translations, imports from Hongkong and Taiwan and a huge variety of pulp publications primarily concerned with sex, violence and the personal lives of famous Chinese. In its time, however, it had much influence and people who had been young during the Cultural Revolution felt it spoke for them. Below, I discuss theme by theme the work of some women writers who wrote about personal issues.

Love, Marriage and Divorce

A striking characteristic of post-reform literature is that in it, love and marriage have returned to centre stage. Two of the most famous stories of the period, Zhang Jie's 'Love Must Not Be Forgotten' (1979) and Zhang Kangkang's 'The Right to Love' (1979), make explicit claims about the pre-eminence of love and the damaging effects of denying it. 'Love Must Not Be Forgotten' is narrated by a woman whose divorced mother was passionately in love for many years with a married man. He returned her devotion, but they both felt that they could never act on their feelings: divorce for such reasons was strongly disapproved both in old China and under the new political morality.

When she learns of her mother's history, the daughter resolves to remain single unless she meets someone she can marry for love. The novella was highly controversial because it insisted that political considerations should not always take precedence over personal life. Critics accused Zhang Jie of undermining public morality by her sympathetic portrayal of extra-marital love (even though it was not consummated) and claimed that it reflected her 'petty-bourgeois mentality'. Only a few years earlier such as accusation might have landed the author in the wilderness but Zhang Jie was not intimidated and continued to publish.

Zhang Jie's next book, *Leaden Wings* (1987), though focusing on industrial management and modernization, again took up the subject of unhappy relationships continued only because those in them fear the public condemnation that a break-up would produce. Out of the six marriages in the book, only one is happy; the others are preserved by couples prepared to pay the price in order to retain their social and economic positions. Zhang Jie's women disappoint more than they inspire. Autumn, the most positive, is a journalist, an idealist, still single because she will not marry without love. She appears to others as a social misfit. Despite her independence and her work, she lacks personal confidence. Zhang Jie allows us to see her as incomplete and wasted. She is not presented as a role model.

Another character, Joy, is a model of traditional female virtue. A widow, she has a hard struggle to bring up her son after her husband's suicide. She is virtuous and passively resigned to her fate – and her death in a tragic accident seems to confirm her status as a victim. Grace and Bamboo, married women of the official class, are typical of the women Zhang Jie loves to hate. They are greedy, selfish and self-righteous: protectors of China's moral and social order that has so privileged them.

Zhang Kangkang's 'The Right to Love' is the story of a sister and brother whose parents, both victims of political persecution, have died. Theirs has been a family which loved Western classical music and played it professionally. The children, called Bei and Mo after Beethoven and Mozart, were taught to play musical instruments when they were very young. However, on his deathbed their father told them that since classical music had brought them nothing but trouble since the onset of the Cultural Revolution, they should give it up. He also urged them to choose politically 'safe' partners. Bei, the daughter, has accepted his admonitions. Life has taught her that love is too dangerous, especially as the one she loves, although only recently rehabilitated, still has dangerously independent ideas. Denying her love for him, she sends him away. She ignores her brother's protest that 'a citizen in a socialist society has the right to love'. It is interesting that Zhang Kangkang gives this line to a man. Self-assertion, she seems to imply, is difficult for everyone in China, but especially for women.

In another early story, 'The Tolling of a Distant Bell' (1980), Zhang Kangkang combines the motif of the denial of love's primacy by an earlier generation with that of the insistence on it now. A boy from an impoverished intellectual's family falls in love with the daughter of a well-to-do official. His widowed mother tries to persuade him to give her up. Only when she meets the official, who also wishes to put a stop to the young people's relationship, does she recognize him as a long-lost love of her own, now grown pompous and dislikeable. The realization persuades her to accept her son's right to decide for himself in love, a right that had been denied to her.

Attitudes to divorce in the People's Republic have long tended to be ambivalent. The marriage law introduced in 1950, by offering both men and women the right to divorce, was said to have made it possible to end many unhappy arranged matches. For a short time, divorce – at least in certain circumstances – was seen as progressive. However, divorce as a common social practice constituted a threat to traditional family values. As the regime became more and more puritan and came increasingly to see the family as a unit that maintained social discipline and order, official attitudes towards divorce changed. It became regarded as undesirable and in practice more difficult to obtain; any increase in divorce rates aroused official concern. Although social and legal changes after the reforms created a somewhat more liberal attitude to divorce and the new marriage law of 1980 made it easier to obtain divorce, divorced people are still frequently treated with suspicion.

Zhang Jie's 'The Ark' (1983) is China's best-known treatment of the fate of women after divorce. Three divorced women live together, gaining some mutual support but despised and discriminated against by society. All three are professionals struggling to fulfil themselves through work, but thwarted by the attitudes of male colleagues and bosses. Liu Quan, who has preserved her looks, is sexually harassed by her boss, while the others are despised at work because they are no longer pretty. They are faced with an underlying assumption that a divorced woman is available and indeed desperate for a man. Perhaps just because of its subject matter, three divorced women living together, which is quite extraordinary in Chinese literature (and would be even more unlikely in life), 'The Ark' has often been described as a feminist work (Honig and Hershatter, 1988, p. 310). However, its author, Zhang Jie, as we see later, has rejected this label.

Single Women

Historically China had a very high marriage rate and the rate is still extremely high in contemporary society. Almost all Chinese will marry at some time in their lives. Far more than in the West, the unmarried are seen as objects of pity and may also be treated as not quite grown up, or less than full members of society.

For approximately seventeen million young urban people sent to live in the countryside during the Cultural Revolution, marriage was often a problem. Many postponed it while they were in the rural areas, fearing that if they married they would be regarded as settled and would be even less likely to be transferred back to the city. When they did begin to trickle back into the urban areas from the 1970s, they tended to be preoccupied with problems of getting residence permits and jobs and improving their education which had been

aborted by the Cultural Revolution. By the time they were ready to start looking for partners many, especially the women, found it difficult to find one. More of the female returnees seem to have been single. It had probably been easier for the young male urbanites to marry in the countryside first because it was acceptable for an educated man to marry a much less educated woman and second because given the patrilocal marriage system in China, they would not necessarily be seen as permanently settled with their wives' families. Single men who did return to the city could pick women of their own age as partners, but could also choose from among younger cohorts. The age range from which female returnees could choose was restricted. Chinese custom meant that they rarely married younger men but men of a generation above them, whose personal lives had been less disrupted by the Cultural Revolution, would have been already married. Women of thirty, or even in their late twenties, might be rejected as 'too old' by their contemporaries.

Many stories reflect the loneliness and sadness of such women, none more vividly than Xu Naijian's 'Because I'm Thirty and Unmarried' (1981). In this story one woman assesses her prospects:

> The penalty for being choosy has come down on us. We're not in a good position and every extra year means a drop in our standards. We can't delay any longer.

Her friend goes to ring a cousin who has been acting as a matchmaker for her. As she stands at the telephone she sees a shop-window advertisement, 'Clearance of Old Stock – Once Only Cut Price Sale'. She reads it as a comment on her position. When they were young, this generation had worn nothing but the uniform of blue or khaki cotton jackets and pants. Now they were supposed to dress up if someone arranged an introduction for them. She feels uncomfortable about doing this and muses,

> At the age when I should have been dressing up I hadn't, and it made me feel strange to be doing it now that my youth was drawing to a close.

The most poignant comment on the plight of the single woman is perhaps 'Irreproachable Conduct', a piece in which an unmarried schoolteacher in her late thirties talks about her life (Zhang Xinxin and Sang Ye, 1986). From a bad class background with a father in Hongkong, she had been victimized during the Cultural Revolution and for years had lived from hand to mouth. She had managed to get to university when she was thirty-one and had then returned to teach in the secondary school where she had studied and taught previously. In common with other employers in China the school only normally gave rooms to married couples; others had to share a dormitory. After a great struggle this woman had finally managed to get her own room and had bought herself a table. Her neighbours reacted with surprise. She was only a single woman, why did she need that? 'Why should they think I would mark homework on my lap for the rest of my life just because I'm not married?' she asks. She wrote to the paper to protest at the terrible way that single women are treated in China. She received some sympathetic letters (from women) and others which admonished her, but almost all were proposals from men. They had read her letter as a lonely hearts advertisement.

She is not a stable person. She comes across as angry and perhaps a hypochondriac.

> I don't want to marry. I've got cirrhosis of the liver, I've had haemorrhages and viral myocarditis. All I want is rights for single people . . . My only fault is that I am different from other people because I haven't married.

The reader is left with the impression of a neurotic woman, but it is clear that the roots of her neurosis are in the treatment she has received from the society around her.

Work and Family

The conflict between the demands of work and family is, predictably, another theme of contemporary women's writing. It is central to the plot of *At Middle Age*, a short novel by Shen Rong that sold over three million copies and was made into a very successful film. It portrays a conscientious woman doctor, Lu, who struggles to reconcile the demands of work and family. She is shown as imbued with superhuman selflessness. For example, when her daughter gets pneumonia, Dr Lu finishes seeing her own patients before going to the kindergarten to collect the child and doesn't consider taking time off work to care for the child herself. Although she is overburdened and stressed, when her husband seems to be finding family burdens too much she suggests that he should move into his Institute and leave her to cope with the children.

Sometimes Dr Lu's dedication to duty seems overdrawn, in a style of characterization rather reminiscent of Cultural Revolution writing. Yet when it first appeared in 1980, *At Middle Age* made an impression partly because it flouted so many of the formulaic rules of the years when literature had 'served politics'. The heroine is an intellectual rather than a worker or a peasant. She and her husband recite the poetry of the poet Petofi to each other and although dedicated to her work she comes from a 'bad' class and is not a Party member. Her foil in the story, the wife of a high Party official, conspicuously lacks proletarian selflessness. She is self-important, smug and secure in the confidence conferred on her by her membership of the privileged Party élite. In a sub-plot another doctor and her husband, unable to endure the harsh living and working conditions in China any longer, are preparing to emigrate. By contrast, Dr Lu works herself into a near-fatal heart attack but recovers, not apparently because her husband sits devotedly at her bedside reading her poetry, nor because her sick child needs her, but because she feels she cannot desert her patients. Perhaps Shen Rong could not allow her to die. A happy ending is often tacked on to works of critical realism in China to protect their authors from the charge of negativism.

At Middle Age is clearly a call to improve the treatment of intellectuals. So hazy are the boundaries between literature and life in China that it was sometimes cited as evidence by those campaigning for better pay and living conditions for professionals. It is less clear that it is a call specifically for women to be treated better. Dr Lu is shown as admirable because she is prepared to accept her role as a self-sacrificing superwoman giving all to her work and family. The story seems innocuous enough, but when it appeared in China it provoked a sharp reaction. Political hardliners condemned its satirical depiction of the 'Marxist-Leninist old lady' and its neutral attitude towards the couple who were 'deserting China' by emigrating. Intellectuals were pleased with its vindication of their role in society. Despite the fact that Dr Lu's real problem was her double burden and her sense of guilt that she could perform neither of her roles satisfactorily, the story was read as drawing attention to the difficulties of all intellectuals rather than to those of professional women.

The younger writer, Zhang Xinxin, was fiercer in her commentaries on the conflicts of family, love and career that beset women. Both in 'On the Same Horizon' (1981) and in 'The Last Harbour' (1983) she writes with great sympathy of a young woman's attempt to have her career accorded the same priority as her husband's. In 'On the Same Horizon', the young wife complains,

> He expects me to love him, but what about me? He wants me to supply the family life he expects to enjoy. But when I've given every-thing up for him I'll not be his intellectual equal any more. Then he'll lose interest in me.

She ends up having an abortion, getting a divorce and enrolling in a drama institute.

Abortion

China's strict population policy has a heavy impact on women, who are caught between pressure from the State which restricts each couple to one or at most two children and families who want more. They may be blamed for giving birth to a daughter by husbands and in-laws who long for a son. They take most responsibility for contraception and when it fails must undergo abortion. Many more women than men are sterilized. The ways in which people's lives and especially women's lives have been affected by population policy have been little raised in fiction. It is a delicate area: the government does not welcome criticism of its strict regulations and any honest treatment of their impact on women's lives might well be read as opposition. Perhaps there is another reason. Strict family limitation has been most difficult for peasants to accept as they want larger families. The lives of rural people are now rarely treated in fiction. Population policy is less an issue for educated urban people, who tend to want smaller families and are the main writers and readers of fiction.

However, abortion has been explored in two hard-hitting stories that movingly describe the way in which patients in abortion clinics are treated. Lu Xin'er's 'The Sun Is Not Out Today' (1987) is set in the waiting-room of a gynaecological department of a major hospital. A notice on the door says, 'No male comrades admitted'. This is a world of female pain, fear and suffering but also of support and confidences. The women rail against their husbands and boyfriends and try to tell each other that the operation will not hurt too much. When an actress is refused an abortion because she has neither a letter of approval from her work unit nor her marriage certificate with her, all the other women urge the nurse to make an exception. The actress wants an abortion, even though her husband would not wish her to have it, because otherwise she will have to give up a role that means everything to her in her career. She goes to get hold of some theatre tickets with which to bribe the nurse. By contrast, the protagonist, Dan Ye, is a single woman who has had an affair with a married man. Although she has come to the clinic in search of an abortion, she changes her mind as she waits and the story ends with her leaving to have the child as a single mother. In practice this is an almost impossible choice in China but is presented here as a woman taking responsibility for her own future.

Tang Min's 'Bearing the Unbearable' is an even harsher indictment of an abortion factory.[1] Although presented as a short story it is rather closer to the sort of piece that one might find in the 'First Person' column in *The Guardian*. The authorial voice makes the claim that:

Fear of pregnancy has become the greatest burden of a woman's emotional life. Married and unmarried women alike live in fear of it. This is a great social question which is not allowed as a social question, for this is a kind of bitterness that the male world will never have to taste.

The development of contraceptives, including the pill, the 'super-technological masterpiece of the modern pharmaceutical industry', has made premarital sex easier and less frightening but cannot eliminate mistakes. And so:

for the various accidents, as well as for illicit and rejected foetuses, there is the other way: 'artificially induced miscarriage'. Today as long as it will reduce the birth rate, many hospitals will perform

ortion on demand for pregnant women, whether they are married
or not. And so, pregnancy and abortion have become just a little
affair of women worth little more than a joke.

The narrator talks of waiting in the waiting-room 'with the lower parts of our
bodies naked for the examination so that the self-image changes, and one
becomes seemingly loathsome and ugly'. In an interesting revelation of status,
the only patient allowed to keep her pants on until she reached the operating
theatre was herself a doctor. The narrator observes that the patients 'took on
the air of convicts awaiting sentence, with hang dog expressions. But at the
same time they were also jostling and trying to get to the front just as if they
were in a vegetable queue.' When finally a patient reaches the nurse she is
asked brusquely 'Is it to pull out a foetus or put in an IUD?'

The operation is extremely painful but the humiliation is worse. When it
is over the narrator goes to look for her husband. We already know she feels
she is lucky to have a partner who is considerate. However, she is enraged to
find him laughing and joking about abortion with a friend in the waiting room
and she slaps his face.

Both these stories are set in a world of women. The female characters
extend each other some solidarity, but authority in all its harshness is represented by doctors and nurses who are all women too.

Until very recently, serious literature in the People's Republic maintained
a firm silence on the subject of sex. In the fiction of the 1980s, there were plenty
of allusions but little explicit detail. This was particularly true of fiction written
by women and the few exceptions are therefore all the more remarkable.

Yu Luojin, in her autobiographical novel, A *Chinese Winter's Tale* (1980)
was concerned above all to commemorate her brother, Yu Luoke, an idealistic
student who was first imprisoned for his ideas and then shot as a counter-
revolutionary in 1970. (He was posthumously rehabilitated in 1977.) In this
book, Yu Luojin provides a picture of the Chinese Gulag in which she la-
boured for several years and of the particular suffering of young women in that
setting. Through her description of the heroine's first experience of sexual
intercourse, in the form of rape by her oafish young husband whom abject
poverty had forced her to marry, she attacks the sexual ignorance in which she
and millions of other Chinese girls were brought up, showing that it leaves
them vulnerable to trauma and misery.

Looking back on her 'first night' she makes an impassioned plea for
rational sex education:

> We learned nothing about sex either from our parents, or from our
> schools. The very mention of the word was something shameful and
> immoral, almost a crime. All of us women are going to experience
> that night so why should it be kept hidden and secret from us? Why
> should a motley collection of men be left to teach us instead, each in
> his own particular fashion?

When this novel first appeared in 1980, all the sexually explicit passages were expurgated and other cuts were made on political grounds. The novel was nonetheless severely criticized. In dealing with the theme of marriage the author was said to have acted as 'the handmaiden of the bourgeoisie' and was accused of 'unhealthy political tendencies' and an 'incorrect literary aesthetic'. In 1985, when a new edition was being prepared, Yu Luojin made a passionate protest against censorship:

> If you must insist on removing this passage I would rather that the book was not published at all. You have all read it with the greatest of interest and have not been poisoned, so why are you worrying about the ordinary reader being 'polluted'? . . . Authors should be allowed to bear responsibility for their work . . . it is truly tragic when an author's rights are not respected. If there is no respect for the author, how can we possibly talk about respecting the reader?

She was ignored. Many of the cuts were restored but the rape scene was still severely bowdlerized. Later that year, Yu Luojin sought political asylum in Germany.

All the writers I have discussed in this article are intellectuals, mostly born in the 1940s or 1950s. They wrote for and about intellectuals and their problems. Their self-identification was very much with educated working women. Despite their backgrounds, or one might say because of them, they had not led sheltered lives. The Cultural Revolution dramatically affected this group. Most of these writers spent long years of deprivation in the countryside, often separated from their families. For the younger ones this meant the disruption of their schooling or a premature end to it. In those years all would have had intimate contact with other social groups. Yet this is not apparent in what they wrote in the 1980s. As they moved from reclaiming for literature the territory of marriage, love and physical appearance (described in other than heroic terms), to a consideration of the problems of divorce, abortion, single motherhood and conflicts between the worlds of the family and that of work, they stayed firmly within the contemporary reality of the Chinese city.

Chinese women's literature of the 1980s was not on the whole explicitly or avowedly feminist although it explored women's issues and exposed and condemned discrimination against women and the gender-based suffering of women in Chinese society. Its writers saw themselves as part of a broader project to base literature on humanistic values. The writing of the early 1980s in particular tended to be Utopian in its treatment of love and marriage. It implied that if people were allowed to run their lives free from political interference, they could find happiness.

Later, writers such as Zhang Jie and Zhang Xinxin began to challenge such views and to present women as victims of structures more profound and more difficult to challenge than the changing policies of the Communist Party.

Nonetheless, these two, like Zhang Kangkang and Shen Rong, all reject the feminist tag. Chinese women seem to have a double sense of unease with the word feminist. First, the accusation of 'bourgeois feminist' lingers on from the Maoist years. Feminists, it was claimed, were concerned only with women's rights, not more broadly with socialist revolution. This misconception is strengthened by the fact that the word most usually used to translate 'feminism' in Chinese is 'nuquanzhuyi' which literally means women's rights-ism. More recently the Western media caricature of a feminist as an unattractive, unfeminine, unlovable, manhating figure of fun has also influenced stereotypes in China. Not surprisingly, this is a particularly unattractive image to writers who belong to a generation who accepted a Maoist uniform when young and feels it had to struggle for the right to 'be feminine'.

Note

1 Tang Min was sentenced to a year in prison in 1990 for having libelled an official in another of her stories.

References

(Citations with minor modifications are to English translations whenever these have been available.)

BENTON, G. and HUNTER, A. (Eds) (1996) *Wild Lily, Prairie Fire: China's Road to Democracy, Yan'an to Tiananmen, 1942–1989*, Princeton University Press, Princeton.

DIKÖTTER, FRANK (1995) *Sex, Culture and Modernity in China*, London, Hurst & Co.

GOLDMAN, MERLE (1967) *Literary Dissent in Communist China*, Cambridge, Mass., Harvard University Press.

GOLDMAN, MERLE (1981) *China's Intellectuals: Advise and Dissent*, Cambridge, Mass., Harvard University Press.

GOLDMAN, MERLE, CHEEK, TIMOTHY and HAMRIN, CAROL LEE (Eds) (1987) *China's Intellectuals and the State: In Search of a New Relationship*, Cambridge, Mass., Harvard University Press.

HAO RAN, *Bright Sunny Skies (Yan Yang Tian)* (1964–1966), vols 1–3, Beijing, People's Literature Publishing House.

HONIG, EMILY and HERSHATTER, GAIL (1988) *Personal Voices: Chinese Women in the 1980s*, Stanford, California, Stanford University Press.

JENNER, W. J. F. (Ed.) (1983) *Fragrant Weeds: Short Stories Once Labelled as Poisonous Weeds*, Hongkong, Joint Publishing Company.

LINK, PERRY (1992) *Evening Chats in Beijing*, New York, W.W. Norton.

LU XIN'ER (1987) 'The Sun is not out Today', in ZHU HONG (selected and translated) (1991) *The Serenity of Whiteness*, New York, Ballatine Books.

SCHWARCZ, VERA (1986) *The Chinese Englightenment: Chinese Intellectuals and the Legacy of the May Fourth Movement*, Berkeley, University of California Press.

SHEN RONG (1987) *At Middle Age*, Beijing, Panda Books. Also included in *Seven Contemporary Chinese Women Writers* (1982) Beijing, Panda Books.

TANG MIN (1989) 'Bearing the unbearable', *China Now*, 128, Spring.

XU NAIJIAN, 'Because I'm Thirty and Unmarried', in ROBERTS, R. A. and KNOX, ANGELA (Eds) (1987) *One Half of the Sky, Selection from Contemporary Women Writers of China*, London, Heinemann.

YU LUOJIN (1986) *A Chinese Winter's Tale*, Renditions, Hong Kong.

ZHANG JIE, 'Love Must Not Be Forgotten' and 'The Ark', both included in *Love Must Not Be Forgotten* (1987) Beijing, Panda Books.

ZHANG JIE (1987) *Leaden Wings*, London, Virago.

ZHANG JIE (1991) *As Long as Nothing Happens, Nothing Will*, New York, Grove Weidenfeld.

ZHANG KANGKANG (1979) 'The Right to Love', in ROBERT, R. A. and KNOX, A. *One Half of the Sky*, London, Heinemann.

ZHANG KANGKANG and MEI JIN, 'The Tolling of a Distant Bell', in DUKE, MICHAEL S. (Ed.) (1984) *Contemporary Chinese Literature: An Anthology of Post-Mao Fiction*, Armonk, M.E. Sharpe.

ZHANG XINXIN (1981) 'On the Same Horizon' ('Zai tongyi diping xianshang'), and (1983) 'The Last Harbour' ('Zuihoude tingpodi') in (1984) *Collected Stories of Zhang Xinxin* (*Zhang Xinxin zhongduanpian xioushuoji*) Sichuan, Sichuan Literature and Arts Publishing House.

ZHANG XINXIN and SANG YE (1986) *Beijing Pen*, People's Publishing House, Shanghai, edited and translated as *Chinese Lives* by JENNER, W. J. F. and DAVIN, DELIA, Harmondsworth, Penguin, 1989.

ZHU HONG (Ed.) (1991) *The Serenity of Whiteness: Stories By and About Women in Contemporary China*, New York, Ballantine Books.

Further Reading

DAVIN, DELIA (1996) 'Chinese women: Media concerns and the politics of reform', in AFSHAR, HALEH (Ed.) *Women and Politics in the Third World*, London, Routledge.

DUKE, MICHAEL, S. (Ed.) (1989) *Modern Chinese Women Writers: Critical Appraisals*, Armonk, M.E. Sharpe.

Chapter 5

Reassessing Representations of Emmeline and Christabel Pankhurst, Militant Feminists in Edwardian Britain: On the Importance of a Knowledge of our Feminist Past[1]

June Purvis

The development of recent interest in women's history in Britain may be traced back to the so-called 'second wave' of the women's movement in the Western world from the late 1960s. As feminists at that time and into the 1970s began to research their foremothers, they found that mainstream history was mainly a male affair, written by men about men's activities in wars, politics, business and administration. Women's history was largely invisible or, if represented, located within sex-stereotypical discussions about the family or the effect of women's paid work on their family roles (Purvis, 1995a, p. 5). Although during the last twenty years or so women's history in Britain has become a booming, scholarly activity,[2] many aspects of our feminist past still remain misrepresented. In particular, this is especially the case with those 'first wave' militant feminists, Mrs Emmeline Pankhurst (1858–1928) and her eldest daughter, Christabel (1880–1958) who founded the Women's Social and Political Union (WSPU) on 10 October 1903 with the expressed aim of fighting for the right of women to enfranchisement on the same terms as it was, or may be, granted to men.

My aims in this chapter are to examine the dominant representations of these two key leaders of the WSPU, to offer an alternative assessment and, finally, in my concluding remarks, to discuss why I think a knowledge of our militant feminist foremothers has relevance for feminists today. But first I give a brief account of the foundation of the WSPU and its political strategies and actions.

'Deeds, Not Words': WSPU Motto

During the 1890s, Dr Richard Pankhurst, his wife Emmeline and their two eldest daughters, Christabel and Sylvia, were active in socialist politics in their home city of Manchester. In 1894, for example, Dr and Mrs Pankhurst joined the newly formed Independent Labour Party (ILP) and their children often accompanied their parents to both political and social events organized by the ILP (Pankhurst, 1931, pp. 119, 128). After the death of Richard, on 5 July 1898, Mrs Pankhurst joined the National Administrative Council of the ILP (Glasier Diaries, entry for 23 July 1898) but became increasingly disillusioned with the lukewarm support (and often hostility) towards women's suffrage shown generally by ILP members. Margaret McMillan (1927, p. 85), active in ILP circles in Bradford, endorsed the offical view when she recollected some years later that the ILP 'was not formed to champion women . . . It was born to make war on capitalism and competition.' Only too aware of the difficulties of trying to push the women's issue centre-stage into such an agenda in a political party where men were in the majority and dominant in policy-making, Mrs Pankhurst resolved that the women should form a Party of their own. Thus on 9 October 1903 she advised a small group of ILP women, mostly wives of socialist men:

> Women, we must do the work ourselves. We must have an independent women's movement. Come to my house tomorrow and we will arrange it! (Pankhurst, 1959, p. 43)

The women who gathered at 42 Nelson Street the next day founded a women-only organization, open to all of their sex in any social class and free from affiliation to any of the political parties of the day. The Women's Social and Political Union, as it was called, adopted the motto 'Deeds, not words' as its guiding principle in the campaign for women's enfranchisement.

From that day until the eve of the outbreak of the First World War in August 1914, when Emmeline Pankhurst called a halt to WSPU agitation, she and Christabel were the acknowledged leaders of the WSPU.[3] During its early years, the WSPU had close links with the ILP, engaging in a range of peaceful activities such as speaking at trade-union meetings and debating societies, organizing deputations to the House of Commons and heckling members of parliament at political meetings by shouting out phrases such as 'When will the government give women the vote?' Often the women were roughly handled at these gatherings and, in the commotion that resulted, they were arrested for creating disturbances. At other times, as Hannah Mitchell (Mitchell, 1968, p. 157) found in her home town of Ashton, local ILP men helped to keep order.

Gradually, however, as the government refused to give women the vote or to recognize imprisoned women as political offenders who should be placed in the more privileged First Division rather than in the Second and Third, more aggressive militant actions were adopted. From 1912, in particular, a small band of guerilla activists, probably about a thousand in number, engaged in widespread window-smashing, placing bombs in empty buildings, arson, vandalizing art treasures, pouring acid on golf courses and destroying mail in letter-boxes. The 'suffragettes' as the members of the 'militant' WSPU were called, in contrast to the law-abiding 'suffragists' of the National Union of

Women's Suffrage Societies (NUWSS) which believed in 'constitutional' reform, were particularly harshly treated after the 1913 Cat and Mouse Act which allowed a prisoner ('mouse') weakened by hunger-striking and forcible-feeding to be released on licence into the community in order to regain their health – only to be rearrested (by the 'Cat') in order to complete the sentence.[4]

Mrs Pankhurst's call on 13 August 1914, the eve of the outbreak of the First World War, to end all militancy must have been greeted with relief by many exhausted militants, as well as by that large number of non-militant WSPU members who might, for example, be newspaper-sellers, typists, sales assistants in WSPU shops and non-active, fee-paying subscribers (Purvis, 1995d, p. 920). In 1918, about eight and a half million women became eligible to vote under the Representation of the People Act which gave the vote to women over thirty years of age if they were householders, wives of householders, occupiers of property with an annual rent of £5 or more, or graduates of British universities (Atkinson, 1988, p. 39; Rosen, 1974, p. 266). Women had to wait until 2 July 1928 to be granted the vote on equal terms with men, at the age of twenty-one. By a cruel twist of fate, however, Mrs Pankhurst had died some weeks earlier, on 14 June. By this time, too, the enfranchisement of women on equal terms with men meant less to Christabel than it might have done: she had lost interest in the women's movement and become a Seventh Day Adventist, preaching the second coming of Christ. She died on 13 February 1958 in California where she lived for the last twenty years of her life.

Representations of Emmeline and Christabel Pankhurst

Although Emmeline and Christabel Pankhurst were represented in a wide variety of cultural forms during their years in the WSPU, such as in songs, drama, poetry, fiction, on postcards, badges, in paintings and cartoons,[5] in this chapter I concentrate on the ways in which they have been represented by historians in written texts.

Observers and participants of the women's suffrage movement, as well as social commentators, wrote histories of the events. Some of the earliest accounts include those by W. Lyon Blease (1910), Sylvia Pankhurst (1911), Millicent Garrett Fawcett (1912), Bertha Mason (1912), Ethel Snowden (1913) and A. E. Metcalfe (1917). However, the most popular and widely read suffrage histories first appeared in 1928 and 1931 respectively, namely Ray Strachey's *'The Cause': A Short History of the Women's Movement in Great Britain* and Sylvia Pankhust's *The Suffragette Movement, An Intimate Account of Persons and Ideals*. Both books were subequently reprinted in paperback editions in the 1970s and 1980s by Virago, a major feminist publishing house, and have consequently been widely read and widely cited. These two texts, written from differing political perspectives which we may broadly classify as liberal feminist and socialist feminist,[6] helped to establish a dominant narrative about the Pankhurst leaders that at best, ignored their women-centred approach to politics and, at worst, misrepresented their views.

Liberal Feminist Influences

Ray Strachey had been a keen supporter of the so-called 'constitutional', non-militant NUWSS.[7] A follower of Mrs Fawcett's liberal feminist, reformist approach to women's suffrage, Strachey endorses her mentor's emphasis on 'the unity of interests' between men and women rather than any analysis based on the 'divisive consequences of politics based on gender' (Dodd, 1990, p. 131). Thus, Strachey points out (1928, p. 307), Mrs Fawcett and the NUWSS did not see their work 'as an attack upon men, but rather as a reform for the good of all, and the next step in human progress'. The admired Mrs Fawcett is presented as a calm, rational, quiet, patient and worthy leader who, when her followers grew too emphatic or too much discouraged, 'rebuked them gently enough but very firmly' (ibid., p. 308).

In contrast, the WSPU, Mrs Pankhurst and Christabel are judged harshly. The leaders of the WSPU, claims Strachey (1928, p. 310) brushed aside the 'normal niceties of procedure' and did not care whom they 'shocked and antagonised . . . nor was democracy much to their taste'. Talk of persuasion was laughed at since they believed in 'moral violence'. With such an 'aggressive and headlong' approach they 'deliberately put themselves in the position of outlaws dogged by the police'. Understandably, Strachey (1928, p. 311) continues, the WSPU attracted to its ranks not only those of extreme opinions, but also those whose natural inclination was towards drama, hero-worship and self-surrender. The organization of the WSPU was also inadequate since no thorough membership or financial records were kept. Indeed:

> All was action! action! As fast as money came in it went out again, spent on flags and banners, leaflets, organisers, meetings, parades, bands, shows, ribbons, drums or even bombs – anything, everything with which to made a noise and a stir, and keep enthusiasm burning and the Cause shining in the public eye. (Strachey, 1928, p. 311)

As Dodd (1990) persuasively argues, Strachey uses the political vocabulary of Liberalism to position the NUWSS and Mrs Fawcett as the 'rational' wing of the women's movement that was responsible for the partial enfranchisement of women in 1918 and their full enfranchisement, on equal terms with men, in 1928. The WSPU and the Pankhursts, on the other hand, are cast out 'of the making of women's history because of their reckless activity, their passion for change, their angry propaganda and their autocratic organisation' (Dodd, 1990, p. 134).

The binary oppositions that Strachey employs of constitutional/militant, civilized/uncivilized, democratic/autocratic and rational/irrational helped to establish a framework within which the majority of the future accounts of the lives of the Pankhurst leaders were placed by liberal historians, with the notable exceptions of Antonia Raeburn (1973) and Olive Banks (1985), and especially so by influential liberal male historians such as George Dangerfield (1966), David Mitchell (1966, 1967, 1977) and Brian Harrison (1982, 1987).[8]

Dangerfield's *The Strange Death of Liberal England* first appeared in 1935 and was reprinted at least up to 1972. Not unsurprisingly, since he discusses the suffragette movement as one of the forces of the downfall of the Liberal Party, he stubbornly refuses to consider it as a serious political movement but rather as a 'brutal comedy', a 'puppet show' where the strings are carefully manipulated by the leaders (Dangerfield, 1966, pp. 132, 165). Time and time again Emmeline and Christabel Pankhurst are ridiculed, as in the following passage where it is claimed that in the WSPU:

> its chief actors – say what you please, they are not very lovable. You are forced to ascribe to Mrs Pankhurst and her daughter Christabel certain motives of self-interest, certain moments of exhibitionism, which do not especially commend themselves. They and their associates were courageous enough; some of them stood more physical torture than a woman should be able to bear: but then, as the scene unrolls itself and their sufferings increase, how can one avoid the thought that they sought these sufferings with an enraptured, a positively unhealthy pleasure? They chose to be martyrs. (Dangerfield, 1966, p. 133)

Both women are seen as opportunists, seeking to rise above their impecunious middle-class background in provincial Manchester. Mrs Pankhurst is an obscure Lancashire widow, not interested in 'municipal politics' but single-minded about a cause her husband had bequeathed to her! (ibid., p. 130) Christabel suffered from 'snobbery' and 'delusions of grandeur', fed by mixing with women above her station in life, such as the aristocractic suffragette, Lady Constance Lytton (ibid., p. 132). Unable to understand the notion of a women-only political movement, where networks of friendships were critical, the WSPU is dismissed as a form of 'pre-war lesbianism' (ibid., p. 128).

The derogatory tone of Dangerfield's analysis is continued particularly in the works of David Mitchell who, by the 1970s, was well-known as a popular writer of women's history with such books as *Women on the Warpath, The Story of the Women of the First World War* (1966) and *The Fighting Pankhursts* (1967). In the Preface to the latter, he refers to 'the drama and maenadic aggression of the Pankhursts', and proceeds to make many disparaging comments, such as the following: 'I salute you, Christabel, as an honourable casualty . . . I salute you, Emmeline, Sylvia and Adela, for being such wonderful, crazy, intolerant and sometimes intolerable busybodies' (ibid., pp. 339–

40). However, it is in Mitchell's biography of Christabel Pankhurst that we find his misogyny at its deepest.

Christabel is presented as ruthless, cold, ambitious, autocratic, self-seeking, single-minded, calculating and selfish – as well as charismatic and quick of mind and tongue. But her life as a feminist is filtered through all the former adjectives. On the opening page of his book, for example, Mitchell describes how on 15 October 1905 Christabel Pankhurst and Annie Kenney were arrested and sent to prison for creating a disturbance when they interrupted a Liberal political meeting at Manchester Free Trade Hall by asking the question: 'When will the Liberal Party give women the vote?' Rather than pay a fine, both women chose to go to prison in order to bring widespread newspaper coverage to the women's cause, as well as converts, which Mitchell describes: 'In thousands of impatient feminists this coldly calculated manoeuvre released a warm, quasi-orgasmic gush of gratitude and heroine worship' (Mitchell, 1977, p. 1). This kind of sexual innuendo, as well as 'hints' about lesbianism, is present throughout his account. As Stanley and Morley (1988, p. 79) cuttingly comment, they can picture Mitchell writing 'with one protective hand cupped over his crotch'.

For Mitchell, there is little positive that he can say about Christabel and her mother. On 5 March 1912, the police arrived at the London headquarters of the WSPU to arrest Christabel and the Pethick Lawrences (Mrs Pankhurst was already in prison). Unknown to the police, Christabel no longer lived at Clement's Inn since some months earlier she had taken a flat of her own. When informed of the Pethick Lawrences' arrest, she spent the night in hiding. Fearing for the future of the movement if all its leaders were in prison, she escaped to Paris the following morning. Here she tried to lead the movement and write copy for *The Suffragette*, with all the difficulties involved in living at a distance. Jessie Kenney, who was one of her trusted aides, travelling in disguise between Paris (where she was known as Constance Burrows) and London, recollected:

> Militants in Britain . . . thought C and I in Paris had an easy time of it. But it wasn't so. The tension was terrific. C felt it terribly, though she never showed it much . . . she seldom showed the strain she was under. For make no mistake, she kept the Movement together by sheer willpower. Her output for *The Suffragette* alone was tremendous: she covered pages and pages at tremendous speed in her almost illegible scrawl (how the printers coped I don't know), and then I would post the copy from near the Gare du Nord about midnight or early hours of morning. (Jessie Kenney interview, 23 March 1964)

This interview was conducted by David Mitchell and although he does quote it in his book (Mitchell, 1977, p. 218), it is framed with such unsavoury comments that the account is lost. It was Christabel's fate 'to sit, well-dressed and

well-fed, in a comfortable apartment' (p. 205). By comparison with other political exiles 'she did not exactly pig it' (p. 206). Christabel and her mother drove about 'in a barouche looking like visiting royalty' (p. 207). She was prominent in 'a Sapphic or androgynous circle' which included Romaine Brooks whose 'lesbianism seems to have been rooted in incestuous feelings of love-hatred for a neurotic mother – an experience which, one feels, was not unknown to Christabel' (p. 207).

By now the die has been cast and we come full circle with Brian Harrison's 1987 essay comparing the leadership styles of Millicent Garrett Fawcett and Mrs Pankhurst. Although Harrison is a fine scholar, with none of the scathing comment so rife in Mitchell, for Harrison, too, Millicent Fawcett is everything good and wholesome, Emmeline Pankhurst everything irrational, compulsive and autocractic. Mrs Fawcett had faith 'in British parliamentary institutions and in the basic good sense of the people . . . [but] There was nothing meek and mild about Fawcett's feminism; moderate tactics by no means indicate lukewarm commitment' (Harrison, 1987, p. 19). She discouraged hero-worship, possessed reason, found time to publish several books and never grumbled during all her long years of leadership (ibid., pp. 24–5). By contrast, Mrs Pankhurst is a 'subversive firebrand' with an interest in clothes, a zest for window-shopping and a love of Paris (ibid., p. 30). The relationship between Christabel and Mrs Pankhurst is described as 'strange', with the mother as 'the extremist, the idealist whom those in the know nicknamed "enfant terrible", whereas the daughter was cautious, calculating, and in some respects cynical' (ibid., pp. 32–33).

Overall, in these liberal histories the 'good' feminists are those women who are non-militant, patient and controlled, prepared to work within the structures of society rather than seeking to transform them. The founders of the WSPU are outside this frame. Neither are they within the frame constructed by socialist feminists for whom class relations and class conflict reign paramount, irrespective of the power relationships between men and women.

Socialist Feminist Influences

If Ray Strachey's *The Cause* has been the key text for establishing a dominant liberal narrative about Emmeline and Christabel Pankhurst, a similar role for socialist feminist accounts must be allocated to Sylvia Pankhurst's monumentual work *The Suffragette Movement* (1931). Although usually classified as 'history', this book is also an autobiographical memoir by a participant in the movement, an account, as Sylvia acknowledges in the Preface, 'largely made up of memories'.[9]

Memories of disagreements with her mother and Christabel float throughout the book; in particular, her socialist feminist outlook was often at odds with the women-centred views of the leaders of the WSPU. The first public acknowledgement of the split among the Pankhurst women came in

November 1913 when the *Daily Mail* reported on Sylvia's appearance on a Herald League platform with the socialist, George Lansbury, commenting that 'every day the Industrial and the Suffrage rebels march nearer together'. In the 14 November 1913 edition of *The Suffragette*, Christabel strongly denied that the WSPU was marching nearer to any other movement or political party, especially the Herald League which was a 'class organisation': the vote would be won, she emphasized, through women of all social classes fighting together. Expelled from the WSPU, Sylvia now devoted her time to working among poor women associated with the East London Federation of Suffragettes (ELFS), an organization with close links to socialist groups.

The differences in political outlook between Sylvia, on the one hand, and her mother and Christabel on the other were exacerbated by the fact that Christabel had always been her mother's favourite child, 'the apple of her eye' as Sylvia vividly remembered (Pankhurst, 1931, p. 267). Such lenses undoubtedly coloured how Sylvia represented the two women and herself. Her mother and sister are both seen as abandoning the socialist cause Dr Richard Pankhurst had so faithfully served and moving further and further to the political right. After the Cockermouth by-election in August 1906, when Christabel announced that henceforth the WSPU would be independent of the ILP and not only oppose all Liberal and Conservative candidates, irrespective of their views on women's suffrage, but also be impartial to all socialist candidates, Sylvia speaks scathingly of her 'incipient Toryism' (Pankhurst, 1931, p. 221). When the First World War broke out, Mrs Pankhurst and Christabel supported the old enemy, the government, advocating a form of 'patriotic womanhood' (de Vries, 1994, p. 80) that stressed not pacificism but devotion to the nation in its hour of need. For Sylvia the humiliation was complete. Thus she recollected:

> When first I read in the Press that Mrs Pankhurst and Christabel were returning to England for a recruiting campaign I wept. To me this seemed a tragic betrayal of the great movement to bring the mother-half of the race into the councils of the nations. 'Women would stand for peace!' How often, how often had they and all of us averred it! (Pankhurst, 1931, p. 595)

As Marcus (1987, pp. 5–6) perceptively notes, in Sylvia's version of the women's suffrage movement she is 'the heroine' who keeps the socialist faith, the Cinderella liberated by a fairy godmother in the form of the socialist giant, Keir Hardie, while her mother and sister are the 'wicked' people, the 'separatist feminists', 'isolated man-haters', and celibate 'unsexed viragoes' who caused split after split within the movement. Emmeline Pankhurst is presented not as the powerful leader of a women's movement but as a mother who neglected her less-favoured children, including a son, Harry, who died. When Sylvia describes the strong influence of Christabel on her mother, she is writing not just as 'an angry socialist' but 'as a rejected daughter' adds Hilda Kean

(1994, pp. 73–4). Variations on these themes have been consistently presented by 'second wave' socialist feminist and male socialist historians. It is the former upon whom I concentrate here.[10]

Sheila Rowbotham's *Hidden from History: 300 Years of Women's Oppression and the Fight Against It*, first published in 1973, is usually regarded as the catalyst for the growth of recent interest in women's history. As a socialist feminist for whom issues of social class relations and capitalist exploitation are central to her analyis, the focus by the WSPU on 'uniting women' through the 'single issue' of the vote is found wanting. 'It is curious', continues Rowbotham (1973, p. 82), 'that at a time where increasing sections of the labour movement were becoming disillusioned with parliament, the women were ready to risk and suffer so much for the vote.' After the Cockermouth by-election (when the WSPU declared independence from the ILP and other political groupings), it is claimed that Emmeline and Christabel Pankhurst had a deliberate policy of 'courting upper-class women'. Thus the leaders of the WSPU are presented as women who moved further away from their socialist roots until they became 'right-wing feminists who . . . supported war' (Rowbotham, 1973, pp. 79, 80, 160). Furthermore, since the only form of valid political organization is that adopted by the Left of mobilizing workers into a mass movement, the WSPU is downgraded to a 'pressure group':

> the use of violent tactics progressively isolated the WSPU and changed the nature of the suffrage campaign from a mass organisation to an elite corps trained in urban sabotage . . . The WSPU for all its militant flurry was a pressure group, albeit a heroic and defiant one. Emmeline and Christabel did not think in terms of building a mass organisation or of mobilising women workers to strike, but of making ever more dramatic gestures. (Rowbotham, 1973, p. 88)

Similarly, Liddington and Norris's (1978) account of the involvement of working-class women in radical suffragist politics in early-twentieth century Lancashire continues the same theme: the only significant form of struggle is that against class exploitation. Christabel Pankhurst in particular is blamed for the 'bitter divisions and destructive splits' that occurred in the suffrage movement: 'Co-operation was not in her nature' (Liddington and Norris, 1978, p. 192). The verdict of Helena Swanwick, a member of the NUWSS, is quoted with approval: Christabel was 'unlike her sisters, cynical and cold at heart. She gave me the impression of fitful and impulsive ambition and of quite ruthless love of domination' (quoted in Liddington and Norris, 1978, pp. 169–70).

By now the narrative is firmly established and repeated at regular intervals. For example, Gifford Lewis in 1988 (p. 9), in wishing to dispel the mists of 'Pankhurst worship', refers to Emmeline and Christabel Pankhurst as 'opportunistic charmers who instantly dropped people no longer of any use to them'. The binary oppositions so powerfully presented in Strachey's *The Cause* appear again: 'Though Mrs Fawcett was dignity personified she was very approachable and was quite understandably revered' (p. 114) while Christabel Pankhurst is 'the agent of division' (p. 92).

Women-Identifed Women

Alternative representations of Emmeline and Christabel Pankhurst to those discussed so far have been few (Holton, 1990; Purvis, 1995b; Sarah, 1983; see Spender, 1982). This is hardly surprising in view of the fact that liberalism in Britain from the 1960s has been the dominant interpretive framework in history writing generally and socialist feminism the dominant perspective shaping and influencing the growth of women's history from the 1970s (Purvis, 1995c, p. 10). Radical feminism, on the other hand, which emphasizes the power relationships between men and women as the key to an understanding of women's subordinate position in history, was very much a 'minority voice' (Rendall, 1991, p. 48) in women's history in this country, despite its influence within the broader field of women's studies. Yet, as Elizabeth Sarah (1983) forcefully points out, we cannot understand Emmeline and Christabel Pankhurst unless we see them as feminists who, some decades earlier, voiced a number of the concerns that were so central to radical feminism from the 1970s: the importance of a women-only movement, the power of men over women in a male-defined world, the commonalities that all women share, despite their social class differences.

In 'reading' Emmeline and Christabel Pankhurst from this perspective, I do not with to represent them as 'feminist heroines with no blemishes' (Mayhall, 1995, p. 337). In particular, as Antoinette Burton (1994) has ably shown, feminist Edwardian discourse often reinforced rather than challenged 'racist' assumptions since it appropriated imperial ideology and rhetoric to justify women's right to equality. However, I claim, like Dale Spender (1982) and Elizabeth Sarah (1983) before me, that in order to appreciate Emmeline and Christabel Pankhurst *as feminists* we must examine their own rationale for their actions. Since I do not have the space within this chapter to develop this analysis in full, I focus on two key themes: the worldview of Emmeline and Christabel Pankhurst and their style of leadership.

Both Mrs Pankhurst and Christabel believed that the injustices generally which women experienced in Edwardian society, including exclusion from the political franchise, could be attributed to the power of men. Thus in a manmade and male-dominated society, men were the cause of women's subordination and inferiority. As Christabel Pankhust thundered in 1913:

> The vote is the symbol of freedom and equality. Any class which is denied the vote is branded as an inferior class. Women's disfranchisement is to them a perpetual lesson in servility, and to men it teaches arrogance and injustice where their dealings with women are concerned. The inferiority of women is a hideous lie which has been

enforced by law and woven into the British constitution, and it is quite hopeless to expect reform between the relationship of the sexes until women are politically enfranchised. (Pankhurst, 1913, pp. 117–18)

Since the slogan of the WSPU was 'Deeds, not words', militancy represented a 'moral critique of male-ordered society' (Holton, 1990, p. 21), a means whereby women could fight man's power and claim their dignity as women. The notion of a 'sex war' formed the 'crux' of the WSPU campaign (see Kingsley Kent, 1987, p. 5). Emmeline Pankhurst (1914, p. 35) put the matter in a nutshell when she asserted: 'Men regarded women as a servant class in the community, and . . . women were going to remain in the servant class until they lifted themselves out of it.'

Such views differed fundamentally from liberal feminists who emphasized that women's inequality was due to their exclusion from certain rights, such as education, and who advocated gradual, constitutional, piecemeal reform. It also differed from socialist feminists who emphasized social class inequalities under capitalism, including class conflict between women. Indeed, Emmeline and Christabel Pankhurst believed that women's interests transcended those of social class and that in a manmade world there was more that united women than divided them. In an article called 'The sisterhood of women' (*Votes for Women*, 20 May 1910, p. 550) Christabel outlined how women can learn to cast class distinctions aside and how the grand procession organized by the WSPU for 18 June 1910 was open to 'every woman who wants the vote', whether a militant, a non-militant or non-member of a suffrage society. It was the social conditioning that women had experienced in a manmade world, she insisted, that had led women to believe that sisterhood between all women, despite their differences, was impossible:

June 18 will be something more than a political demonstration; it will be a festival at which we shall celebrate the sisterhood of women. According to the old tale of men's making, it is not in women to unite and to work with one another. Women have only now discovered the falsity of this, and they are rejoicing in their new-found sisterhood. (Pankhurst, 1910, p. 550)

Having now given a brief outline of the worldview of Emmeline and Christabel Pankhurst we can reassess some of the other critical points made in liberal and socialist feminist histories about their leadership qualities and especially their style of leadership.

What is not emphasized in the accounts we considered is Christabel Pankhurst's political flair, her genius for leadership, especially in the earlier years of the movement, before she fled to Paris, when she was seen as the 'supreme tactician' (Stanley with Morley, 1988, p. 176) and a 'resourceful and imaginative strategist-in-chief' (Pankhurst, 1987). Of key importance here is

Christabel's decision to introduce the strategy of women heckling male politicians about votes for women as a way of attracting publicity to the cause. As we saw earlier, when she and Annie Kenney used this tactic at a Liberal Party meeting on 13 October 1905, they both refused to pay a fine but chose instead to go to prison – which attracted the widespread attention of newspaper reporters. This was a brilliant move. As Jane Marcus (1987, p. 9) points out, before the WSPU initiated this tactic on a large scale, women had been expected to sit quietly in political debate, listening to the men speak. From Christabel Pankhurst, however, they learned 'not only to speak in her own voice for her own cause, but to split asunder patriarchal cultural hegemony by interrupting men's discourse with each other' (ibid., p. 9). Thousands of suffragettes from all social classes learned to heckle, often the first stage in becoming a political activist for the women's cause (Purvis, 1994, p. 322).

Mrs Pankhurst, on the other hand, a small, frail-looking woman, was especially well-known for her magnetic oratory. On a political platform she had a forcefulness and a driving energy not usually associated with a woman described as 'so feminine', recollected Cecily Hamilton (1935, p. 77). She was vibrant, asserted Rebecca West (1933, pp. 479–80): one felt, as she lifted up her hoarse, sweet voice, that she was 'trembling like a reed. Only the reed was of steel and it was tremendous.' Even some members of the NUWSS, such as Mary Stocks, were fascinated by Emmeline Pankhurst's dignity and mastery of oratorial skills:

> Mrs Pankhurst was, in very truth, a hero. Nobody who can recall her physical presence or hear, in memory, echoes of her very beautiful voice, can fail to experience a reminiscent thrill of excitement. I often heard her speak to great crowds in the Albert Hall, a thing few people could do effectively in that pre-microphone age, and to small groups or in the hurly-burly of a street scuffle ... When I describe Mrs Pankhurst as a spellbinder I know what I am talking about. (Stocks, 1970, p. 70)

Indeed, in Rebecca West's view, Mrs Pankhurst was the last popular leader to act on inspiration derived from the principles of the French Revolution: Liberty, Equality and Fraternity. 'In the midst of that battle for democracy,' she continues, 'she was obliged, lest that battle should be lost, to become a dictator' (West, 1933, p. 500).

As this makes evident, the representation of Emmeline and Christabel Pankhurst as ruthless and autocratic leaders who 'manipulated' their followers requires closer investigation. True, people were expelled from the WSPU in a dictatorial way, such as Emmeline and Frederick Pethick Lawrence in 1912 when they objected to the further extension of militancy. The move shocked many WSPU supporters since Emmeline Pethick Lawrence was another key figure in the WSPU and both she and her husband had not only been close friends with the Pankhursts but also brought money and organizational skills to the movement. But, as Vicinus (1985, pp. 262, 153) highlights, 'autocracy' contained a strange paradox: any suffragette who accepted militancy to the full was following the policies of the leaders although, at the same time, she was making her own independent judgement about in which acts she should engage it. Furthermore, as Stanley and Morley (1988, pp. xiii, 153) make clear, one cannot maintain a case for the Pankhurst leadership manipulating their followers like puppets on strings. The WSPU, they point out, was a loose coalition of women whose opinions, analyses and actions differed enormously and who might try out new tactics without discussion with or the approval of Mrs Pankhurst and Christabel.

On the evening of 30 June 1908, for example, after a meeting in Parliament Square when many suffragettes were brutally treated by both the police and gangs of young men, Mary Leigh and Edith New took a cab to 10 Downing Street. Armed with a bag of stones, they broke two of Prime Minister Asquith's windows, not only in protest about the turn of events that evening but also in exasperation at his refusal, yet again, to meet a deputation that afternoon. Once such action was initiated, the leadership was quick to support its membership. Thus some days later, Christabel Pankhurst pointed out:

> There is no doubt that this act of theirs has convinced some who before were sceptical on the point that women suffragists mean business, and are more likely to increase the vigour of their methods in order to match the strength of the Government's resistance to their demand . . . Everyone must admire the courage and devotion which prompted the act, and recognise the surprising fact to be, not that the thing has been done now, but that it has not been done before. Certain it is that if voteless men had been treated as women are being treated by the Liberal Government, they would not have been so moderate or so patient (*Votes for Women*, 9 July 1908, p. 297)

Similarly, the first hunger strike, begun on 5 July 1909 by Marion Wallace Dunlop as a protest against being denied the status of a political prisoner, was another tactic initiated without the foreknowledge of Emmeline and Christabel Pankhurst, although welcomed by both.

The representation of rank-and-file members as cultural dopes who somehow mindlessly followed their autocratic leaders is, to say the least, troubling. In particular, it denies feminist women agency for their own actions. The obvious point needs to be stated that membership of the WSPU was *voluntary* not compulsory. As Mrs Pankhurst (1914, p. 59) emphasized, 'It is purely a volunteer army, and no one is obliged to remain in it.' Furthermore, in a rousing speech given at a WSPU meeting after the departure of the Pethick Lawrences in 1912, Mrs Pankhurst pointed out the variety of militant acts that could be engaged and how women members of the WSPU *did* have a choice:

Be militant each in your own way. Those of you who can express your militancy by going to the House of Commons and refusing to leave without satisfaction, as we did in the early days – do so. Those of you who can express militancy by facing party mobs at Cabinet Ministers' meetings, when you remind them of their falseness to principle – do so. Those of you who can express your militancy by joining us in our anti-Government by-election policy – do so. Those of you who can break windows – break them. Those of you who can still further attack the secret idol of property, so as to make the Government realise that property is as greatly endangered by women's suffrage as it was by the Chartists of old – do so. (Pankhurst, 1914, pp. 265–6)

Conclusion

We can make two key points here. First, as feminists today we need to be aware of the way in which the stories on which we rely for knowledge about key feminist figures in the past have been socially constructed and culturally produced (Burton, 1992, p. 26). The representations by liberal and socialist feminist historians alike of two prominent 'first wave' militant feminists, Emmeline and Christabel Pankhurst, have become the dominant textual representations, rarely questioned and commonly cited. As a result, there has been an almost silencing of alternative narratives and alternative interpretations. Yet these dominant representations must be subjected to careful scrutiny, since they are filtered through particular perspectives which are fundamentally at odds with those of the militant leaders themselves. An examination of the rationale which Emmeline and Christabel Pankhurst articulated for their actions reveals that in many ways they were forerunners of some of the ideas voiced by radical feminists of the 'second wave'.

Second, as feminists today we should pay attention to our history. As Anna Davin (1972, p. 224) once noted, we need to know our past since historical understanding of the struggles of earlier generations of women can help us to win our own. Furthermore, as feminists today, we have a responsibility to capture the lives of our feminist foremothers in all their complexities as well as to reveal the variety and diversity of their number (Caine, 1994, p. 25). In particular, I claim that a study of Emmeline and Christabel Pankhurst, pioneer militant feminists in Edwardian Britain, can help us to recover a tradition of autonomous feminist thought and action that has been obscured from our view.

Notes

1 This chapter was first published, in a slightly different form, with the title 'A "pair of . . . infernal queens"? A reassessment of the dominant repre-

sentations of Emmeline and Christabel Pankhurst, First Wave feminists in Edwardian Britain' in *Women's History Review* 6 (2), 1996.

2 For useful accounts that give an overview of this research see Rendall (1991), Hannam (1993), Purvis (1995a) and Purvis (1995b).

3 The other main leader was Emmeline Pethick Lawrence. Keir Hardie, who had a high regard for her executive skills, persuaded Mrs Pankhurst early in 1906 to offer Mrs Pethick Lawrence the post of treasurer of the WSPU. Both she and her husband, Frederick, were staunch supporters of the Union until ousted by Mrs Pankhurst and Christabel in 1912. They were the joint editors of its first newspaper, *Votes for Women*, which was inaugurated as a threepenny monthly in October 1907. *The Suffragette* was founded after the split with the Pethick Lawrences and inaugurated in October 1912, edited by Christabel who was then living in exile in Paris. See Rosen (1974, pp. 93 and 175).

4 I am following the common usage of referring to women in the 'militant' WSPU as 'suffragettes' and to those who were members of the 'constitutional' NUWSS as 'suffragists'. However, the very terms 'militant' and 'constitutional' are themselves imprecise, as Holton argued in her 1986 book *Feminism and Democracy*, p. 4. If 'militancy' involved a preparedness to resort to extreme forms of violence, few 'militants' were 'militant' and then only from 1912 (this point is elaborated in the following paragraph in the main text of this chapter). If, on the other hand, 'militancy' involved a willingness to take the issue on to the streets, then many 'constitutionalists' were also 'militant'. Furthermore, many women belonged to both militant and constitutional societies, especially at the local level: see Stanley with Morley (1988, p. 152). For an account of the prison experiences of the suffragettes see Purvis (1995c).

5 For example, two works by WSPU member Elizabeth Robins – the play *Votes for Women!*, first produced in London in April 1907, and the novel *The Convert*, published in the same year – feature the suffrage struggle. In the Elizabeth Robins Collection at the Humanities Research Center at the University of Texas, Houston, there are letters from both Emmeline and Christabel Pankhurst discussing the drafts of these two works and, in particular, suggesting that the name of the heroine should be changed so that no sexual scandal would be associated with Christabel. The description of another woman suffragette in *The Convert*, namely Ernestine Blunt, is said to resemble Christabel: 'Almost dull the round rather pouting face with the vivid scarlet lips; almost sleepy the heavy-lidded eyes (p. 110 of reprint edition, 1980, London, The Women's Press). For discussion of Robins as a feminist playwright and novelist of the suffrage era, see, respectively, Chapter 1 in Stowell (1992) and Chapter 8 in Sypher (1993). For a superb account of the imagery of the suffrage campaign – including banners, posters, postcards and the orchestration of mass demonstrations – see Tickner (1987).

6 Such classifications of Western feminist theory are never neat and clear-

cut: see Maynard (1995) for an insightful and lucid discussion. However, despite the differences within these broad categories, we may say generally that liberal feminists emphasize gradual, piecemeal reform as a way to gain equal rights for women and stress the importance of women and men working together to attain equal rights. Socialist feminists, on the other hand, emphasize that the subordinate position of women in society may be attributed both to the nature of capitalism and to the control that men exercise over women. They also stress the importance of men and women working together as comrades in the building of a socialist society. Feminist theory is not static but changes its shape and emphases over time so that what we might term 'liberal feminism' and 'socialist feminism' in the Edwardian era will take a different shape in the 1990s. Maynard (1995) questions whether the 'Big Three' labels of liberal feminism, socialist feminism and radical feminism are still useful in the 1990s since feminist theory today is much more pluralistic than in the early days of 'second wave' feminism.

7 See note 4.
8 See also Fulford (1957), Harrison (1982) and the chapter on 'Mrs Pankhurst' in Brendon (1979).
9 It is interesting to note that Sylvia paints a more sympathetic picture of her mother in *The Life of Emmeline Pankhurst: The Suffragette Struggle for Women's Citizenship* published four years later, in 1935. However, this has not been reprinted in a widely accessible paperback edition and is difficult to acquire. In contrast, as Marcus (1987 p. 5) notes the *The Suffragette Movement* provided the basis for George Dangerfield's influential 'analysis' so that the Sylvia Pankhurst/George Dangerfield version has become 'the standard reading' of the suffrage movement, 'stubbornly held and hardly challenged'. For a fascinating account of the ways in which Sylvia Pankhurst's writings were socially constructed and culturally produced, at particular moments in time, see Dodd (1993) 'Introduction' to her edited collection of Sylvia's writings.
10 See, for example, Garner (1984), Pugh (1990) and Bullock and Pankhurst (Eds.) (1992).

References

ATKINSON, D. (1988) *Votes for Women*, Cambridge, Cambridge University Press.

'BANKS, O. (1985) *The Biographical Dictionary of British Feminists Vol. 1: 1800–1930*, Brighton, Wheatsheaf Books.

BLEASE, W. LYON (1910) *The Emancipaton of English Women*, London, Constable & Co.

BRENDON, P. (1979) *Eminent Edwardians*, London, Secker and Warburg, Chapter 4 'Mrs Pankhurst'.

BULLOCK, I. and PANKHURST, R. (1992) (Eds) *Sylvia Pankhurst, From Artist to Anti-Fascist*, London, Macmillan.

BURTON, A. (1992) '"History" is now: feminist theory and the production of historical feminisms', *Women's History Review*, 1 (1).

BURTON, A. (1994) *Burdens of History, British Feminists, Indian Women, and Imperial Culture, 1865–1915*, Chapela Hill and London, University of North Carolina Press.

CAINE, B. (1994) 'Feminist Biography and Feminist History', *Women's History Review*, 3 (2).

DANGERFIELD, G. (1966) *The Strange Death of Liberal England*, London, MacGibbin and Kee (first published 1935).

DAVIN, A. (1972) 'Women in History', in WANDOR, M. (Ed.) *The Body Political, Writings from the Women's Liberation Movement in Britain 1969–72*, London, Stage 1.

DODD, K. (1990) 'Cultural politics and women's history writing: the case of Ray Strachey's *The Cause*', *Women's Studies International Forum*, 13 (1/2), Special Issue *British Feminist Histories*, Ed. by L. Stanley.

DODD, K. (1993) 'Introduction' to DODD, K. (Ed.) *A Sylvia Pankhurst Reader*, Manchester, Manchester University Press.

FAWCETT, M. GARRETT (n.d. but 1912) *Women's Suffrage, A Short History of a Great Movement*, London, T. C. & E. C. Jack.

FULFORD, R. (1957) *Votes for Women, The Story of a Struggle*, London, Faber & Faber.

GARNER, L. (1984) *Stepping Stones to Women's Liberty, Feminist Ideas in the Women's Suffrage Movement 1900–1918*, London, Heinemann Educational Books.

GLASIER, B. (1898) *Bruce Glasier Diaries*, Sydney Jones Library, University of Liverpool.

HAMILTON, C. (1935) *Life Errant*, London, J.M. Dent & Sons.

HANNAM, J. (1993) 'Women, history and protest', in RICHARDSON, D. and ROBINSON, V. (Eds) *Introducing Women's Studies*, London, Macmillan.

HARRISON, B. (1982) 'The act of militancy, violence and the suffragettes, 1904–1914', which is Chapter 1 of his *Peaceable Kingdom, Stability and Change in Modern Britain*, Oxford, Oxford University Press.

HARRISON, B. (1987) 'Two models of feminist leadership: Millicent Fawcett and Emmeline Pankhurst', in his *Prudent Revolutionaries, Portraits of British Feminists between the Wars*, Oxford, Clarendon Press.

HOLTON, S. STANLEY (1986) *Feminism and Democracy, Women's Suffrage and Reform Politics in Britain 1900–1918*, Cambridge, Cambridge University Press.

HOLTON, S. STANLEY (1990) 'In Sorrowful Wrath: Suffrage, Militancy and the Romantic Feminism of Emmeline Pankhurst', in SMITH, H. (Ed.) *British Feminism in the Twentieth Century*, Aldershot, Edward Elgar.

KEAN, H. (1994) 'Searching for the past in present defeat: the construction of historical and political identity in British feminism in the 1920s and 1930s", *Women's History Review*, 3 (1).

KENNEY, JESSIE (1964) Interview conducted by David Mitchell with Jessie Kenney, 24 March 1964, David Mitchell Collection, Museum of London.

KENT, S. KINGSLEY (1987) *Sex and Suffrage in Britain, 1860–1914*, Princeton, New Jersey, Princeton University Press.

LEWIS, G. (1988) *Eva Gore Booth and Esther Roper, A Biography*, London, Pandora.

LIDDINGTON, J. and NORRIS, J. (1978) *One Hand Tied Behind Us, The Rise of the Women's Suffrage Movement*, London, Virago.

MARCUS, J. (1987) 'Introduction' to her edited *Suffrage and the Pankhursts*, London, Routledge & Kegan Paul.

MASON, B. (1912) *The Story of the Women's Suffrage Movement*, London, Sherratt & Hughes.

MAYHALL, L. E. NYM (1995) 'Creating the "Suffragette Spirit": British Feminism and the Historical Imagination', *Women's History Review*, 4 (3).

MAYNARD, M. (1995) 'Beyond the "Big Three": the development of feminist theory into the 1990s', *Women's History Review*, 4 (3).

McMILLAN, M. (1927) *The Life of Rachel McMillan*, London and Toronto, J.M. Dent.

METCALFE, A. E. (1917) *Woman's Effort, A Chronicle of British Women's Fifty Years' Struggle for Citizenship (1865–1914)*, Oxford, B.H. Blackwell.

MITCHELL, D. (1966) *Women on the Warpath, The Story of the Women of the First World War*, London, Jonathan Cape.

MITCHELL, D. (1967) *The Fighting Pankhursts, A Study in Tenacity*, London, Jonathan Cape.

MITCHELL, D. (1977) *Queen Christabel, A Biography of Christabel Pankhurst*, London, MacDonald & Jane's.

MITCHELL, G. (Ed.) (1968) *The Hard Way Up: The Autobiography of Hannah Mitchell Suffragette and Rebel*, London, Faber & Faber.

PANKHURST, C. (1910) 'The sisterhood of women', *Votes for Women*, 20 May 1910.

PANKHURST, C. (1913) *The Great Scourge and How To End It*, London, E. Pankhurst.

PANKHURST, DAME C. (1959) *Unshackled: The Story of How We Won the Vote*, London, Hutchinson.

PANKHURST, E. (1914) *My Own Story*, London, Eveleigh Nash.

PANKHURST, E. S. (1911) *The Suffragette, The History of the Women's Militant Suffrage Movement 1905–1910*, London, Gay & Hancock.

PANKHURST, E. S. (1931) *The Suffragette Movement: An Intimate Account of Persons and Ideals*, London, Longmans, Green.

PANKHURST, E. S. (1935) *The Life of Emmeline Pankhurst: The Suffragette Struggle for Women's Citizenship*, London, T. Werner Laurie.

PANKHURST, R. (1987) 'Introduction' to the 1987 reprint of Dame C. Pankhurst *Unshackled*, London, The Cresset Library.

PUGH, M. (1990) *Women's Suffrage in Britain*, London, The Historical Association.

PURVIS, J. (1994) 'A lost dimension? The political education of women in the suffragette movement in Edwardian Britain', *Gender and Education*, 6 (3).

PURVIS, J. (1995a) 'Women's history in Britain: an overview', *European Journal of Women's Studies*, 2, pp. 7–19.

PURVIS, J. (1995b) 'From "women worthies" to poststructuralism? Debate and controversy in women's history in Britain', in PURVIS, J. (Ed.) *Women's History: Britain, 1850–1945*, London, UCL Press.

PURVIS, J. (1995c) 'The prison experiences of the suffragettes in Edwardian Britain', *Women's History Review*, 4 (1).

PURVIS, J. (1995d) ' "Deeds, not words": the daily lives of militant suffragettes in Edwardian Britain', *Women's Studies International Forum*, 18 (2), pp. 91–101.

RAEBURN, A. (1973) *The Militant Suffragettes*, London, Michael Joseph.

RENDALL, J. (1991) ' "Uneven developments": women's history, feminist history and gender history in Great Britain', in OFFEN, K., ROACH PIERSON, R. and RENDALL, J. (Eds) *Writing Women's History, International Perspectives*, Basingstoke, Macmillan.

ROBINS, E. (1980) *The Convert*, London, The Women's Press (first published 1907).

ROSEN, A. (1974) *Rise Up Women! The Militant Campaign of the Women's Social and Political Union 1903–1914*, London, Routledge & Kegan Paul.

ROWBOTHAM, S. (1973) *Hidden from History: 300 Years of Women's Oppression and the Fight Against It*, London, Pluto Press.

SARAH, E. (1983) 'Christabel Pankhurst: reclaiming her power', in SPENDER, D. (Ed.) *Feminist Theorists, Three Centuries of Women's Intellectual Traditions*, London, The Women's Press.

SNOWDEN, E. (1913) *The Feminist Movement*, London and Glasgow, Collins.

SPENDER, D. (1982) *Women of Ideas and What Men Have Done To Them*, London, Routledge & Kegan Paul, Part IV, section (B) 'Militant and maligned'.

STANLEY, L. with MORLEY, A. (1988) *The Life and Death of Emily Wilding Davison*, London, The Women's Press.

STOCKS, M. (1970) *My Commonplace Book*, London, Peter Davies.

STOWELL, S. (1992) *A Stage of Their Own, Feminist Playwrights of the Suffrage Era*, Manchester, Manchester University Press, Chapter 1 'Elizabeth Robins'.

STRACHEY, R. (1928) *'The Cause': A Short History of the Women's Movement in Great Britain*, London, G. Bell and Sons.

SYPHER, E. (1993) *Wisps of Violence, Producing Public and Private Politics in the Turn-of-the-Century British Novel*, London, Verso, Chapter 8 'The novel and women's suffrage'.

TICKNER, L. (1987) *The Spectacle of Women, Imagery of the Suffrage Campaign 1907–1914*, London, Chatto & Windus.

de VRIES, J. (1994) 'Gendering patriotism: Emmeline and Christabel Pankhurst and World War One', in OLDFIELD, S. (Ed.) *This Working-Day World, Women's Lives and Culture(s) in Britain 1914–1945*, London, Taylor & Francis.

VICINUS, M. (1985) *Independent women, work and community for single women 1850–1920*, London, Virago.

WEST, R. (1933) 'Mrs Pankhurst', in *The Post Victorians*, with an Introduction by the Very Reverend W. R. INGE, London, Ivor Nicholson & Watson.

Chapter 6

Gender, Nation and Scholarship: Reflections on Gender/Women's Studies in the Czech Republic

Jitka Malečková

The participation of women in our history is so important that it truly deserves more attention than has been devoted to it till now. Only in the most recent times has the effort to evaluate the contribution of Czech women to our national culture started to revitalize and an interest in this new topic has made its way also to the wider public. (Stloukal, 1940, p. 7)

The future is not enough for the feminists, they want to get hold of the past as well and newly interpret it from a women's point of view. (Šmahel, 1993, p. 147)

Stloukal's satisfaction with the scholarly and public interest in women's history, legitimate in 1940 in the introduction to a six-hundred page collection of fifty-nine articles devoted to Czech women in history by twenty-eight scholars would hardly be shared today. A feminist reinterpretation of (world) history, worrying Šmahel half a century later, does not yet threaten Czech academia. And this is not only the case with history; none of the social and human sciences have reason to fear a feminist attack. Taking into consideration the prevailing views of students and scholars, such disciplines as Women's or Gender Studies do not exist in the Czech Republic. Nevertheless, on the periphery of mainstream academic life, works on women are often written and gender issues are discussed.

This article characterizes the current state and problems of research and debates on women and gender and their roots. It deals with a subject which the academic community does not recognize and with authors who mostly refuse a classification under such labels as feminism or Women's Studies. In a situation when everything, including research and teaching, is still changing quite rapidly, this contribution does not aim at a systematic description, theoretical summary or thorough explanation of the results and shortcomings of the discourse about gender issues. It merely offers some reflections on this topic, representing the personal views of a Czech scholar who, as an historian, tends to emphasize history more than other disciplines.

The first section of this chapter briefly mentions the construction of gender relations in Czech society, from the efforts to achieve national independence from the Habsburg rule and recognition by Western powers in the nineteenth and early twentieth centuries, to the claims of the communist regime after 1948 to have created a society of gender equality; it also looks at works on women in this period. In the second section two different approaches to the study of women in the Czech Republic after 1989 are characterized. The last section articulates some problems facing those scholars who, in the mid-1990s, are trying to establish Gender Studies as a discipline in Czech academia.

The Roots: Czech Women in History

Modern Czech history presents an interesting example of the intercourse between the national and the women's questions. From the early stage of the Czech national revival, women were addressed as potential and potent saviours of the nation, not only through their role as mothers, but also as active participants in the national awakening. Women heard this call. In the first half of the nineteenth century, women in their poems celebrated the country and nation similarly to men. When, in the later part of the century, the women's question started to be discussed, women placed gender interests after those of the whole nation.

A number of Czech men, leading Prague intellectuals as well as educated men in smaller towns, viewed the emancipation of women as a substantial part of the emancipation of the Czech nation. Although different opinions appeared, limiting women's roles to the family, the idea of women's equality and the priority of national (and all-human) interests was expressed and accepted by both men and women. This concept implied a persuasion that the fulfilment of national demands would enable and bring about the solution of the women's question.[1]

In 1910, Teréza Nováková, a prominent Czech female writer, author of scholarly works on women and representative of the turn of the century Czech women's movement, wrote an article called *Women's Unions and Nationalism* (published in 1912) in which she described the state of the women's movement in the world from a Czech perspective. Nováková established three issues of particular relevance to Czech women. Her reflections, unjustly forgotten yet still topical today, deserve to be presented in her own words.

First, Nováková mentioned the dissolution of an original sisterhood and the development of an unequal relationship between representatives of small nations and women belonging to world powers:

> The female members of a world nation instinctively looked down at a nation the language of which was not known and which did not exceed ten million inhabitants: women of the latter, on their part, felt hurt, offended, that they, who followed the activity of their luckier

sisters with a devoted interest, were not found worth the slightest study, the most modest effort for understanding. (pp. 357–8)

Generally, it seemed that the female creators of the World Union of Women, the International Council, American and English women, having looked at the map of the world only superficially and knowing nothing in detail, apart from their own conditions and perhaps also those of French and German women, dictated to the all-women's movement some general laws which could hardly have been carried out. (p. 360)

Second, Nováková emphasized national interests and specificities in the women's question, including differences among East European Slavic nations. In the International Council, Czech women were supposed to join the section of Austrian women – who 'despised or at least ignored them' – or form a union with other Slavic women.

Although this second alternative, which has never become more than a vague possibility, anyway, seemed more acceptable and pleasant, a person knowing deeply the conditions of various Slavic tribes immediately sensed the danger of an early dissolution. (p. 360)

[F]eminist tasks in various countries and nations cannot be solved according to patterns or, if expressed more politely, general rules . . . women of various countries, if they want to benefit their cause, have to do first what is most needed and to do it in a way appropriate to the nation and environment in which they live. The women's question is not on the same level everywhere: what in one region is a pressing life's problem has in another region lost its topical relevance. (p. 361)

Finally, Nováková criticized the image of men as women's enemies and acknowledged their role in the struggle to improve the position of women:

The women's movement gets its validity not by undertaking a stubborn opposition quand-meme, not from a front against men, but by bringing benefit to the female sex, by strengthening it and raising it to a higher level. (p. 362)

It is necessary to change the front! Yes, even to abolish it, where the adversary does not face it: it is necessary not to change camps but to connect the lines of similarly thinking workers into one camp, disregarding sex. The happiness, advancement, cultural unification and moral deepening of a nation is a common interest of all its members. (p. 363)

Such a joint work will fasten mutual knowledge and thus mutual respect: it is unthinkable that a woman, working and struggling on a man's side, would not establish in him – if he is not of a limited or unhealthily obstinate spirit! – a persuasion about her full and equal value and thus make him help her to acquire what she, as a member of a long neglected sex, lacks. (p. 364)

When Nováková wrote her article, the Czech women's movement had gone through a comparatively successful history and discourses about the social roles, position and achievements of women, as well as feminism, had acquired an important place in the life of Czech society. The three factors which Nováková considered to be substantial for the turn of the century Czech women's movement – the relationship to the West, Czech specificities and the role of men – reappear a hundred years later in debates on Gender Studies in a society where feminism is mentioned mostly in a negative sense, if at all.

Nováková also published the *Pantheon of Czech Women*, an extensive work on female creators and martyrs of the Czech past (Nováková, 1894). Despite the limitations of the time and of the erudition of the author, it presents to this day one of the most detailed studies of the role of women in Czech history. Czech intellectuals of the late nineteenth and first half of the twentieth century have also dealt with other aspects of women's lives, experiences and expectations, extending their interest beyond the national framework. In the first two decades of the twentieth century, Nováková's son wrote a series of women's biographies, including such figures as Elizabeth Barrett-Browning and Charlotte Stieglitz (Novák, 1940). Particularly noteworthy is a monumental enterprise by the famous poet Stanislav Kostka Neumann, a four-volume *Women's History. Popular Sociological, Ethnological and Cultural-Historical Chapters*, describing the social habits of women all over the world from the ancient civilizations until modern times (Neumann, 1931–1932).

During the Second World War, when the nation was endangered, the role of Czech women in the fate of the country came under yet more attention. In 1940, apart from the volume edited by Karel Stloukal (1940), a series of lectures organized by the Women's Centre of the Czech National Council (Česká žena v dějinách národa, 1940) or a collection of articles on women in the Czech drama (Žena v českém umění dramatickém, 1940) emphasized the contribution of women to the progress of the Czech nation. Then 1946 witnessed, for example, the publication of a study about women as the eternal inspiration for the arts (Blažková, 1946) and Pavel Eisner's *The Temple and the Fortress* (1992). The latter still fascinates linguists and translators for its observations on language, general readers for its witty style and present-day feminists for the chapter about 'The Czech language and the woman', displaying the 'sexual discrimination' inherent in the Czech language and in other 'European languages [where] the domination of men over women has been assured for a long time' (Eisner, 1992, pp. 366–7).

After 1948, the women's question was claimed to have been solved. The communist regime pursued the policy of equality in its own way: first, by really improving the position of many lower-class women and second by making women in general as unfree and oppressed as men. The opposition against the regime was led from all-human and not gender-specific positions. In the new society, the women's question and the women's movement, limited to the official and extremely unpopular Women's Union, were separated from the research devoted to women.

Works on women published in this period were of two kinds, both conspicuously lacking any connection with the current situation and problems of Czech women, not to mention the questions raised by Western feminism since the 1960s. The aim of many books was primarily ideological: to show the achievements and prove the superiority of the socialist system over capitalism. Such works often dealt with contemporary women 'in the struggle for the happiness of the people' or with 'the position of women under socialism'. Unable or not allowed to admit that the life of women in socialist countries was not all roses, however, they could do little but illustrate Gustáv Husák's statement that

> in the framework of the new socialist social order it is, for the first time in history, possible to resolve the equal position of women in production, in society, in political and public life, to create for women the same conditions for work and for their irreplaceable role in the family and in the education of the new generation. (Žena a společnost, 1975, p. 51).

A selection from the works by Marx, Engels and Lenin 'on the women's question', translated from Russian – one of many similar selections on various topics – had a similar goal. Its introduction criticized the non-Marxist efforts for women's emancipation for being 'in their consequences directed against the interests of the working-class movement' (Marx-Engels-Lenin, 1973, p. 10). In the atmosphere of the period, even an attempt to acquaint the public with examples of women's journals since the late-nineteenth century was intended only to 'depict the activity of the women's movement struggling during all this time for the realization of the ideas of socialism', thus circumscribing and distorting the image of the Czech women's movement (Vaníčková, 1984, p. 1).

Other works, even if they often had to pay lip-service to the superiority of Marxism and socialism, presented serious scholarly studies on women. They did not deal with women from a women's or feminist point of view, but as a subject of research like any other. Thus, a prominent historian wrote about *Women in the History of Mankind*, emphasizing that 'the greatness of a human being lies probably somewhere deeper in the human mind and therefore the sex should not matter so much' (Polišenský, 1972, p. 7). A pioneering work on witch-hunts mentioned the misogynist implications of 'Hexenhammer', yet concentrated on the sufferings of 'hundreds of thousands of *people* [my italics] directly affected by the inquisition' (Kočí, 1973, p. 19). Apart from other individual studies in various disciplines, literary historians, in particular, have produced a number of works on Czech female writers noteworthy for their empirical research as well as for their literary analyses (Mourková, 1975; Moldánová, 1976).

Two Different Approaches:
Research on Women and Gender Studies

Unlike in the West or in the former Yugoslavia,[2] scholarly interest in women in the contemporary Czech Republic does not result from a women's movement. Today, the women's question is apparently non-existent. No need is expressed for either Women's or Gender Studies. The reaction of both men and women, the public as well as academics, towards the very terms feminism, women's movement and Women's Studies is generally negative.[3] The symptoms of this attitude have been described in a number of writings on Czech or East European women. Serious attempts by local scholars to explain the roots of this attitude from a sociological, philosophical or historical point of view are also available in English (Havelková, 1993; Šiklová, 1993; Šmejkalová-Strickland, 1993; Tatur, 1992).

In the context of this article, it is more important to ask why, given the lack of public demand, women are studied at all? There is no single answer to this question. With a certain amount of simplification and leaving aside a few individuals who defy such a classification, it is possible to distinguish two main approaches to women's and/or gender issues.

The first stream can be considered as a continuation of the research carried out in the past, namely of the non-ideological works on women from the communist period. Women are studied not as women, but as a part of the experience of mankind. Such works are often a 'by-product' of the research within the academic disciplines. The reasons for writing on women vary. Scholars may discover some interesting sources or data while dealing with another topic and use such materials in an article about women. In other cases, they write when asked to participate in a conference or to give a lecture connected with women. Sometimes a women's subject is chosen because it is found attractive or exotic, such as witchcraft, Oriental women or a biography of famous female artists. Or the selection may be haphazard.

Although it is impossible to establish the exact proportion, both men and women contribute to these studies to a similar extent that they are represented in various disciplines. Apart from a few exceptions, for example in demography or in sociology, scholars deal with women rather than with gender.[4] Books on 'attractive' topics are intended for the wider (Czech) public, while the majority of works on women are presented to (Czech) colleagues within the same discipline. Rather than for any theoretical contribution to the discussion on women and gender, an aspect which is usually completely missing in this stream of research, these works are worth appreciation for their professional qualities. Moreover, they often analyse sources which have not been used before and thus are able to provide relevant information on both the history and present-day condition of Czech women.

This approach was exemplified by the conference on 'The role and position of women in the life of Prague', organized by the Archive of Prague on 5–6 October 1993. The contributions covered the life of women from various social strata from the early Middle Ages to the twentieth century, including the first female monasteries in Bohemia, information on women available in legal and other medieval sources, images of women in early modern literature, the social and economic conditions which influenced women in the nineteenth century as well as various aspects of the women's movement. These often revealing papers have shown the richness of sources and the 'human potential' of scholars who could contribute to the compilation of Czech women's history. However, this is not usually the aim of their research. Although Czech scholars, to a varying extent, are acquainted with Western feminism and women's studies, their reactions are quite diverse.

Pavla Horská and Jaroslava Pešková, a well-known historian and a philosopher respectively, both participants of the Prague conference, noted in a published dialogue the contrast between the attention paid to feminism by the Czech public in the late-nineteenth century and the relative absence of this subject in the current mass media and in research. They emphasized the specificity of Czech thinking on the women's question when compared to other countries. Although they are persuaded that both past Czech feminism and current Western feminist theories have little to offer to contemporary Czech women, unlike other authors they do not refuse the inspirations offered by feminism and Women's/Gender Studies (Horská and Pešková, 1992). In extreme though not infrequent cases, scholars can 'decide to open the theme of women's history, the theme of the position, role and self-reflection of women in society before [female] feminists disgust us – men as well as the women collaborating with men – or drive us away from this theme', as the organizer of the conference mentioned in the opening address without any objections from the audience (Pešek, 1993).

Can works on women written by scholars who deliberately avoid any connection of their research to women's experiences and efforts to change gender relations (not to mention those who are explicitly anti-feminist) form a part of or at least contribute to Women's Studies? In the Czech context this question is not a major one. More important, as far as this stream of work is concerned, is that random or unsystematic studies cannot and do not even try to change the basically male-oriented disciplines. Thus scholarly works, university lectures and reading lists will continue to create the image of the world in which women simply do not appear. Undertaken and presented as an addition to or diversion from 'more serious' research, such works may even reconfirm the marginal status of women's topics.

Another approach to the study of women's and gender issues is promoted by a group gathered around the Gender Studies Centre in Prague.[5] Consisting of a couple of journalists, editors, representatives of freelance professions and scholars and students, the group aims to establish Gender Studies in the Czech Republic as an academic discipline. Inspired by their personal experiences and/or by an acquaintance with Western feminism, they want to introduce the gender aspect into public consciousness and debates, into research and teaching.

Among the scholarly activities of the group, priority is given to education, public lectures in and outside Prague, as well as to lectures and seminars for university students. The biggest achievements so far are the regular courses on 'Social problems from a gender point of view' at the Department of Social Work, the Charles University, and on 'Gender, culture, society' at the School of Social Sciences, organized by Jiřina Šiklová, Jiřina Šmejkalová (and currently Hana Havelková) respectively, where other members of the group participate as guest lecturers. The Gender Studies Centre is also helping to organize courses at other faculties and plans to set up similar courses at universities outside Prague.

Scholars and students, as well as those making their living outside academia, also write on women and gender, explaining to the Czech public why it is important to deal with gender issues and why not to be afraid of feminism; and to the Western public why there is no feminism in our country and how the gender relations here differ from the West.[6] Sociology, with several students concerned with gender issues and with a couple of interesting projects already finished or near completion, seems to be the most advanced among the disciplines.[7] Czech women's history, particularly the women's movement, also attracts the attention of both history students and representatives of other disciplines. In this, as in most other cases however, research is only in an initial stage.

In a way, Czech Gender Studies are experiencing a 'golden age' which Western feminists now remember with a certain nostalgia. The discipline is young, the tasks are numerous and the number of people involved is very small. There seems to be a place for everybody and, indeed, every newcomer is warmly welcome. Even in research, there is (still) no rivalry. This idyllic image has its reverse side though, particularly the disproportion between the countless duties and noble aims and the limited number of people available for their fulfilment. On a theoretical level, there are also still many questions to be solved and the rest of this article is devoted to them.

Identity, Message and Audience: Why Deal with Gender Issues?

In February 1994, the Prague Gender Studies Centre and the Slovak-Czech journal *Aspekt*,[8] published in Bratislava, organized a round table 'Feminism, Why Not?' The debate exposed several features characteristic of the current thinking on women in the two parts of the former Czechoslovakia. The title hinted at the doubtful attitude of the two publics towards feminism. A great deal of attention was devoted to a comparison of women's movements and Women's Studies in the West with the Czech and Slovak situations, including the question as to whether a different kind of feminism could develop in Slovak and Czech societies. The participants agreed that current activities should take into consideration the specificities of Czech and Slovak women's history and of the development of gender consciousness.

The discussion also revealed a substantial difference in approaches towards the role of men in Gender/Women's Studies. While Slovak women claimed that men's experiences, but not men themselves, should be included in the emerging discussions on the women's question, according to most Czech representatives both the subjects of research and those carrying it out should respect the category of gender (Hradílková, 1994, p. 2).

At first sight this debate brings to mind the turn of the century discourse on the women's movement. In the framework of this article, it is not possible to analyse this – real or illusory – similarity and its possible reasons.[9] The following pages will show, though, how the issues emphasized by Teréza Nováková permeate the efforts to establish Gender Studies in the late-twentieth century Czech Republic. Given the general lack of interest, the main question is: Why try to establish Women's or Gender Studies at all? For whom, to whom and about what should we speak?

Identity

A gender-based identity – or at least its reflection in public discourse – seems to be missing in Czech society.[10] As one of the first activists for Gender Studies in Prague has put it:

> Even those who have not been passive and who are thinking about these 'hot' topics [gender issues and feminism] still hesitate to verbalize their problem as a 'problem', since they feel very unsure about its specifics. They only feel vaguely that there might be some 'gender' problem either in public or in private life. (Hradílková, 1993, p. 20)

For the group around the Gender Studies Centre the question of identity has a different form. Do they speak as individuals, as women or as Czechs? Should they represent the group or Czech – and maybe even East European – women?[11] In theory it is emphasized that both women and men should express men's and women's experiences. Indeed, one man has been taking part in the activities of the Gender Studies Centre. However, it is not the case that women from the Centre speak for women and the man for men. While he explicitly presents his well-thought-out feminist views, the women mostly hesitate to define themselves as feminists.

This reluctance can be followed on the levels of content and terminology. Avoiding the term 'feminism' means more than a mere tactic, taking into consideration the prejudices of the Czech public, or a way to distance oneself from stereotypical image/s of feminism and from some Western feminists who came to Prague after 1989. Dealing with women simply does not seem to require the use of a specific label, especially if the label is felt to be imposed from outside.

The attitude towards feminism also reflects a search for an approach corresponding to Czech conditions, which do not encourage a separation along gender lines. Thus even:

> contemporary theoretical thought evinces a reluctance to treat this [women's] problem in isolation, putting general human problems above that of sexed identity, and showing a relatively high degree of acceptance and entrenchment of the idea of the equality of the sexes. (Havelková, 1993, p. 62)

'Women particularly,' as Jana Hradílková (1993, p. 20) has observed:

> strongly refuse to be separated from men, for various reasons including, perhaps, that they are afraid of categorization, of being defined, separated and observed as something that needs special care – because special care automatically presumes the presence of oppression.

Two points should be emphasized in this context: the unwillingness to separate oneself from society as a whole, which is also valid for the women (though maybe not for the man) from the Centre[12] and the generally accepted superiority of all-human matters over the interests of any group, including women.[13] At the same time, however, the experience of the past, when somebody constantly spoke for others (in the name of the working-class, progressive citizens or socialist women), has created a feeling that one has no right to represent anybody but oneself, or maybe a group of close friends who share the same views.

Although the stress put on the particularity of Czech conditions recalls Nováková's views, the parallel does not reflect a similarity in national feelings, but rather in the reaction towards Western feminism or feminists: an unwillingness to be considered as little (undeveloped) sisters. While Western students of the women's position in the former Eastern bloc often still see Eastern and Central European countries as a compact whole and even speak about a 'uniformity of the Eastern European experience' (Watson, 1993, p. 71), women in Central and Eastern Europe, on the other hand, tend to overestimate the past and present differences among their societies. It is 'the West' that matters while the Czech identity is in a sense interchangeable with a Czechoslovak or an East European one. This does not mean that Czech women see themselves as East Europeans, but rather that the emphasis on local – be it Czech, Czechoslovak or East European – specificities is primarily directed to the West. We Czech and other East European women do not have to emphasize that our countries differ from each other. We 'know' it . . .

Message

The promoters of the new discipline mostly agree that its subject should be gender, rather than women. This decision reflects both the above-mentioned views of those who conduct research and the sensitivities of the Czech public. If the work is to have any sense and impact it seems that it should concentrate both on the particular and the common problems of the two genders without preference. Although the existence of discrimination against women is acknowledged it is felt that it must not be solved by an opposed extreme, such as 'positive discrimination'. The focus on gender is expressed not only in the name of the Centre, but also in reflections about feminism and gender relations in the Czech Republic.

All this can be seen as symptomatic of an early stage of women's awareness and of research, the analysis of the past and present relations among genders forming a necessary precondition for understanding women's specific problems. Or the introduction of the problem of gender identity into public discourse and the development of Gender Studies can be considered as a goal, with research on women as an initial step. Hana Havelková (1993, p. 72) referred to the latter alternative when she wrote that 'The female problem, if grasped by women, will at last open questions of gender relations, and could become the model for analysing the general problem of identity in post-socialist society.

Despite the proclaimed focus on gender, the mainly female members of the group appear to be primarily interested in women. Leaving aside the already-mentioned articles on the current state of gender awareness in Czech society, research into history, philosophy, sociology, or film, art and literary history deals with women more than with gender, not to mention the somewhat overlooked experiences of men.

Another dilemma of the emerging Gender Studies concerns the relationship towards Western feminism and Women's and Gender Studies. Can Western feminist theories be applied to Czech conditions? To what extent can the results of Western research be used by Czech scholars? The answer to this question would hardly be unanimous. Students of women's issues may appreciate the achievements of Western feminism and admit that it is possible to find inspiration in Western works. At the same time, they will probably agree that the Czech situation has been and still is different from conditions in Western countries and therefore requires a specific approach. Their views about the validity of the theoretical claims of feminism, however, differ substantially.

In this situation, it is not clear whether the new discipline should be based on translations of the 'classical' and recent texts from Western languages or on local works which would take into consideration 'specific' Czech conditions. There is no doubt that Czech students of gender issues should be acquainted with the most important Western works. However, if because of the lack of financial resources, only a few texts can be translated, then the problem of selection criteria emerges. Which disciplines and currents of thought should be given preference?

To rely on local sources is no less problematic. Given the limited number of Czech scholars dealing with women's and gender issues, some fields of research and approaches would be completely excluded. It would be hard if not impossible to secure a sufficient quality in the published works. Even more contradictory is the question suggested by the round table on feminism in the former Czechoslovakia: can or should a specific Czech (or Slovak) or East European feminism develop?

Audience

Scholars dealing with gender cannot ignore the lack of knowledge and interest and even the prejudices of Czech society concerning the concepts and terminology of feminism and Women's Studies. The experience of the communist period and the conviction of the proponents of Gender Studies, resulting at least partly from this experience, preclude any campaigns aimed at persuading the public about a certain 'truth'. Even when the audience is ready to listen and to learn, the general level of knowledge and consciousness requires that the same terms and basic conceptions are explained again in each lecture or interview. Teaching also implies a certain amount of simplification and, because of the newness of the subject, often does not offer a chance to benefit from discussion.

What then are the possibilities for Czech scholars concerned not only with 'enlightening' the public, but also with producing serious scholarly works, to obtain feedback on their hypotheses and conclusions? They may write for their small group of friends interested in gender and women's topics, but dealing mostly with other fields of research. They may also present their works to colleagues working in their disciplines. The latter, however, often do not take research on women seriously, especially if it has any connection with feminism.

The last alternative, sometimes chosen by Czech as well as other East European scholars, is to write for a Western public. This makes sense, especially if the aim of the work is to describe the current Czech situation in gender relations and the reaction of Czech society towards feminism or in the case of such disciplines and subjects which require special knowledge and would not find a sufficient readership in the Czech Republic.

Writing for the West, however, is not always the best or even a possible solution. When describing women's experiences, especially under the communist regime and to a certain extent even in the present one, some East European scholars tend or have to write what the Western audience or editors want to hear. How many works on Czech women would Western publishing houses and periodicals produce anyway? Even if all the works on gender written by Czech scholars could be published abroad, one aspect still has to be taken into consideration: especially in this period, when the questions of gender relations and identities and of women's experiences have only started to be (re)introduced into Czech society, research on Czech women is relevant and should be presented particularly to the Czech public.

As for the future, let us return to Nováková's vision from 1912. For her, the joint effort of women and men:

> on a worldwide scale according to some general rule is still, under current conditions, impossible, impossible at least in some fields. Certainly its time will come with a culture that is constantly deepening, with a humanity that is always being refined; when it comes, then this activity, which will encompass the diversity of millions within its cycles, will appear as something natural, without struggles between sexes, tribes, political actors. Then there will be no fortifications, no contempt, no envy.
>
> I think that this day is still very far away; meanwhile, in the half-light of these defensive times, let us not, we women and men, twiddle our thumbs and give up but let us all fulfill our cultural tasks. (Nováková, 1912, p. 364)

Notes

1 Unlike women in some of the other East European countries who had supported men in the national struggles, Czech women were indeed 're-warded' for their assistance by the comparatively favourable legislation of the first Czechoslovak Republic, gaining for example the right to vote in 1918 (David, 1991, p. 41).

2 In a sense, this was also the case for the Czech society of the nineteenth and first half of the twentieth century.

3 'Gender Studies' is accepted with less aversion and even with some interest or curiosity, not only because such a discipline is less well known than women's studies, but also because it implies equality and not animosity between the sexes.

4 Research on specific men's views, experiences or problems seems to be completely non-existent in the Czech human and social sciences.

5 The Gender Studies Centre was founded by Jiřina Šiklová in October 1991, with the support and encouragement of the Network of East-West Women, as a library, education and consulting centre dealing with gender issues. It is currently financed by the German Frauen Anstiftung. The Centre (with originally two and today with three co-ordinators and a librarian, with some assistance from volunteers) runs and expands its library, publishes a Czech-English Bulletin, provides information about women's organizations and about activities and publications concerning women and gender, presents women's issues in the mass media, maintains contacts with Czech and foreign institutions and supports and encourages special projects, such as the prevention of violence against women. One of the most popular enterprises are language courses with debates on gender. The activities of the Centre also include organizing popular and scholarly lectures and seminars and local and international conferences and supporting university courses and publications of Czech and translated works on gender, women and feminism. A similar centre is being established in the Moravian town of Brno.

6 For example, the above mentioned articles in *Bodies of Bread and Butter* (Hradílková, 1993) and the special issue on 'women in philosophy' of the *Philosophical Journal* from 1992.

7 One of the projects, led by the sociologist Marie Čermáková, is carried out by members of the group working in other fields.

8 *Aspekt* is a quarterly journal devoted to women's issues and intended for both the scholarly and the wider public.

9 A lack of research on the current situation and on the history of the Czech women's movement does not allow for any conclusions. If the resemblance is really based on a specificity in Czech thinking about women, its roots can be looked for in the process of the formation of gender relations, from the emergence of modern Czech society, with the intercourse of the national and women's questions, to the atmosphere of equality typical of the communist period. It is also possible to suggest that some structural similarities exist between the two seemingly contradictory situations. Although the Czech nation no longer has to struggle for its independence, society is going through a period of transformation when old identities are being redefined and new ones searched for. From the perspective of a small State, striving to be included 'into Europe', the role of Western countries can appear similar to the period when the nation was trying to achieve world recognition and the right for an independent State. In both cases, the emphasis on local specificities may be a reaction to the impossibility of influencing the decisions of the powerful States.

10 Although one encounters some clearly gendered jokes, remarks or behaviour every day, these are not conceived as gender-based either by men or women. A good example is publicity: women are not offended by the use of female nudity in advertisements and when a sequence with sexual con-

notations mocking men appeared, women rather than men confessed that they felt uncomfortable watching it.
11 This dilemma presents a difference between the current situation and the nineteenth and early-twentieth centuries, when the representatives of the women's movement mostly acted and wrote as *Czechs*.
12 The roots of this phenomenon can be traced back to the communist period when to differ was 'wrong', both in the eyes of the regime (and thus potentially dangerous) and of the public which, to some extent at least, internalized the official view.
13 Here, too, the impact of the shared oppression and resistance to it under the communist regime can still be felt. Concurrently, this attitude is connected to the tradition of the idea of equality of both sexes which survives to this day.

References

BLAŽKOVÁ, J. (1946) *Woman, The Eternal Inspiration of Arts: Woman in the Arts from the Stone Age until Picasso* (*Žena, věčná inspirace umění: Žena ve výtvarném umění od doby kamenné až po Picassa*), Prague, Symposion.

The Czech Woman in the History of the Nation (1940) (*Česká žena v dějinách národa*), Prague, Novina.

DAVID, K. (1991) 'Czech feminists and nationalism in the late Habsburg monarchy: "The first in Austria"', *Journal of Women's History*, 3 (2), pp. 26–45.

EISNER, P. (1992) *The Temple and the Fortress. A Book about the Czech Language* (*Chrám i tvrz: Kniha o češtině*), Prague, Lidové noviny (first published in 1946).

Filosoficky Časopis (Philosophical Journal) (1992) Special Issue on Women in Philosophy, 40 (5).

HAVELKOVÁ, H. (1993) 'A few prefeminist thoughts', in FUNK, N. and MUELLER, M. (Eds) *Gender Politics and Post-Communism: Reflections from Eastern Europe and the Former Soviet Union*, New York/London, Routledge, pp. 62–73.

HORSKÁ, P. and PEŠKOVÁ, J. (1992) 'A dialogue between a female historian and a female philosopher about the women's question in Bohemia', (Rozhovor mezi filosofkou a historičkou o ženské otázce v Čechách) *Filosofický časopis*, 40 (5), pp. 757–68.

HRADÍLKOVÁ, J. (1993) '(Re-)building the house of gender studies', in TRNKA, S. and BUSHEIKIN, L. (Eds), *Bodies of Bread and Butter: Reconfiguring Women's Lives in the Post-communist Czech Republic*, Prague, The Gender Studies Centre, pp. 19–22.

HRADÍLKOVÁ, J. (1994) Round Table Report: 'Feminism, Why Not?', *Bulletin of the Prague Gender Studies Centre* (Summer), p. 2.

Kočí, J. (1973) *Witch-Trials: From the History of the Inquisition and Witch-Trials in the Czech Lands in the 16th–18th Centuries* (*Čarodějnické procesy: Z dějin inkvizice a čarodějnických procesů v českých zemích v 16.–18. století*), Prague, Horizont.

Marx-Engels-Lenin (1973) *To the Women's Question* (K ženské otázce), Prague, Svoboda.

Moldánová, D. (1976) *Božena Benešová*, Prague, Melantrich.

Mourková, J. (1975) *Růžena Svobodová*, Prague, Melantrich.

Neumann, S. K. (1931–1932) *Women's History. Popular Sociological, Ethnological and Cultural-Historical Chapters* (*Dějiny ženy: Populární kapitoly sociologické, etnologické a kulturně historické*), Prague, Melantrich.

Novák, A. (1940) *Portraits of Women* (*Podobizny žen*), Prague-Brno, Novina (first published in 1918).

Nováková, T. (1894) *Pantheon of Czech Women, I, From the Most Ancient Times Until the Rebirth of the Czech Nation* (*Slavín žen českých, I, Od nejstarších dob do znovuzrození národa českého*), Prague, Libuše.

Nováková, T. (1912) 'Women's unions and nationalism' in Nováková, T. *From the Women's Movement*, Prague, Jos. R. Vilímek, pp. 354–64.

Pešek, J. (1993) 'Women's history – A both historical and topical theme' (Dějiny žen – téma historické i aktuální). Paper presented at a conference 'Women of the Prague towns from the middle ages to the twentieth century', Prague, October 1993.

Polišenský, J. (1972) *Women in the History of Mankind* (Ženy v dějinách ľudstva), Bratislava, Obzor.

Šiklová, J. (1993) 'Macdonalds, terminators, Coca Cola ads – and feminism? Imports from the West', in Trnka, S. and Busheikin, L. (Eds) *Bodies of Bread and Butter: Reconfiguring Women's Lives in the Post-communist Czech Republic*, Prague, The Gender Studies Centre, pp. 7–11.

Šmahel, F. (1993) 'Review of Katherine Walsh: Ein neues Bild der Frau in Mittelalter?' *Český časopis historický*, 91 (1), p. 147.

Šmejkalová-Strickland, J. (1993) 'Do Czech women need feminism? Perspectives of feminist theories and practices in the Czech Republic', in Trnka, S. and Busheikin, L. (Eds) *Bodies of Bread and Butter: Reconfiguring Women's Lives in the Post-communist Czech Republic*, Prague, The Gender Studies Centre, pp. 13–18.

Stloukal, K. (1940) (Ed.) *Czech Queens, Princesses and Great Women* (*Královny, kněžny a velké ženy české*), Prague, Jos. R. Vilímek.

Tatur, M. (1992) 'Why is there no women's movement in Eastern Europe', in Lewis, P. G. (Ed.) *Democracy and Civil Society in Eastern Europe: Selected Papers from the Fourth World Congress for Soviet and East European Studies*, London, Macmillan Press, pp. 61–75.

Vaníčková, B. (1984) (Ed.) *A Collection of Selected Extracts of Women's Journals* (*Sborník vybraných ukázek ženských časopisů*), Prague, MONA.

Watson, P. (1993) 'The rise of masculinism in Eastern Europe', *New Left Review*, 198 (March–April), pp. 71–82.

Jitka Malečková

The Woman in the Czech Dramatic Art (1940) (*Žena v českém umění dramatickém*), Prague, Topič.

Woman and Society: A Contribution to the Problematics of the Women's Movement (1975) (*Příspěvek k problematice Žena a společnost ženského hnutí*), Brno, Knihovna Jiřího Mahena.

Chapter 7

Possibilities for Women's Studies in Post-communist Countries: Where Are We Going?

Svetlana Kupryashkina

When given the wings, fly! (Lesya Ukrainka, 1901)

The word 'studies' when translated into Ukrainian is homonymous with the word 'studio' meaning an artist's place. When a group of enthusiastic Kiev scholars was going through the registration process to obtain legal status for the first Ukrainian Centre for Women's Studies, the most commonly asked question was: 'Where will this place be where women can come and draw pictures?' This reflects both the novelty of the field and the inapplicability of the term 'Women's Studies' to the current discourse, as well as the confusion people experience when they encounter it. The picture, however, that can be drawn of the emergence of Women's Studies as a discipline, a research field or just a simple notion in Ukraine is lacking in perfection. Many details are still missing of this picture. Who embodies the ideas? What can be considered an academic base for development? Whose needs and interests might such an approach articulate? What target groups and politics are to be influenced? And finally, is this novel approach in any way generated by or connected with any of the existing social and political movements? My intention here, therefore, is to draw a sketch rather than a complete picture of the possibilities for the development of Women's Studies and feminist organizations in Ukraine and, more generally, in other Republics of the former USSR.

'Socialist Emancipation': What Preceded It

The breakdown of the Soviet Union did not eliminate dangerous tendencies in that society but, on the contrary, made them more visible. Among such tendencies were the almost complete distrust of women's leaders and the women's movement in general, not to mention the classic socialist ideals of solidarity and collective action. Now, at a time when women, more than ever before, need the unity and power of collective decision-making and action, these ideas appear irrelevant, unimportant and are rejected and despised by the majority of women. Women tend to be the first to refuse themselves the right to decide their own fate. Several public opinion studies carried out at various periods of time in Ukraine steadily show that at least one third of Ukrainian women would deny women the right to be in the government, joined by one quarter of men questioned for the same purpose. The majority of those remaining, while having nothing against the right as such, would still raise doubts about the appropriateness of such a measure.[1] It is, therefore, no surprise that the first free elections for Verkhovna Rada (Parliament of Ukraine) held in 1990 and the recent one in March 1994 reflected the same tendencies and showed a definite decline in women's political representation. Women who were coming to the polls did not trust other women with power; instead they preferred to vote for men. Moreover, despite the fact that there were no specific women's needs formulated in most of the electoral programmes, women still preferred to vote for those candidates.

The reasons for this appear deeply embedded both in Soviet and further back in Ukrainian and Russian pre-revolutionary history and culture, as well as in the development of intellectual thought. First, there is the model of power. Power was never anything but authoritarian and totalitarian both in Russia (which only abolished serfdom in 1861, although in practice it remained for decades afterwards) and in the USSR. No form of government other than 'one-man rule' (which normally assumed a form of unrestricted monarchy or, later, 'dictatorship of the proletariat') has been popular and effective in an area so vast and diverse as Russia has been (Ukraine was incorporated into Russia for most of its history). Russia has never, in any form, experienced what might be called 'democratic rule' and, thus, it lacks any historic precedent in this regard.[2]

Second, there are economic reasons. Remaining an agrarian, rural country before and well beyond the 1917 revolution, Russia's economic output and growth largely depended on the smallest farming production unit: the nuclear, extended family. The pressure on maintaining the nuclear family withstood all the 'liberal deviations' of the first years of Soviet rule with its ideas of 'free love', the abolition of marriage and the adoption of children by the State. Restrictive anti-abortion Stalinist legislation was aimed at reinforcing the family, making it the smallest constituent of the transforming industrial State. Within the family, the same authoritarian model was being reproduced at the micro-level.[3]

Third, Russian Orthodoxy, which for many years remained a State religion and, what is more important, practically the only one, prescribed all power to the male family members, leaving women only with devotion, obedience and lots of work to perform. This combination of almost 95 per cent illiteracy, a rigid political system, restrictive religion, the absence of any form of middle-class, the dominance of the agrarian sector of the economy and the problematic economic system resulting from it: this is what Russia was at the beginning of the twentieth century, leaving women among the poorest and the least educated, without passports and legal rights – in fact, almost completely neglected. Nothing even remotely resembling the Reformation in Europe, bourgeois revolutions, the War of Independence in America, the rise of a middle-class, the development of the philosophy of individualism with its positive outcomes leading to the growth of public and, eventually, feminist consciousness, ever occurred on Russian soil where Peter the First (1672–1725) may still be considered as one of the greatest reformers of all times.

Moreover, what is considered as the 'height of Russian intellectualism' in the nineteenth century, which was represented mostly in the works of revolutionary Russian democrats and liberal progressive writers, also failed to incorporate the women's question into its agenda. This is the context for the later development of socialist feminist ideas in Russia, which subsumed the question of female emancipation under the broader and comprehensive issue of social justice and connected 'the woman question' and the full liberation of women with the victorious social revolution. Dmitrij Pisarev (1956), Nikolai Dobrolyubov (1956) and Nikolai Chernyshevsky with his famous *Chto Delat? (What Is To Be Done?)* (1982) remain among the few sympathetic to women's needs and advocates of equality between sexes. But the latter's book showed more of a Utopian model of relationships between man and woman in an imaginary socialist community than anything close to existing reality.[4] In practice, women were later equally incorporated into all the revolutionary activities in Russia, starting with 'The People's Will' and its stunning terrorist activities[5] and ending with Left Socialist-Revolutionaries who, in their attempt to assassinate Lenin in 1918, were incapable of finding anyone among their ranks but semi-blind Fanny Kaplan, equally devoted and ready to self-sacrifice, to perform the task.[6] Thus women remained omnipresent, instrumental, but never in full power in decision-making even among their most progressive, enlightened 'socialist brothers'.

In Ukraine during the nineteenth century, however, all progressive intellectuals were operating under the idea of Ukrainian national emancipation from the Russian Tsarist regime. This united their efforts and made other contradictions less relevant. Women appeared to be relatively more visible in intellectual and public spheres, starting with figures such as Lesya Ukrainka,[7] Marko Vovchok, Olga Kobylanska, going well into the twentieth century with the names of Milena Rudnytska, Olga Kobrynska and even to the next generation of intellectuals in the 1930s and 1940s whose tragic fate was to be torn between battling against Bolshevism and collaborating with the Nazis in their struggle for independence. Overall, individual rights and freedoms for a woman could still be considered only within the framework of the total success of the national cause and were only seen to matter when they coincided with that cause. Any ideas that women intellectuals produced which appeared to be separate from mainstream thinking were considered alien and not treated seriously, often labelled as 'irrelevant', 'pretentious' or 'unimportant' by fellow-intellectuals. Intellectuals' greatest scorn was always aimed at women intellectuals who stood apart from what was generally accepted, with the most common accusation that of 'élitism'. True, women intellectuals of pre-revolutionary Russia, Ukraine and then of the USSR belonged to an educated, relatively well-to-do class but, at the same time, in the absence of what might be called a women's movement, they alone could articulate women's needs and problems by using the privileges their relatively higher social status provided for them.

The biggest blow to the women's movement and to the formation of a feminist consciousness in Russia has been to isolate educated women from other women, accusing them of 'élitism' and a lack of understanding of 'ordinary' women's lives and needs. At the same time, this has pushed them on to the margins of male intellectual society which, in its turn, did not represent any major political force and operated in a country ruled by populist stereotypes, where the mere word 'intelligent' could be used in derogatory terms. In general, in the USSR the role of the intelligentsia has been reduced to that of a 'technocratic workforce', scientifically and ideologically legitimizing the system and laying sophisticated scientific grounds for almost all the Party directives. This might partially explain the confusion and frustration felt by many Soviet intellectuals after the demise of the Communist regime.

The niche which educated women were finally forced to find for themselves still remains the same. It is small but comfortable enough for them to realize some of their intellectual ambitions and potentials. At the same time it is as distant as ever from contributing to the general cause of the liberation of all women. Some of these women are really turning into individual reactionaries, more concerned with maintaining their controversial but still to some extent privileged status, sometimes assuming the worst characteristics of bourgeois upper-class attitudes, thus remaining alienated from the majority of other women.

The Soviet Period: Equality or Loss of Gender Identity?

The pledge that the communist regime made after 1917 to build an egalitarian State was ambitious and unrealistic to the extreme. Having ideologically exploited 'the most progressive ideas elaborated by humankind', as Lenin was always putting it, the Bolsheviks failed to create adequately corresponding legislative and political systems and were eventually swallowed by the same monster they had created. The fundamental postulates of socialism, having been fitted into the old Russian bureaucratic administrative system combined with traditional, if not rural values, became unrecognizable and started to work in the reverse. Thus, the right to work turned into an unbearable duty, sometimes for as long as fifty years, performed for symbolic pay. The right to housing turned into the shameful 'propiska' residence permit: this has survived in the former USSR region until the present day and its loss could also mean losing all other socially attached benefits.[8]

The tenet of women's liberation, in a similar way, turned into the most wicked and sophisticated form of exploitation. Never relieved from the heavy burden of housekeeping – many regions still remain what may be described as underdeveloped, with people getting their water from wells and heating their houses with wood – women had imposed on themselves a new burden of full-time work and political participation. A crucial breakthrough in the development of the 'young socialist State' was, therefore, achieved by attracting millions of women into the workforce. The political stakes of such actions were high. In exulting the victories of socialist ideology, women were especially important and were made especially visible. The world will not easily forget the women fighter-pilots of the Second World War, women metalworkers, millions of women university graduates, the first woman cosmonaut, Valentina Tereshkova, who was then made the Head of the Soviet Women's Committee. These were the examples of the supremacy of one ideology over another personified in particular living examples. Only by consolidating the efforts of millions of low-paid and unpaid workers (millions of camp prisoners also count) and expropriating the products of their labour was the State able to achieve huge surpluses in production and maintain its international status. Thus women's share in all of this great property accumulation appears large, although unrecognized. No one has yet recognized the cost women paid for their full-time lives.

One of the most tragic consequences of the greatest social experiment in history was that outside and, very often, inside the family sphere, an almost complete loss of gender identity for both men and women was occurring in the USSR. This is not as paradoxical as it seems. Cynically proclaiming gender equality, the system at the same time tried to erase whatever diversities existed between the sexes, making everyone service the 'great socialist Motherland' and subordinating all other needs to this ultimate goal. The State thus assumed almost ultimate control over its citizens.

The state in this instance acted as a 'great patriarch' towards its citizens, both men and women, granting rights, taking away rights, acting on its own discretion. The situation was such that virtually no man could remove any individual rights and freedoms from a woman which the State had not already taken and used at its discretion. No one belonged to anyone. Everyone belonged to the State. And the State was very, very protective. The degree of State interference in the private sphere acquired an immense scale during Soviet times when almost everyone was encouraged to spy on their family members, workmates, friends, neighbours and/or report on their own private life. This attempt to erase gender identity was thus planned as the most powerful means of social control, penetrating deep into the human value system where nothing else mattered but survival. It made the images drawn in Orwell's *Animal Farm* pale into insignificance when compared to actual reality.

Male identity has also undergone a serious transformation under the Soviet system. Men (along with women) have been deprived of any decent source of income. They have been forced into mandatory army service whose militant ideology demands full sacrifice of its disciples and is often based on the demonstration of crude force. Homosexuality was always treated as a crime. Male members of society have been deprived of whatever might constitute power. They have been reduced either to mere 'combat force' or, more correctly, 'gun fodder' at war or a huge army of hard manual labour on the construction sites of the 'great socialist Motherland'. They have, therefore, often been taken away from their families or killed. The demographic imbalance created in the course of 'The Great Terror', and following it, the Second World War, was so huge that it only started to level by the 1960s. (In my grandmother's generation almost half the women remained widows and she became one at the age of twenty-nine.)

There is a strong argument, developed by some Eastern European feminists, that their role in the family provided some autonomy for women (in bringing up children and other tasks, for example) and thus lessened the direct interference of the State in their lives.[9] Being male, on the other hand, always required full-time participation in military, industrial or political activities. Maybe this explains the fact that life expectancy for men is ten years lower than for women in countries of the former USSR – and the gap is growing – while the rate of suicides among men exceeds that of women five times.

The task, therefore, remains one of carefully restoring and, at the same time, developing gender identity on a more egalitarian basis, creating new paradigms for the egalitarian co-existence of all diverse social groups and securing these in the new legislation and policies of the new democratic societies. Unfortunately, the process which is now going on in post-communist societies seems to be focusing more on restoring or preserving old traditional cultural and religious values and protecting them from any outside influences, than considering the actual needs and aspirations of their members. In such circumstances, no progressive legislation by itself will be able to introduce major changes into societies where basic human rights still remain a luxury or are unknown, unless all the particularities of their historic and social development are taken into consideration. The gap which may appear between progressive legislation and the current historical and social realities can subvert or dramatically postpone democratic developments in our region. Qualitatively new approaches are now needed to fully understand the situation in the region. Gender research, in this regard, presents a unique opportunity for such an analysis. Currently, there are no obvious indicators that this will become popular in the near future.

Women's Studies in Ukraine: Current Trends

There is a long history of women's community organizing (including academic groups and organizations of women) in pre-revolutionary Ukraine and then in Western Ukraine before 1939. Organizations such as the Ukrainian Society of Women with Higher Education had a certain impact on the country's intellectual life and their representation at the International Federation of University Women enhanced the status of Ukrainian women in general. Many of the women involved did not use the term 'feminist' to describe themselves, while in reality the issues they addressed were genuine women's issues.[10] However, in Soviet historiography all records of this period were later carefully erased along with many other names and organizations labelled 'nationalist'. The starting point in the history of the women's movement was, therefore proclaimed to be 1917. The real history remained hidden.

Ukraine proclaimed its independence on 24 August 1991, after the failed coup in Moscow. Immediately, new women's groups and organizations started to form and more than a dozen all-Ukrainian organizations with various agendas now exist. However, they are not always cognisant of their predecessors and if they are, mainly only of their old names and rhetorics. Many of these organizations have raised environmental concerns which have been particularly acute since 26 April 1986 – the day of Chernobyl – a black date in the Ukrainian calendar. It is because of environmental and health issues that women's issues have initially emerged and only gradually have women's organizations developed.

In intellectual circles, feminist ideas have started to circulate because of more freedom in foreign travel, access to literature and the ending of censorship. More women academics are using the opportunities to attend international conferences on women and feminism. They can now gather together to discuss ideas and try to adapt them to the Ukrainian situation. This is how the feminist seminar at the Institute of Literature of the Ukrainian Academy of Sciences came to be organized, headed by Solomiia Pavlychko. Women are also active in public life and the first collection of essays, a feminist literary critique of Ukrainian literature, has appeared in the journal *Slovo I Tchas* (*Word and Time*).[11] There is also some conventional research on women within a more traditional sociological framework and although it does not draw very much on feminist research methods, it still provides a great deal of factual material. However, with the collapse of regular State funding for the collection of statistics, most official statistics on women are no longer available: the most recent are dated 1991. With the current availability of grants, some surveys are being done regionally but a more systematic approach, with regular funding, is needed.

The Ukrainian Center for Women's Studies began as a public organization of women-scholars 'to enhance the position of women in Ukrainian society, promote research on women and disseminate feminist ideas'. The group has now won several small-scale grants to conduct various research projects. It has a small library of feminist literature and publishes a bilingual newsletter.

The year 1992 was significant for women's studies in the region. Feminist groups and research began to develop and the first two Western scholars from Women's Studies' courses came to Kyiv on Fulbright fellowships. Dianne Farrell from Moorhead University, Minnesota, taught a course on 'The History of Women in Europe' at the Department of Mass Communication and Journalism at Kyiv State University. Martha Bohachevsky-Chomiak from the US National Endowment for Humanities came to teach at the History Department of Kyiv University and then at Kyivo-Mohyla Academy – the first private university in Kyiv financed by the Soros Foundation and government funds. The appearance of such a novel discipline as Women's Studies is unprecedented in Ukraine and both scholars found it difficult to fit into the standard university curricula which, naturally, did not contain Women's Studies or women's history. The audience was very receptive to the ideas presented, although some students did not hide the fact that they enrolled mostly because they wanted to hear lectures delivered in English or just to learn more about America. This situation is common all around Ukraine and many Fulbrighters and other Fellows do not feel at ease with the Ukrainian educational system which is only now beginning its restructuring.[12]

The experiences of these two American scholars as academics and teachers in Kyiv again remind us how incongruent are most of their approaches with the Ukrainian system of education. They also point towards confusion in the terms used, especially how women who develop research on women, whether inside or outside the academic institutions, try to omit the term 'Women's Studies' or 'feminism', replacing them instead with 'gender research' which they think is more neutral. More knowledge of Western literature about these issues is needed but, with most of it available only in English, it can only be acquired by people who read English since very few translations are available.

However, another large source of material remains undiscovered by many modern feminists. This comprises the writings of our own women-activists and feminists of the past, although most of this is still unattainable by the wider public. If this could be incorporated into contemporary discourse, it could change it dramatically and help it to acquire a truly national scope. For the time being, however, feminist discourse in Ukraine, as well as in other countries of Eastern Europe and the former USSR, remains influenced and controlled by Western concepts. No matter how hard the attempts to change this, progress is slow.

To the outsider, feminism appears mostly as a sort of 'intellectual ghetto'. Its ideas do not appear to be having any impact on the political and social developments in the country. The new grassroots women's groups and organizations which are emerging often dismiss notions of equality and women's issues as unimportant, associating them with the legacies of the old system which was responsible for imposing a double burden on women. It is not just their lack of understanding of feminist issues which keeps women unaware of the great potential of these ideas. The systematic abuse of terms such as 'feminism' by Soviet propaganda and the cynical use of women for Party purposes has generated a deep distrust of women, women leaders and feminism in general. It will take a long time to restore positive connotations to all of these. However, I have faith in the great human potential of Ukrainian women. The question is how to make the word 'zhinotstvo' ('womankind') which exists in the Ukrainian language acquire its true meaning and value.

Notes

1 One particular survey carried out in 1992 by a group of sociologists at the Institute of Sociology, Ukrainian Academy of Sciences, questioned 1900 men and women representatively all around Ukraine. Since then, there has been no all-Ukrainian systematic study on the status of women and their political representation.

2 Western parts of Ukraine, formerly Halychyna, remained under Austrian-Hungarian and then Polish rule until 1939–1940 when they were incorporated into the USSR. Austrian rule may be characterized as less rigid in relation to national language and culture. It allowed Ukrainians to have schools and publish in Ukrainian, practise religions other than Russian Orthodox and reserved for them the right of community-organizing. This resulted in women having self-governed community organizations as early as the second half of the nineteenth century (see Martha Bohachevsky-Chomiak, 1988).

3 More can be read on the position of women in rural Russia in Dunn (1978) and Farnsworth and Viola (1992).

4 'O, human degradation! Depravity! To possess! Who dares possess a human being? One may possess a pair of slippers, a dressing-gown. But what am I talking about? Each of us, men, possesses some of you, our sisters! Are you, then our sisters? You are our servants. There are, I know, some women who subjugate some men; but what of that? Many valets rule their masters, but that does not prevent valets from being valets' (Chernyshevsky, 1982, pp. 41–2).

5 For more knowledge about female radicals and revolutionaries see Broido (1977) or Engel and Rosenthal (Eds) (1977).

6 The Socialist Revolutionary Party had a long history of enrolling women as terrorists. The most famous was Maria Spiridonova who shot General Luzhenovsky of Tambov province. Her trial won international fame and she was spared the death penalty. Fanny Kaplan (revolutionary pseudonym of Feiga Roidman) was chosen by the Socialist-Revolutionaries to assassinate Lenin while he was delivering a speech at one of St Petersburg's large factories in August 1918 (see Stites, 1978b, ch. 7).

7 Lesya Ukrainka (literary pseudonym of Larysa Kosach, 1871–1913) is the most famous Ukrainian poetess and playwriter. Her name, along with that of Taras Shevchenko, serves as a symbol of the Ukrainian nation.

8 The 'Propiska' or residence permit was a law according to which everyone was supposed to have a permanent residential address and there was a page in your passport marking it. Mostly, these were the apartments which the State leased at symbolic rent and people obtained them through their place of employment. But the arrangement was that you could not move out unless you found a job in another area. This measure effectively tied people to the workplace and some waited many years to get their apart-

ments from the State. Ironically, nothing is permanent now. With restitution going on in some countries of Eastern Europe, people have to surrender their places if old owners come back.

9 See for example, Havelkova (1993) or Pavlychko (1992b).

10 One of the best descriptions of this historic period may be found in Bohachevsky-Chomiak (1988).

11 Solomiia Pavlychko gives a vivid description of her turn to feminism in *Letters from Kiev* (1992a), which is also a wonderful diary of the events in Ukraine at that time. She also talks about the change in attitudes it brought to her within academia.

12 The humanities as a field were most strongly affected by ideologization during Soviet times. A whole new discourse has to be created, both in research and instruction. Martha Bohachevsky's impressions of the Ukrainian educational system, the treatment of women in academia and her experience of work with Ukrainian students is widely discussed in her 1988 and 1994 publications.

References

BOHACHEVSKY-CHOMIAK, MARTHA (1988) *Feminists Despite Themselves: Women in Ukrainian Community Life 1884–1939*, Edmonton, Canadian Institute of Ukrainian Studies, University of Alberta Press.

BOHACHEVSKY-CHOMIAK, MARTHA (1994) 'Rediscovering the Humanities in Ukraine', *Humanities: The Magazine of the National Endowment for the Humanities*, 15 (3), pp. 30–4.

BROIDO, VERA (1977) *Apostles into Terrorists: Women and the Revolutionary Movement in the Russia of Alexander II*, New York, Viking.

CHERNYSHEVSKY, N. G. (1982) *'Chto delat?' What is To Be Done? Tales About New People*, London, Virago Russian Classics, Virago Press.

DOBROLYUBOV, NIKOLAI (1956) *Selected Philosophical Essays*, trans. J. FINEBERG, Moscow, Foreign Languages Publications House.

DUNN, ETHEL (1978) 'Russian rual women', in ATKINSON, DOROTHY, DALLIN, ALEXANDER and LAPIDUS, WARSHOFSKY, GAIL (Eds) *Women in Russia*, Hassocks, Harvester Press, pp. 167–87.

ENGEL, BARBARA and ROSENTHAL, CLIFFORD (Eds and trans.) (1977) *Five Sisters: Women Against the Tsar*, New York, Schocken.

FARNSWORTH, BEATRICE and VIOLA, LYNNE (Eds) (1992) *Russian Peasant Women*, Oxford, New York, Oxford University Press.

FUNK, NANETTE and MUELLER, MAGDA (Eds) (1993) *Gender Politics and Post-Communism*, New York, Routledge.

HAVELKOVA, JANA (1993) 'A few pre-feminist thoughts', in FUNK, NANETTE and MUELLER, MAGDA (Eds) *Gender Politics and Post-Communism*, New York, Routledge.

ORWELL, GEORGE (1945) *Animal Farm*, London, Secker and Warburg.

PAVLYCHKO, SOLOMIIA (1992a) *Letters From Kiev*, trans. MYRNA KOSTASH, New York, St Martin's Press in association with the Canadian Institute of Ukrainian Studies, University of Alberta.

PAVLYCHKO, SOLOMIIA (1992b) 'Between nationalism and feminism', in BUCKLEY, MARY (Ed.) *Perestroika and Soviet Women*, Cambridge, Cambridge University Press.

PISAREV, DMITRIJ IVANOVICH (1956) *Realisty*, Moscow, Goslitizdat.

STITES, RICHARD (1978b) *The Women's Liberation Movement in Russia: Feminism, Nihilism, and Bolshevism 1860–1930*, Princeton, New Jersey, Princeton University Press.

UKRAINKA, LESYA (1901) *Vybrany Ivory*, Moscow, Progress Publishers.

Further Reading

ATKINSON, DOROTHY, DALLIN, ALEXANDER and LAPIDUS, WARSHOFSKY, GAIL (Eds) (1978) *Women in Russia*, Hassocks, Harvester Press.

BIDA, KONSTANTYN (1967) *Lesya Ukrainka: Life and Work*, trans. by VERA RICH, Toronto, Women's Council of the Ukrainian Canadian Committee, University of Toronto Press.

BUCKLEY, MARY (Ed.) (1992) *Perestroika and Soviet Women*, Cambridge, Cambridge University Press.

GLICKMAN, ROSE (1978) 'Russian factory women, workplace and society, 1880–1914', in ATKINSON, DOROTHY, DALLIN, ALEXANDER and LAPIDUS, WARSHOFSKY, GAIL (Eds) *Women In Russia*, Hassocks, Harvester Press.

STITES, RICHARD (1978a) 'Women and the Russian intelligentsia: Three perspectives', in ATKINSON, DOROTHY, DALLIN, ALEXANDER and LAPIDUS, WARSHOFSKY, GAIL (Eds) *Women In Russia*, Hassocks, Harvester Press.

YEDLIN, TOVA (Ed.) (1980) *Women in Eastern Europe and the Soviet Union*, New York, Praeger Publishers.

Section II

*Women in Movement: Identity, Migration
and Nationalism*

Chapter 8

Resituating Discourses of 'Whiteness' and 'Asianness' in Northern England: Second-generation Sikh Women and Constructions of Identity

Jasbir K. Puar

A South Asian friend of mine born in Guyana, raised in Canada and living in England once said to me, 'It always comes down to the same one question: "Where do you come from?"' The psychological impact of encountering this question for those of us who do not necessarily come from anywhere or, perhaps more precisely, come from many places, should not be underestimated. As a second-generation South Asian Sikh woman born and raised in the United States, I, along with many others, have struggled long and hard to answer this question satisfactorily – to no avail. In time I began to see that it is actually the question, not the answer, which is problematic. Exclusionary and ultimately racist through its denial of self-definition, this question imposes criteria on its respondent: you must come from somewhere. Some *one* where that is most probably not from here.

Immigration is not a onetime movement; it is a complex shifting of physical, mental and emotional states, which begins much before and extends far beyond the actual event. As children of immigrants we are denied these realities by Western society, yet constantly reminded of them. The actuality and validity of our displaced 'outsider' identities are hence negated. Why else would this question be asked? It is to remind us that do not really fit in:

> When a white person asks a Black woman where she comes from, the implicit assumption is that she does not belong here. The implicit threat is that she should go back to where she belongs. (Grewal *et al.*, 1988)

As theoretical positions often stem from autobiographical history, I feel it is important to clarify my self and my influences. I write with a sense of urgency, fuelled by painful definitions that I did not create, understand or fulfil. This pain was exacerbated when I arrived in Britain and my relationships to racial constructions shifted from what they had been in the US. My politicized identification against racism, imperialism, sexism, homophobia and classism

.d remained clear; however, my positioning relative to the differing terms of struggle had undergone many changes. The necessity to relocate was eye-opening; the denial of self-definition was inevitably familiar.

I began this project to examine racism in the lives of second-generation Sikh women within the British context.[1] I felt that my 'outsider within' position as a Sikh woman raised in another Western country would provide me with an unusual combination of access and critical distance.[2] It became more clear as my research progressed that notions of identity provide an important way to evaluate the binary constructs within which white, Western and feminist thinking is still constructed, despite attempts to theorize otherwise. This essay attempts to illuminate why Western dichotomies of white/black, East/West and oppressor/oppressed consistently reinscribe 'identity' as a fixed, static and boundaried state. Such an understanding of identity continues to define qualifiable 'difference' in terms of 'sameness', as in 'not the same as'. Such definitions remain fixed in comparative, never absolute constructs and maintain the focus on exclusionary politics by marginalizing those with multiple alliances.[3]

What is 'Asianness?': The South Asian Other

The construction and maintenance of an oppositional South Asian stereotype that is mutually exclusive of white British society is facilitated by the reluctance of dominant white gazes to acknowledge some form of interdependence on the other. The use of the term *white gaze* is not to suggest that whiteness is a monolithic entity devoid of multiple ideologies and configurations. Rather, the concept of gaze acknowledges the power that voyeuristic positionings have to define modes of objectifications and delineate 'difference' as the most different difference possible. The insistence on oppositional boundaries clearly marked and upheld as mutually exclusive realities mythologizes a cohesive white identity.[4] The privileging of the white side of the binary ensures that the other is consumed, assimilated, cannibalized and left unable to claim subjectivity.

Dominant white gazes facilitate the discourse of the relational difference of Asianness in Britain in three ways. First, perceptions of 'brownness' imbue South Asian communities with a false homogeneity – particularly compared to dominant white society.[5] Second, extreme culturalist explanations deny 'sameness' (*vis-à-vis* white society) by pre-empting the possibilities of drawing parallels, for example, along the lines of class, gender and migratory experience. Finally, the second generation is constructed as 'cultural conflict-bound'. Substantiated through theories of assimilation, supposed cultural conflict places this generation within an either/or framework.

The perception of an homogenous brownness leads to a reductionist 'colour equals culture' equation that denies specificity. Tariq Modood points to indications that South Asians are the most disliked 'group' in Britain today because 'they are insufficiently inclined to adopt English ways'; South Asians are associated with fear-based ideas of a unified and 'alien' culture (Modood,

1991, p. 185). In turn, the link between racial discrimination and socioeconomic disadvantage is fixed, ignoring vast economic distinctions between Muslims and other South Asians, for example. Modood points to the usage of the word 'Paki' and the Salman Rushdie affair to illustrate how South Asians suffer from generalized discrimination.

Through colour equals culture, the Black woman becomes a victim of her own repressive, 'sexist' culture.[6] Chandra Talpade Mohanty refers to this construction as the 'monolithic Third World Woman' (Mohanty, 1991, p. 51). For South Asian women this construction is manifest in stereotypes of passivity, docility and helplessness. This image is signified by the wearing of the *salwaar kameez* (the customary South Asian long blouse and baggy trousers) and veil, arranged marriages, domestic violence, female educational aspirations (or lack thereof) and sexism (seen as a wholly cultural phenomenon) in South Asian communities.[7] The histories and nuances within each of these practices are ignored. For instance, an image of the 'universal' arranged marriage, from the most traditional modes of partnership-matching in working-class communities, does not indicate the diversity of actual practice dictated primarily by class; this in turn is highly shaped by such factors as religion, migratory experiences and regional settlements. A focus on cultural practices, in conjunction with an essentialized concept of culture, allows dominant white gazes to perceive Asianness as more patriarchal. Although this perception is problematic for many reasons, it specifically fixes culture outside the impact of immigration and racism. These factors influence the desire to reconstruct notions of home, to reaffirm religious and ethnic identities within communities that offer protection, as well as mediate the ways in which class disadvantage limits economic and hence life options of South Asian women. Culture is thus understood as only a source of oppression and the only source of oppression.

If they are visible, South Asian women are seen only in Eurocentric ways, through the critique of problem areas like arranged marriages, clitoridectomy and the veil. This in turn fixes these women as 'naturally' passive because their modes of resistance are not understood within the economic, political, social and ideological structures that shape their lives within Britain. Rarely are South Asian women portrayed in the context of their own self-agency, of resistance constructed and functioning within specific social contexts.

The Second Generation

How is the victim image altered, continued, reinforced or dismissed for second-generation South Asian women? Much of the literature on second-generation South Asians either ignores or does not differentiate the experiences of girls and women.[8] Additionally, there is little written by second-generation South Asians. Media representation and academic scholarship invariably return to the question of cultural conflict. Most portrayals characterize second-generation South Asians as involved in intense, soul-searching battles over their identities, loyalties and feelings of belonging. Many representations locate them floundering between opposing definitions of white/black, East/West, South Asian/British. The assumption is that these polarized identities are mutually exclusive and that eventually anyone struggling with cultural conflict must choose either one side or the other, primarily for the sake of mental and emotional well-being.

For the second-generation South Asian woman, her assumed identity conflict constructs her as a victim, this time not only of her oppressive, patriarchal, backward culture and 'extended' family but also of her supposed longings to assimilate into white society and the racism she faces within it. This Eurocentric view is applied particularly to perceived restrictions on dating and relationships, suggesting that 'it is a source of desperate frustration' that she is denied the 'intense experiences' her (white) friends are having (James, 1974, pp. 89–90). She is seen to crave all that the West has to offer, but according to dominant white gazes, her culture holds her back and only the 'rebels' succeed. Naturally, the rebels are perceived to be far more emancipated than their dutiful counterparts, who 'lack the courage to face the risks and responsibilities that go with an independent existence' (Hiro, 1973, pp. 168–9). Whereas the first-generation immigrant South Asian woman may identify primarily with her birthplace, the second-generation South Asian woman is completely and directly 'identified' by relational discourses of difference – white/black, South Asian/British, East/West; and timid/independent and freedom/security.

Thus, the oppositional poles of white/black, East/West, South Asian/British acquire social significance and meaning through an assumed experience based on dominant representation, thus rendering the second-generation South Asian other without voice, space or autonomy in terms of class, religion, culture and history. She is either repressed by her patriarchal culture or co-opted by a racist white society into benefiting from the so-called freedom of the West, despite the loss of familial support and protection. The either/or equation freezes the South Asian other without political or social agency or the room to negotiate subjectivity.[9] The South Asian other is thus the object, not the subject, of her own cultural identity. The South Asian other's identity is thus defined as directly oppositional to white culture – defined not by the self but by the dominant white other.

Assuming that the experiences of the second-generation are inadequately reflected by the oppositional either/or constructs, how do second-generation South Asian women function strategically in the politics of everyday life? Recent literature points to a growing South Asian 'subculture' that synthesizes South Asian and British culture. *Bhangra* music, a combination of Punjabi folk music and house/dance music, has arisen entirely from British-Asian culture (Banerji, 1988). Parminder Bhachu (1991a) points to another form of synthesis between 'Black' music, such as reggae and hip-hop, and Bengali lyrics to create another innovation of British-Asian culture, *Bangla* music. She also maintains that a constant 'engagement with and transformation of cultural frameworks' results in the internalization of material and regional cultures; some examples include new styles of *salwaar kameezes* that mix Eastern and Western fashion trends, a growing population of Sikhs with yuppie consumption patterns and the changing contents of the *daaj* – the gifts of the dowry (Bhachu, 1991a, p. 408).

Cultural conflict resolution through synthesis may not always be possible or desirable. The presumed preoccupation with conflict resolution for second-generation Sikh women overlooks the fact that generational conflict exists in all cultures (Ballard, 1979; Stopes-Roe and Cochrane, 1989). The emphasis on conflict resolution also assumes a final, fixed end – a finite solution – when the ability to transcend duality is actually facilitated by flexible and fluid notions of identity. Thus the tension of contradictions is neither resolved nor dissolved; instead, it is played with, manipulated (for empowerment and subversion), and enjoyed.[10] Mutuality and interdependence replace oppositional difference and exclusivity.

Bargaining with Racism: Oppositionally Active 'Whiteness'

Racial and cultural identity that is not merely assimilatory must be strategically reactive. I term such identity formation 'oppositionally active'. Such a notion of identity suggests a complete alliance with neither South Asian nor white society; rather, it resists both. It is oppositional in its unwillingness to be consumed by the white pole; activity in this arena results not from racism or rejection by white society. It is instead the product of critical evaluation and appreciation of one's own culture. Furthermore, it entails a strategic comprehension of the fractures, disjunctions and intersections of 'whiteness', as well as which constructions are predominating and when.

Moreover, the deconstruction of polarized identities allows a re-examination of traditional ideas of resistance – those equating consciousness with activity. Because dominant, Western definitions are applied to the social construction of South Asian women, their resistance is rendered invisible and presuppositions are affirmed; the circle is thus complete. Rethinking the 'consciousness equals activity' configuration would suggest that all resistance is not immediately and obviously apparent; compliance and resistance may coexist in the form of subversion. That is, oppressed peoples do not necessarily learn dominance. They learn about dominance from a position of inequality. Perhaps second-generation South Asians learn not about whiteness but about the different constructions of whiteness and their points of intersection. Being from a subordinate position necessitates strategizing to maximize the benefits of this knowledge. Oppositionally active whiteness is about manipulating the 'terror of whiteness', changing the oppressive discourses of whiteness to discourses of subversion and power and breaking down oppressor/oppressed dichotomies (hooks, 1992, p. 344).

I think of oppositionally active whiteness as a process of 'bargaining with racism'.[11] It is understood that certain racist stereotypes that lead to assumptions of being a 'coconut', an 'oreo', a 'sellout' or 'whitewashed' provide protection from the very same racism from which they originate. Meaning can be altered by shifting context and content; empowerment is obtained through subversively insisting on culturally informed self-definition. Ultimately, oppositionally active whiteness represents the self to one's self; one stands in solidarity with, without assimilating to, the stereotypes of difference. Problems occur when, in recognizing the representation to one's self, one becomes that representation.

Receiving and Returning the 'Double Gaze'

Recently I watched *Mississippi Masala* for the fourth time.[12] I find this movie problematic in many ways. At first glance Mina, a second-generation South Asian woman raised in the US, transcends the docile/rebel oppositional definitions by being a strong-willed woman still on good terms with her parents. However, she is dissatisfied with her existence as a hotel cleaner and finds 'freedom' only through a love affair with an African-American man and the rejection of her family. The film, utilizing an unusual scenario – most South Asians involved in interracial relationships tend to have white partners – proposes a very dangerous and unrealistic solution for the identity 'problems' of the South Asian woman. The message is 'run away with your non-South Asian lover and you will be free and your problems will be solved'.

Even more disturbing is the fact that the film is directed by a South Asian woman. Mira Nair, and the leading actor, Sarita Choudhury, feels that she is providing South Asian women 'trapped in their own cultures' with a strong role model (Lloyd, 1992, p. 14). The movie stereotypes South Asians in the US as hotel-owning, bad-English-speaking, patriarchal communities.

I only view this movie in protected environments with non-South Asians who know my politics or South Asian friends because it invariably leads to long and complex discussions. With my South Asian friends, we can laugh, relish the accents and gestures and recognize and share in the all-too-familiar scripting of our lives. The movie is funny and comforting, if highly exaggerated for humour's sake.

However, in creating the forum for our enjoyment, this movie sanctions the amusement of other audiences by saying, 'Look, this is the real story.'[13] It is funny to hear South Asian migrants speaking English and so one must laugh. It is only natural according to white liberal interpretations of ideologies of Western love that Mina must 'follow her heart' and run off with her unacceptable lover. With white people present, I cannot laugh and must analyse others' laughter. It is difficult to decipher . . . is one laughing at the parody of the stereotypes or actually laughing at the stereotypes themselves, because they lend themselves to ridicule so easily? And invariably I ask the questions: Why are the stereotypes funny? Is it because the humour itself is constructed in a racist way? If they are funny to me, does that sanction the laughter of other audiences?[14]

These issues of reception imply a critical analysis of 'who is comprehending this movie how and from what positioning'. Many white, middle-class, politically correct ideologies would answer that we can all be part of the joke – we are all human beings regardless of our differences. This attitude seems to deny others' rights to exclusion through an assumption of automatic inclusion. It also assimilates difference into sameness. It attempts to capture the 'double gaze' or 'outsider within' position that simply cannot be mirrored by white people, for whom race can only be lived as white. The dominant white gaze is a metaphor for the means by which white society oppresses through its use of objectification as a voyeur. Politically correct ideologies sanction the voyeur. I don't; what is funny and politically sound for some is simply not so far others. For example, when I use the word *Paki*, I make it clear that the usage is only for those who need to reclaim it to subvert and to escape its oppressiveness; I expect no others to appropriate this language. Similarly, when I imitate migrant English, I do so only in front of people whom I know understand the political resonance. These acts are a form of comfort, solidarity and remembrance. They are not for the voyeuristic pleasure of dominant white gazes and certainly not because I am making fun of or degrading my culture.

Mississippi Masala panders to the situated double gaze of white and South Asian societies, a gaze experienced by only a few – for example, second-generation Sikh women who have the knowledge and resources to critically view both South Asian and white societies yet who are also objectified by these two poles. The double gaze, a form of oppositionally active whiteness, can facilitate creative subjectivity as well as negotiate objectification, which in turn enable subject positioning by the self. Thus a second-generation Sikh woman simultaneously receives and returns the double gaze; they double gaze as well as are double gazed at. The two processes are interdependent; objectification is a disembodied, visual experience that in specific moments of struggle necessitates an embodied, subjective experience.

How do South Asian women negotiate the constant interplay of subject/object relations? Through oppositionally active whiteness – giving an appearance of conformity while maintaining identity through subversion of dominant white gazes – one can manipulate and empower subjectivity yet retain internal identity. To demonstrate these manipulations in practice. I shall use excerpts from in-depth interviews with six second-generation Sikh women living in Leeds, a city in Northern England. The interviews focused loosely on racism and culture to pursue the women's varied interests. The interviewees ranged in age from twenty to thirty-three and came primarily from working-class backgrounds; all have completed some higher education.

Before continuing I should like to emphasize that I do not equate Sikh identity with South Asian identity. The nature of oppression in India and subsequent South Asian diasporic hierarchies make the terms *Indian* and

South Asian problematic. (Detailing Sikh history is beyond the scope of this chapter). Rather, I will present Sikh identities as the site of embodied subjectivity inscribed in disembodied, visual objectification *vis-à-vis* a monolithic interpretation of South Asian identity. I will also treat these women's words as neither generally representative of second-generation Sikh women nor representative of themselves; rather, I present their words as representations of my understanding of these specific women's lives. In doing so I present no facts or concrete conclusions. My intentions are to complicate issues of identity, suggest certain possibilities and trends and offer these women's experiences to substantiate alternative methods of theorizing.[15]

I will briefly summarize my participants' identification with Sikhism (which influences the uses of oppositionally active whiteness) and then explore the subversion of external definitions (outward appearance, language, and interracial relationships) that are incorporated into identity and subjectivity. Although I am focusing on the negotiation of different constructions of whiteness and their applications to second-generation South Asian women, I have introduced the concept of 'double gaze' to demonstrate that the problematization of the privileged position is not possible without illuminating the interactive nature of oppressor/oppressed binaries.

The Politicization of Sikhism

How is one to know and define oneself? From the inside – within a context that is self defined, from a grounding in community and a connection with culture that are comfortably accepted? Or from the outside – in terms of messages received from the media and people who are often ignorant? Even as an adult I can still see two sides of my face and past. I can see from the inside out, in freedom. And I can see from the outside in, driven by old voices of childhood and lost in anger and fear. (Noda, 1989, p. 244)

What are the relationships between a self-identity and a social, external, objectified identity that one struggles to subjectify? An internal identity must work in conjunction with racialized objectifications to negotiate the ground between identity and subjectivity. For second-generation Sikh women who may identify religiously, ethnically and/or culturally as Sikh, this means navigating racialized objectifications of gender and class.

For the purposes of this chapter, I shall provide a brief summary of Sikh immigration patterns to Britain; numerous sources provide further accounts.[16] Mass migration of South Asians from India, primarily men, began in the mid-1950s and filled the postwar labour demands for unskilled and semiskilled workers. In the early 1960s South Asians employed in Kenya and Uganda to build the national railroads joined the migration to Britain. (They thus became 'twice-migrants'.) Though many came from East Africa, the vast majority of

Sikhs immigrated from India. They made up about 20 per cent of the South Asian population in 1984. By the late 1960s many families were reunited and settled in the urban areas of England, particularly London and the Midlands; the 1970s were characterized by the emergence of the second generation.

An overarching status as Sikh has developed as a universal awareness and identity in the face of opposition and adversity. Within Britain, Sikh identity developed through extending community networks, dissolving the 'myth of return', strengthening familial and generational ties and reviving Sikh symbols such as the turban for men and the *salwaar kameez* and uncut hair for women. This national identification with Sikhism was also part of an international Sikh movement precipitated by the 1984 attack by Indira Gandhi's military on the holy Golden Temple at Amritsar, India (Bhachu, 1991b). Resulting media coverage and popular discourse regarding the liberation struggle in Punjab incorrectly and one-sidedly represented the Sikhs as terrorists. Thus Sikh identity is highly politicized on the national level as an immigrant identity solidifying against and within hostile conditions. On an international level the politicization comes within the context of *Khalistan*, the movement for independence from India to establish a Sikh homeland.

According to the tenets of Sikhism, it is a casteless religion that accords equality to men and women. Ideology, however, is never fully replicated in practice and in Britain the importance of caste within Sikh communities is monumental, in some cases determining which temple one attends, whom one can marry and so on. Sikhism also functions to distinguish Sikhs from other South Asians and from white society. This appearance of unity can easily be undermined internally within caste contexts, whereby class and subclass become foregrounded.

Sikhism can be far more complex than simply a cultural or religious identification. In its stance against oppression by the Indian government it is a unifying politicized movement, signalling a possible shift in communal identification with Sikhism. For the second-generation women of my research, identification with Sikhism is described in varied ways that point toward forms of symbolic ethnicity focused less on culture and traditions and more on maintaining a feeling of being (Gans, 1979). All interviewees identified themselves as Sikhs; Satinder, Harpreet and Manpreet retained outward symbols of Sikhism – particularly uncut hair – and all of them still attend *gurdwara* (Sikh temple). Their attendance varied from occasional special functions to weekly.[17] None of them, however, seemed particularly attached to Sikhism as a religious identity. Satinder stated that the only reason she went to *gurdwara* was to see people: 'I don't have any other reason to go really.' Rajinder was highly critical of what she perceived as the abuse of the socialist principles of Sikhism. She also disregarded traditions such as the caste system, the dowry, and the keeping of long hair: they 'should be eradicated . . . Why should one need an identity like that? If you believe in something, you believe in it inside; you don't need an outward token to show other people what you are.'

Similarly, Inderpal considers herself religious yet does not maintain Sikh traditions; she cuts her hair, smokes and is also angered by the caste system: 'I am religious but in a different way. Sikhism to me is not religion; it's tradition.' Gurjeev also mentioned her belief in god but did not connect it to Sikhism. Only Harpreet expressed an interest in actually praying: 'I just go to *gurdwara* whenever I feel like it, and I feel afterwards like I've really gotten something out of it . . . I pray at home, when I feel like it – religion is important to me.' Collectively these women reflect religion as a concept that shifts to suit political and social needs. Each of them must navigate the spaces between subjective, lived experiences and discursive, applied definitions.

Masala-itis

> Clothing for us has had so much to do with the nature of underclass exploited reality. For we have pleasure (and the way this pleasure is constituted has been a mediating force between the painful reality, our internalised self-hate, and even our resistance) in clothing. Clothes have functioned politically in Black experience. . . . I am particularly interested in the relationship between style as expressed in clothing and subversion, the way the dominated, exploited peoples use style to express resistance and/or conformity. (hooks, 1990, p. 217)

Appearance and sexual imagery are pivotal areas where manipulations of dominant white gazes occur. White and South Asian populations often interface in this arena (Wallman, 1978). Since the amount of direct communication between dominant and minority societies may be minimal in comparison to the power to oppress, this interface is particularly important (Saifullah Khan, 1982). Stereotypes are one primary force of objectification and operate as a potent method of maintaining exclusionary and inclusionary definitions. South Asian women's sexuality is curiously stereotyped as passive, submissive, licentious and available. Avtar Brah summarizes the three primary objectifications of South Asian women in Britain: (1) the 'exotic, oriental woman – sensuous, seductive, full of Eastern promise' typically portrayed by airline advertisements showcasing compliant hostesses; (2) the 'dirty, ugly' South Asian woman; and (3) the 'sexually licentious' South Asian woman-on-the-rampage.[18]

The exotic South Asian other is further manifested in the image of the westernized South Asian woman: ethnic, exotic. The submersion in such an image has been termed 'Masala-itis' by Sayantani DasGupta (1993). While she points to the very real pitfalls of Masala-itis via racist ideologies of exoticism, a subversion of such stereotypes means the joke is on the voyeur. Masala-itis can be a forum within which desire is used to protect subjectivity through shifts of meaning and context of objectified constructions. This may happen through either a subversion of certain stereotypes based on desire, a challenge to explicitly racist stereotypes or a combination of both processes.

Racialized gender constructions operate differently in various class and generational contexts. The 'dirty, ugly South Asian woman' is typically embodied as a working-class woman who wears the customary *salwaar kameez* and is often veiled. Interestingly, the *salwaar kameez* has undergone a revival of sorts in Britain, especially among second-generation Sikh women. The popularity of the *salwaar kameez* cannot be entirely attributed to Sikh societal imposition. Satinder, who used to wear mostly skirts and dresses, explained, 'I feel more comfortable in Asian suits, you see a lot of girls wearing them now, so it's okay, you don't feel like an outcast.'

Satinder actually prefers to wear *salwaar kameezes*. Others might accord her attire as a restriction imposed on her by her father and/or husband. The popularization of indigenous clothing can also be explained by the value placed on ethnicity in today's fashion industry. The ability to capitalize on ethnicity has been sustained by market demand. White investment in and desire to be the exotic South Asian other allows for commodification, consumption and possession of the other; dominance is maintained through appropriation and assimilation. Manpreet noted this shift, saying that when she was younger, 'You'd get your friends saying, "Oh, you look like a Paki." . . . But now the trends have changed so much, everybody's prepared to wear multi-coloured clothes, Jamaican clothes, Chinese clothes; Asian clothes.'

The popularity of *salwaar kameezes* has been further enhanced by the fashionable and expensive ones worn primarily for weddings and special occasions. When asked, 'Do you ever notice any adverse reactions when you wear a *salwaar kameez*?' Rajinder answers, 'No, because all my Indian clothing is beautiful.' using the word 'beautiful' (meaning fashionable and expensive), Rajinder implies that wearing an unbeautiful *salwaar kameez* can leave one open to adverse reactions. The stereotype of the dirty, ugly South Asian woman thus becomes exoticized through middle-class consumption. Thus Masala-itis can act as a strategic way to minimize the daily impact of racism, through refuting the ugly South Asian woman stereotype and subverting, for example, 'politically correct' interest in 'exotic' and 'ethnic' clothing.

Masala-itis also challenges images of assimilation and westernization. South Asian women are aware that they present a different image – a reminder and a jolt to dominant white gazes. Gurjeev, who is very light-skinned, expressed annoyance that white friends often forget that she is Indian. 'They say [when she wears a *salwaar kameez*] "I didn't realize . . . you look really nice, I'm really glad you did that".' Rajinder says, 'My non-Asian friends like [the *salwaar kameez*]. . . . they make silly comments, like "You look like a little Indian girl, you look like you're about to get married." I find it amusing.' Her use of the words 'silly' and 'amusing' indicates a certain amount of condescension toward her non-Asian friends.

Rajinder explained that in white-dominated workplaces, people assume she is very Westernized. She feels no need to refute this: 'I could be really "Indian".' I could put on Indian clothes and an Indian accent and seem Indian for their benefit, but I'm not interested.... It's a certain mentality that it's based on – it doesn't impress me. I'm more Indian than I look. I don't mean having Indian friends or listening to Indian music; I don't think that makes you Indian.... I'm aware. I know where my roots are.'

Masala-itis also challenges stereotypes of the 'downtrodden South Asian woman' through confident, assertive and sexual self-presentations. Gurjeev explained, 'If I'm going to a real big evening with my English friends, I'll wear it then, because it's quite stunning for people who don't normally see it, just to look a bit different when I go out with my friends ... not to a pub, but to a private party maybe. I always like to wear my national dress.' Satinder states, 'if I go for a job interview I like to wear a skirt or a dress ... sometimes, you know, people, they might look at you and they're thinking, she might not be able to wear a uniform, if the job requires one – if you're wearing trousers they know you can.' Both Gurjeev and Satinder *receive* the situated white gaze and *respond* with renegotiations of the contested images. They recognize the operation of racism through different constructions of the South Asian woman; Satinder understands the nuances between 'I will not hire a South Asian woman' and 'I will not hire certain kinds of South Asian women.'

Finally, in certain situations the ability to confuse and to contradict static constructions can be enormously threatening. Inderpal related a story about a South Asian friend who works for a primarily white women's organization. The woman, who normally wore Western clothing to work, showed up to a board meeting in a *salwaar kameez*. The few other South Asian women present were also attired in *salwaar kameezes*. During the meeting a white coworker said that the white women found the South Asian women's attire 'oppressive'. Reflecting on a similar situation, a meeting at her workplace, Inderpal said, 'It's the notion of whatever is white, whatever whites do is right. I suppose it [wearing a *salwaar kameez*] can be threatening because I suppose it shows strength, it shows a strong cultural identity.' I asked, 'When you wear a *salwaar kameez* to work, are you making a statement?' Inderpal responded, 'Yes, maybe on Friday I think I was ... [pause] Actually I don't think so, I think white people might take it that way, but I don't think I meant it like that.'

The South Asian women I interviewed all expressed disdain and pity toward white friends and colleagues who insisted on 'comparing tans' after a holiday. The popularity of tanning can be seen as another attempt by the dominant white gazes to appropriate the qualities of and therefore 'normalize' or define the non-white other. Interviewees mentioned that a stereotypic rebel or an exotic party girl image – as one who rejects and has been rejected by her own community – was another effective way of combating stereotypes of South Asian female passivity. Several participants pointed to the frequent use of the word *Paki* in their presence as an indication of white co-workers' assumptions that Westernized dress or behaviour indicated whiteness, yet another attempt to assimilate sameness into difference. The other, however, was not subsumed as subject. The women always made a point of confronting such assimilative behaviour, 'often much to people's surprise' (Gurjeev).

Strategic appearances of compliance and challenges to racist stereotypes can thus help to create and to maintain one's own subjectivity. Masala-itis may function as oppositionally active whiteness through the process of reception and response. Whiteness is received and distinguished, then altered to recapture a subjectivity that contradicts, synthesizes with or remains ambivalent to one's identity. It is important to note that all women, regardless of culture and race, often find themselves negotiating with manipulations of image. These negotiations not only exist within the realm of visual interpretation but permeate the realm of language.

Language as Resistance

At first I did not speak because of her order; later I found not speaking to be a useful form of resistance. I would stand mute before her, even when being questioned, which added to her rage and frustration. (Dillion, 1989, p. 216)

Language retention has been a highly emotive issue for ethnic minorities; it is one of the most visible and powerful (exclusionary) symbols of a distinctive identity (Taifel, 1982). As a form of solidarity, it also openly threatens the dominant society. (Note the heated debates over multilingual education.) Knowledge of the mother tongue facilitates retention of other forms of cultural identity and practice; for South Asians, this means reading *gurbani* (Sikh prayers), singing *shabads* (religious hymns), watching Punjabi films and so forth.

All my participants considered themselves bilingual in English and Punjabi; all were ashamed of speaking Punjabi when they were younger but now view it as extremely positive. (This change is probably due to maturation and the resurgence of Sikhism as an ethnic identity.) All six women were raised in families that encouraged them to speak Punjabi. All had access to Punjabi classes at *gurdwaras* and night schools. Three of the women used Punjabi at their workplaces anywhere from very occasionally to everyday. All of the women I interviewed switched back and forth from one language to the other often with no immediate recollection of doing so. Rama Kant Agnihotri refers to this as a 'Mixed Code' that randomly interchanges English and Punjabi (Agnihotri, 1987).[19]

Diglossia and the use of a Mixed Code could reflect the subconscious ambivalence of the second generation. Language retention and an appearance of assimilation are not necessarily at odds. Language can function as a means not only of exclusion but also of subversion. The women I interviewed use language as strategic resistance (oppositionally active whiteness): 'Sometimes when you go into a shop and you know they're really snobby – they're really short with you . . . they're just chatting away to each other as if you're not even there and somewhere in the middle of it you say something and they just kind of jump up and think "God, she speaks English, she must've been listening to what we were saying"' (Gurjeev). This is clearly a manipulation of the 'dumb' South Asian stereotype – that is, the woman who is unable to speak English. When asked about the advantages of being bilingual, many brought up the ability to manipulate dominant white gazes through exclusion: 'The advantages? When you're with English people you can swear and they don't know what you're talking about' (Rajinder). Bilingualism is a form of protection. On hearing racist comments, for example, some people are 'able to put up a front that you don't understand something but you know you can' (Gurjeev).

When asked how non-South Asians reacted to Punjabi, an element of disdain characterized the responses: 'Well, they can either find it very amusing, or they can find it offensive because they might think you're talking about them' (Rajinder). A co-worker overheard Gurjeev on the phone with her mother: 'He said, "God, I didn't know you could speak Punjabi" and I said to him, "Well, what do you think I speak at home then?" . . . I don't know whether it's surprise. I always think like what do they expect me to speak when I'm at home? I don't know if it's maybe a bit of jealousy that they can't do it.' Two participants who felt that speaking Punjabi was an asset at work also discussed jealousy; their skills were called upon in situations involving other Punjabi-speakers. They were often positively singled out when white co-workers were at a loss.

During one interview we discussed the use of a South Asian accent while speaking English. I asked Rajinder what she thought her parents wanted and expected for her future. In accented English she responded: 'Be a good little Indian girl, marry an Indian boy.' This parody of migrant English is common among many South Asians I have met. It seems to be an act of solidarity and exclusion; dominant white gazes are unable to participate in the parody. Reclaiming this 'language' renders the objectifiers impotent. We were sharing in the solidarity of the double gaze; she used this accent primarily to express resistance to the perceived social restrictions of her family and the Sikh community.

As with Masala-itis, language can be used as a navigational tool between identity and subjectivity. Clearly, language openly threatens dominant society and is a subversive, hidden provocation. Stereotypes of South Asian women based on clothing and other visual indicators are complicated by acts of silence (such as pretending one does not understand English), open displays of language as signs of cultural pride and the usage of Punjabi for exclusionary purposes.

Interracial Relationships and Cultural Autonomy

Interpersonal relationships are often used to suggest that cultural identity can be measured by the colour of one's primary contacts. Interracial marriages have symbolized a final assimilation into white society.[20] The strict, inflexible, patriarchal, extended South Asian family is seen by the white gaze as the scapegoat; Westernized daughters are rebelling against their own culture.[21] At the time of my research two of the interviewees were involved with white partners. Gurjeev is married; Harpreet is unmarried but living with her partner. Interracial relationships raise questions about access to privilege and protection from racism. Does this, however, automatically imply assimilation? Clichés found within popular white discourses describing relationships between white British males and South Asian females (which are different from discourses on South Asian men and white women) demonstrate contexts within which autonomous culture and racial identities complement without subsuming each other.

Women engaged in interracial relationships are widely understood to be rebels; they seek out white partners as acts of rebellion against their families and view white men as more desirable and 'better' catches. It follows that these women, along with their less 'liberated' counterparts, view arranged marriages as horrifically debilitating and oppressive. Consequently, the rebels are either thrown out of their family or run away, never to return, and are completely ostracized from their community. Ultimately, South Asian rebels are frozen into assimilated white wanna-bes who have abandoned their religious, cultural and racial identities. If this categorization does not fit neatly within the assumptions, her partner is ultimately conceptualized as a 'Paki-lover'.

These clichés about second-generation South Asian women are substantiated, reinforced and reproduced through a complex process. External Masala-itis-type indicators compose the rebel imagery and reflect essentialized notions of identity constructions: 'modern' dress, cut hair and 'Western' appearance. Despite having such indicators, Gurjeev and Harpreet's statements do not reflect rebellious seeking of white partners: 'It wouldn't have mattered whether he was white, black, Indian or what, I don't think it would've mattered, not to me anyway . . . I didn't go out looking for a partner, I just fell in love with him' (Gurjeev). 'Before I met him, it was something that happened to other girls, though I didn't have anything against it . . . then I found myself in the situation' (Harpreet).

These comments do not support the common assumption that South Asian women who work and live in predominantly white environments search for and desire only white partners. Harpreet was involved in arranged marriage proceedings at the time she met her partner. These conclusions are also based on the incorrect premise that South Asian partners and arranged marriages are not viable options – that any free, independent and progressive thinker would not participate in such a process. Again, the attitudes of the respondents do not reflect the assumptions. Harpreet and Gurjeev had ambivalent feelings about arranged marriages, citing both positive and negative aspects. Harpreet said that although at times, when being introduced to potential partners, she felt as if she was on a 'conveyor belt', she had no urge to break out of it and had no problems with the system.[22]

The notion that these rebels eventually leave or are expelled by their family gains currency from the proliferation of South Asian women's shelters in Britain. The mainstream media and tabloid press propagate the stereotype by sensationalizing rare cases to be the norm. This is not to say that familial relationships remain unchanged when these situations arise. Both Harpreet and Gurjeev recognized that Sikh women are more restricted than Sikh men in similar situations. Both have endured major upheavals in their familial relationships.

Gurjeev patiently attempted for two years to negotiate a meeting between her family and her partner. 'When my mum met him, I don't know if she was shocked or pleased or what, but she had this idea of what white men were like, and when she met him, she said to me, "He's got such good manners and he's got such a good personality, I can't believe it, I always thought white men were this and that," etc. Well, I said, even white people can be acceptable to us.' Harpreet was willing to compromise in almost any way before she eventually left her family. 'I would've done it; I would've stayed home and said right, you want me to go through the normal rigmarole and a normal Indian wedding, but with him, I'd go with it, I would've done that. And lots of people said to them [her parents] that you've got to give and take ... but they weren't giving.' Now after several months without communication, she maintains a sort of clandestine relationship with her parents. Her relationship with her partner is never discussed. 'Basically my mother and father feel ashamed, disgraced, whatever you want to call it. . . . I mean, if my dad would be really ill one day and I said "Look, I'm here with a car out there, I'll take you." "No, there'll be other Indian people there that we know," they'll say.' When I asked her why she still wanted to maintain a relationship with her parents when they were ashamed of her, she responded, 'I've got to . . . I'm the closest one to them, without me they wouldn't cope. The family is important. I know it sounds silly, coming from me, in my position, but it is important, and it is closer, ours, than, I guess some British people's, I don't know.'

Harpreet's reconceptualization of family also extends to community. Her negotiations within the Sikh community contradict the assumptions of dominant white gazes. When asked how she feels she is perceived by the Sikh community at large, Harpreet says she maintains contact with several people from her former *gurdwara*, which she no longer attends because of her parents. 'It was my own family that was walking past and ignoring me, and all of a sudden, people that I knew, they came charging up to you ... to talk, very friendly, and next time you see your own cousin walking by, you see your own nephew up the road – they wouldn't cross the road over, they'd walk past you.'

She now attends *gurdwara* in another city where she is quite friendly with everyone. The people there know of her white partner but do not know her family. Harpreet has strategically redefined her community to suit her own needs and priorities. Gurjeev is similarly involved in creating and building her own community with relatives and friends; she no longer participates extensively in her former religious communities and said, 'So long as my own family thinks it's fine, I don't care what the others think.'

Both women seem unwilling and unable to give up their Sikh identities. Harpreet still prays daily, attends *gurdwara* regularly and plans to raise her children as Sikhs. 'I'd hope they'd [her former Sikh community] still see me as the kind of person I was when I was at home . . . as far as I'm concerned I haven't changed one bit since I left.'

She expresses disdain toward Western society: 'All the qualities I've got, all in me, all the things my mother and father brought me up with, when you see white people you think, oh my god, now I know why they taught me the way they did.' This seems to imply that she does not see her white partner in the context of whiteness or Western values (perhaps she disconnects her partner from certain groups of white people) and could only be with a certain type of partner who shared her moral standards: 'I mean, a lot of Asian girls I know are lovely girls and they do exactly what their parents say and then all of a sudden, you'll go into town and you'll see them smoking.'

Interestingly, though Harpreet has maintained certain concepts about her identity within her relationship with her partner, the objectifications imposed upon her seem to have shifted. She described her work situation where she met her partner, who was at that time her supervisee: 'In a way, since I've gotten together with [him], they're [co-workers] a bit more friendly, I don't know why . . .' cause I think all of them went through the motions I was going through, all the hassle with my family.' Harpreet attributes this attitudinal shift to emotional involvement; it must be asked why her white co-workers responded this way. 'Did this response entail a shifting of racial and cultural constructions?' Clearly her battles with her family disrupted her Asianness and facilitated rebel and white constructions. Her association with a white partner implied her Westernization, resulting in dominant white gazes' ability to assimilate difference into sameness. Harpreet was unable to recognize this assimilation because, in this case, she was no longer acting in oppositionally active whiteness; she had become subsumed as its subject.

Gurjeev also seems to maintain her own racial identity by disconnecting her partner from his own identity: 'I don't really refer to him as white, I think of him as light-skinned.' If the woman remains within South Asian frameworks, the white partner is labelled a Paki-lover and the desire that otherwise is inexplicable is fetishized. Harpreet, however, does not describe her partner's participation in her cultural identity as appropriative or obsessive. When I asked 'How does [he] fit into this, how does he feel about the whole thing?' Harpreet answered, 'He's all right about it . . . he just goes along with whatever . . . they [non-South Asians] don't always understand everything of your way of life. I don't know . . . he tries to understand, but there's only so much a person can take in, I guess . . . He makes an effort, he tries to get books out of the library and what have you, he certainly did more than he did, say two years ago.' Harpreet's partner had little knowledge of South Asian and/or Sikh culture before she entered his life – something which seemed to exist without too much difficulty in her relationship. Gurjeev acknowledged that there were some things a white partner could not understand. When asked about racism she said, 'To us it's huge, but to someone white, how would they ever understand what it's like?'

The process of negotiating autonomous space among interracial couples is not monolithic; few generalizations can be made. Clichés effectively freeze South Asian culture while giving unwarranted legitimacy and status to Westernization; yet the South Asian woman as rebel white wanna-be, however, is ultimately disdained because, inherently, 'South Asians can't be like us [the white gaze].' The privileging of whiteness validates assimilation. Assimilationist beliefs about interracial relationships presume differences between the two cultures to be so great that the minority culture must submit to the dominant. This does not take into account the cultural capital endowed to anyone raised in Britain (as contrasted with raised as British). This terrain (which for some Sikh/South Asian communities may consist only of knowledge gained from television) may include knowledge about food, accents, educational system and media.[23] Cultural capital does not necessarily detract from a Sikh identity; cultural capital can enhance identity – providing tools with which to better negotiate British society and forging the common ground within interracial relationships for autonomy.

Similar to and intersected by processes of Masala-itis and language, clichés objectify in a way open to reinterpretation and manipulation. Those attempting to maintain subjectivity are in some ways protected from racism by white partners (as well as friends, contacts, etc.). Negotiating one's subjectivity with a white partner may not necessarily be opposing, contradictory, or vastly different from negotiating subjectivity with a South Asian/Sikh partner. They are both forms of insulation against racism.

Conclusion

There is no monolithic experience for second-generation Sikh women in Britain. In presenting a sampling of the intersections of struggle and their possible meanings, I hope to have demonstrated the contradictory and complex nature of identity that, by necessity, must be negotiated to survive. My research indicates that a South Asian woman's identity is a resistant identity when it is defined *on its own terms*. The mechanisms of cultural conflict that I describe defy the terms of identity by maintaining Asianness as a distinct category functioning only in relation to whiteness – that is, without one category there would not be the other. The application of such a colonialist notion of cultural conflict is inherently racist. These discourses are based on the assumption that the desired and ultimate goal is to be as Westernized as possible. If that Westernization does not occur it is the fault of 'culture'. Inadequacies stem from expectations based on relational differences (e.g. East/West, white/ Black) rather than from individual identity. My participants generally expressed an ability to function quite 'normally' in worlds which perhaps do not seem so incredibly distinct, or simply are not because contradictions have been negotiated through conscious and necessary thinking.

Oppositionally active whiteness re-evaluates fixed difference/sameness and oppressor/oppressed categories; the oppressed, forced to be flexible, create new ways of subverting, challenging and resisting. I am not suggesting that these second-generation Sikh women are free from oppression. Rather, I believe they manipulate and maximize the (potential) power of their powerlessness subversively. There is no clearer demonstration of the flexibility of an emerging generation adept at the usage of marginalized positions than the double gaze. The double gaze allows for amazing creativity; in its supposed curse it can be a blessing in disguise. Dominant white gazes that see through monolithic eyes have no access to the double gaze and perceive no need for it.

Oppositionally active whiteness is a process of fluctuating and reciprocating the subject/object positionings that are in constant negotiation. To successfully navigate between the binaries of identity and objectivity and maintain subjectivity, oppositionally active whiteness must be paired with an internalized Sikh identity. Masala-itis redefines the meanings imposed by objectifying voyeuristic gazes through manipulating desire and exoticism; language is similarly used in exclusionary resistance to interrupt the visual and disembodied act of objectifying. A white partner entails that negotiation of the Sikh pole is subversive to dominant white gazes; popular discourses accord whiteness where there may be none and assume assimilation where the opposite may be happening.

The skills with which one manipulates subjectivity *in the particular ways that I have described* increase as knowledge of and contact with different parts of white society expand. These skills utilize shifts of racial and class constructions. What is oppositionally active for some arenas may not be so for others; different spaces of whiteness sometimes co-opt the same positioning. For example, a politically correct position influenced by ideologies of multiculturalism might support the wearing of *salwaar kameezes* as an embracing of diversity; a liberal position might object to what is perceived as a lack of 'freedom of choice'; a conservative position may ambivalently agree as it supports racialized constructions of South Asian women as passive victims. Despite the varied rationalizations, all three positions converge at the point at which the South Asian woman is 'otherized'.

Ultimately, the complexities of identity must not be reduced, defied or transcended. In today's world of transition, of transnational mass migration and displacement, differing ideas of home, identity and self-definition must emerge. Along with this emergence must follow alternative modes of knowing, conceptualizing and theorizing.

Notes

1 For this article I define 'second generation' as children of immigrant families born in Britain or children who moved to Britain before the age of five – those 'socialized' by the British educational system.
2 See Hill Collins (1991).
3 An extended analysis of the points summarized in the next three sections can be found in Puar (1994).
4 The precedent of colonialism is important in historicizing these boundaries. See, for example, Stoler (1990).
5 For examples of such constructs see Saifullah Khan (1980).
6 The term *Black* has particularly poignant significance in Britain, as it refers to a political coalition of people of colour, primarily African Caribbeans and South Asians. The relationships that South Asians have with this term and with Blackness are varied and complex and subsequently beyond the scope of this paper, though these configurations should be kept in mind.
7 For examples see Parmar (1982).
8 Examples include Taylor (1975); Ghuman (1980); and Thompson (1974).
9 For more work on the 'either/or' approach see Kalra (1980); Kannan (1978); and Ballard (1972–3).
10 Based on Benjamin's concept of 'ambivalence'. See Benjamin (1980).
11 Taken from Kandiyoti (1988).
12 This film stars Sarita Choudhury as a second-generation South Asian woman living in Mississippi. She has an affair with an African-American man (Denzel Washington) which neither the Black nor the South Asian community accepts.
13 Other works which become problematic in the context of reception issues attempt to document the 'authentic' and 'real' traumas and life struggles of South Asian women. Ultimately, this flatters the West and renders South Asian women as victims. See Wilson (1978); various contributors (1984); Shan (1985); and anonymous (1982).
14 A more recent example of such racist humour is the Phileas Fogg Punjab Puri Crisps television commercial featuring 'Punjabi Airways'.
15 See the work of Chandra Talpade Mohanty, Gayatri Chakravorty Spivak and Trinh T. Minh-ha – to name but a few who look at feminist theoretical approaches to identity and subjectivity.
16 The following literature that I have not otherwise referenced details immigration patterns: Singh (1992); Ballard and Ballard (1977).
17 The names of the interviewees are pseudonyms.
18 Avtar Brah quotes nineteen-year-old Sunjita to provide an example of all three constructions in oppressive operation: 'If I am with a white boy, say

just on the way home from college, they shout in the street, "What's it like to fuck a Paki?" or if I'm on my own with other girls, it's, "Here comes the Paki whore, come and fuck us Paki whores, we've heard you're really horny." Or maybe they'll put it the other way round, saying that I am dirty, that no one could possibly want to go to bed with a Paki ... I don't think any white person could know what it's like.' (*Guardian*, 5 September 1985, quoted in Brah, 1992.)

19 This work also includes an extended analysis of linguistic behaviour of second-generation Sikhs.

20 See for example Jones (1982) and Stopes-Roe and Cochrane (1988).

21 The most recent media sensationalism regarding Sikh women seems to be Wallis (1993). Wallis introduces the 'authentic' first-person narrative with these words: 'Here Amarjit talks about what it means to be a Sikh woman on the brink of an arranged marriage in 1990s Britain.' The words '1990s Britain' used in conjunction with arranged marriages is significant in this context because it constructs savage/civilized, backward/progressive, oppressed/liberated oppositions.

22 This is part of a larger work in progress on second-generation Sikh women and arranged marriages.

23 This may be the case in cities in England where the concentration of South Asian communities is highly dense. See Singh (1978).

References

AGNIHOTRI, RAMA KANT (1987) *Crisis of Identity: The Sikhs in England*, New Delhi, Bahri.

ANONYMOUS (1982) 'A young Pakistani/British female', in HUSBAND, CHARLES (Ed.) *'Race' in Britain: Continuity and Change*, London, Hutchinson, pp. 185–8.

BALLARD, CATHERINE (1979) 'Conflict, continuity and change: Second-generation South Asians', in SAIFULLAH KHAN, VERITY (Ed.) *Minority Families in Britain: Support and Stress*, London, Macmillan.

BALLARD, ROGER (1972–3) 'Family organization among the Sikhs in Britain', *New Community*, 2 (1) winter, 12–24.

BALLARD, ROGER and BALLARD, CATHERINE (1977) 'The Sikhs: The development of South Asian settlements in Britain', in WATSON, JAMES L. (Ed.) *Between Two Cultures: Migrants and Minorities in Britain*, Oxford, Basil Blackwell, pp. 21–56.

BANERJI, SABITS (1988) 'Transmutations', *Race Today: Black Cultural Expression*, 18 (2).

BENJAMIN, JESSICA (1980) 'The bonds of love', in EISENSTEIN, HESTER and JARDINE, ALICE (Eds) *The Future of Difference*, Boston, G.K.

BHACHU, PARMINDER (1991a) 'Culture, ethnicity and class among Punjabi Sikh women in 1990s Britain', *New Community*, 17 (3) summer.

Jasbir K. Puar

BHACHU, PARMINDER (1991b) 'Ethnicity constructed and reconstructed: The role of women in cultural elaboration and educational decision-making in Britain', *Gender and Education*, 3 (1).

BRAH, AVTAR (1992) 'Women of South Asian origin in Britain', in BRAHAM, PETER, RATTANSI, ALI and SKELLINGTON, RICHARD (Eds) *Racism and Anti-Racism: Inequalities, Opportunities and Politics*, London, Open Univerisity Press/Sage.

DASGUPTA, SAYANTANI (1993) 'Glass shawls and long hair', *Ms*, 5.

DILLION, KARTAR (1989) 'The parrot's beak', in ASIAN WOMEN UNITED of CALIFORNIA (Eds) *Making Waves: An Anthology of Writings by and about Asian American Women*, Boston, Beacon.

GANS, HERBERT (1979) 'Symbolic ethnicity; The future of ethnic groups and culture in America', *Ethnic and Racial Studies*, 2 (1).

GHUMAN, P. A. S. (1980) 'Bhattra Sikhs in Cardiff: Family and Kinship organization', *New Community*, 8 (3) summer, 308–16.

GREWAL, SHABNAM, KAY, JACKIE, LANDOR, LILIANE, LEWIS, GAIL and PRAMAR, PRATIBHA (Eds) (1988) *Charting the Journey: Writings by Black and Third World Women*, London, Sheba.

HILL COLLINS, PATRICIA (1991) 'Learning from the outsider within: The sociological significance of Black feminist thought', in FONOW, MARY MARGARET and COOK, JUDITH A. (Eds) *Beyond Methodology: Feminist Methodology as Lived Research*, Bloomington, Indiana University Press, pp. 35–56.

HIRO, DILIP (1973) *Black British, White British*, Harmondsworth, Penguin.

HOOKS, BELL (1990) *Yearning: Race, Gender and Cultural Politics*, Boston, South End Press.

HOOKS, BELL (1992) *Black Looks: Race and Representation*, London, Turnabout.

JAMES, ALAN (1974) *Sikh Children in Britain*, London, Oxford University Press.

JONES, PETER (1982) 'Ethnic intermarriage in Britain', *Ethnic and Racial Studies*, 5 (2), pp. 223–8.

KALRA, S. S. (1980) *Daughters of Tradition: Adolescent Sikh Girls and their Accommodation to Life in British Society*, Birmingham, Third World Publications.

KANDIYOTI, DENIZ (1988) 'Bargaining with patriarchy', *Gender and Society*, 2 (3), pp. 274–90.

KANNAN, C. T. (1978) *Cultural Adaptation of Asian Immigrants: First and Second Generation*, Bombay, India Printing Works.

LLOYD, ANN (1992) 'Culture shock', *Guardian*, 8 January, p. 14.

MODOOD, TARIQ (1991) 'The Indian economic success', *Policy and Politics*, 19 (3).

MOHANTY, CHANDRA TALPADE (1991) 'Under Western eyes: Feminist scholarship and feminist discourse', in MONHANTY, CHANDRA TALPADE, RUSSO,

ANN and TORRES, LOURDES (Eds) *Third World Women and the Politics of Feminism*, Bloomington, Indiana University Press.

NODA, KESAYA E. (1989) 'Growing up Asian in America', in ASIAN WOMEN UNITED OF CALIFORNIA (Eds) *Making Waves: An Anthology of Writings by and about Asian American Women*, Boston, Beacon.

PARMAR, PRATIBHA (1982) 'Gender, race and class: Asian women in resistance', in CENTRE FOR CONTEMPORARY CULTURAL STUDIES (Eds) *The Empire Strikes Back: Race and Racism in 70s Britain*, London, Hutchinson.

PUAR, JASBIR K. (1994) 'Rethinking identity: Racism, 'whiteness' and the South Asian 'Other', *Diatribes*, 3, summer, pp. 39–58.

SAIFULLAH KHAN, VERITY (1980) 'Asian women in Britain: Strategies of adjustment of Indian and Pakistani migrants', in DE SOUZA, ALFRED (Ed.) *Women in Contemporary India and South Asia*, New Delhi, Manohar, pp. 263–85.

SAIFULLAH KHAN, VERITY (1982) 'The role of the culture of dominance in structuring the experiences of ethnic minorities', in HUSBAND, CHARLES (Ed.) *'Race' in Britain: Continuity and Change*, London, Hutchinson.

SHAN, SHARAN-JEET (1985) *In My Own Name*, London, Women's Press.

SINGH, RAMINDER (1978) *The Sikh Community in Bradford*, Bradford, Faculty of Contemporary Studies.

SINGH, RAMINDER (1992) *Immigrants to Citizens: Sikh Community in Bradford*, Bradford, Race Relations Unit.

STOLER, ANN (1990) 'Making Empire respectable: The politics of race and sexual morality in twentieth-century colonial cultures', in BREMAN, J. et al. (Eds) *Imperial Monkey Business*, Amsterdam, VU University Press.

STOPES-ROE, M. and COCHRANE, R. (1988) 'Marriage in two cultures', *British Journal of Social Psychology*, 27, pp. 159–69.

STOPES-ROE, M. and COCHRANE, R. (1989) 'Traditionalism in the family: A comparison between Asian and British cultures and between generations', *Journal of Comparative Family Studies*, 20 (2), pp. 141–58.

TAIFEL, HENRI (1982) 'The social psychology of minorities', in HUSBAND, CHARLES (Ed.) *'Race' in Britain: Continuity and Change*, London, Hutchinson.

TAYLOR, H. J. (1975) *The Half-Way Generation*, Slough, NFER.

THOMPSON, MARCUS (1974) 'The second generation – Punjabi or English?', *New Community*, 3 (3) summer, pp. 242–8.

VARIOUS CONTRIBUTORS (1984) *Breaking the Silence: Writing by Asian Women*, London, Centreprise Trust.

WALLIS, LYNN (1993) 'Fated attraction', *Guardian*, 6 July, p. 7.

WALLMAN, SANDRA (1978) 'The boundaries of "race": Processes of ethnicity in England', *Man*, 13.

Jasbir K. Puar

WILSON, AMRIT (1978) *Finding a Voice: Asian Women in Britain*, London, Virago.

Further Reading

MODOOD, TARIQ (1992) *Not Easy being British: Colour, Culture and Citizenship*, London, Trentham Books and the Runnymede Trust.

Chapter 9

Women Who Move: Experiences of Diaspora

Magdalene Ang-Lygate

You who understand the dehumanization of forced removal – reloca-
tion – reeducation – redefinition, the humiliation of having to falsify
your own reality, your voice – you know. And often cannot say it.
You try to keep on trying to unsay it, for if you don't, they will not fail
to fill in the blanks on your behalf, and you will be said. (Trinh T.
Minh-Ha (1987) 'Difference: A special Third World women issue',
Feminist Review 25, March, p. 6)

Introduction

Global migration can no longer be seen as an unusual occurrence, nor does it
belong to the realm of a privileged few. It is fast becoming a fact of life in
contemporary Western societies.[1] The globalization of economies and the
migration of ex-colonial populations to the West has created and sustained
new kinds of social formations. The alteration of traditional demographic
and cultural profiles of Western societies challenge current notions of identity
and belonging as communities are becoming increasingly multicultural,
multiethnic or multiracial. Some scholars claim that the subsequent de-
stabilization of Western societies may be attributed to a combination of factors
which include the invasion of superhighway communication technologies and
the neo-imperialisms of transnational corporations and financial institutions.
In tandem, a post-colonial condition that has been engendered by the blurring
and shifting of geographical, cultural, political and economic boundaries has
led to the exposure of the limitations of our social vocabulary. Old styles of
conceptualizing social structure struggle to explain this post-colonial condition
that seems mysteriously volatile and fluid.

Over recent years, ideas formulated within Women's Studies have been
particularly influential in setting a new agenda in terms of social studies.
However, I believe that the time has come for scholars in Women's Studies to
start addressing the under-researched phenomena of immigration[2] from ex-
colonies to the West and to study the impact that this has had on women's lives
and women's movements – nationally and globally. Ex-colonial diasporic[3]

women who have crossed all kinds of boundaries occupy a unique location in the West. Reminiscent of earlier feminist claims that women are only socially constructed as non-men, women of colour located in the West are now rejecting Eurocentric definitions of themselves. For example, feminist debates around the triple concerns of gender, ethnicity and post-colonialism have raised complex issues about the construction of the female Self with the assertion that this is not only a result of sexual socialization but that the Self is equally a product of an individual's location in space and in time, within frameworks of hierarchized power relationships. In the case of women of colour who have immigrated to the West, a similar and simultaneous process of racialization locates them within a complicated matrix of outsider-within social relationships. As they engage socially not only as women but as non-white women – positioned as Other in a predominantly Eurocentric society – everyday social transactions involve a multiplicity of interconnected and sometimes conflicting subjectivities. Moreover, apart from the lack of literal vocabulary to describe them, these women, variously described as 'Black',[4] 'Third World', migrant, immigrant and so on, share a common dilemma: their multilayered identities are often constructed for them by others rather than by themselves.

My research is an ethnographic study centred around the immigration experiences of Chinese and Filipina women who originate from Pacific and South East Asian countries and who have settled in the Glasgow area in the west of Scotland. The research work consists mainly of gathering oral accounts of women's experiences of immigration with particular reference to their notions of 'home' and community, their sense of Self and their sense of belonging. This chapter is not about the empirical processes of my research work. Rather it is with the hope that more dialogue, discussion and debate be generated that it seeks to outline some of the difficulties I have encountered.

Who is She? Where is She? Woman-as-Other, Native-as-Other, Woman-Native-Other

The concept of *woman-as-Other* is a familiar one in feminist research. The main assertion is that an androcentric and phallocentric culture inevitably defines 'woman' negatively – as Other in relation to the male Self. However, while some feminist scholars contest the universality of an homogenous category 'woman', others propose that there is an essential 'feminine' – common to all women – which has been silenced or denied. Although there appears to be a conflict between these two different points of view, what has emerged from this curious tension is the general acknowledgement that there are vast areas of female subjectivity yet to be rendered visible and charted.[5]

It is now widely recognized that female subjectivity is culturally constituted because the realities or experiences of women only make sense when these are contextualized within given historical social frameworks. While feminists questioned the conditions for the production of a male-biased know-ledge, cultural theorists who challenged the conditions for the production of Western knowledge pointed to the Eurocentric and imperialistic definitions of the native or colonized Other.[6] They further argued that the deconstruction of Western narratives reveal hitherto hidden dimensions of imperialism in Western culture and philosophy, thereby accounting for hegemonic notions of non-European peoples. In particular, Said's (1978) term *Orientalism* has been used to describe the ways with which traditional European narratives of an-thropology and colonialism view and construct negative images of the oriental Other as 'uncivilized', 'heathen', 'pagan', 'barbaric' and so on. However, more importantly, Said suggested that the preservation of this Orientalist discourse was in fact fundamental to the identity of the European Self – a Self that claimed an identity by defining the 'native' as everything that Self was not. Hence the task of dismantling any colonial and imperialist biases, whether in knowledge production or in culture, was also inevitably a direct threat to European identity. So it was and is not in the interest of dominant Eurocentric, androcentric and phallocentric Western societies to explore the kinds of issues that feminists and post-colonial scholars want to examine. Unless we actively work against the grain of hegemonic scholarship, such biases will remain in place. Or as Audre Lorde puts it, 'The master's tools will never dismantle the master's house' (1984, p. 110).

The title of an anthology of Black women's writings edited by Hull, Scott and Smith (1981) *All the Women Are White, All the Blacks are Men, But Some of Us Are Brave* very aptly described the position of those women who did not conveniently fit into either mainstream feminist or anti-racist discourse. The 'brave' risked accusations of treachery by both white feminists and by Black men who could not see that gender politics and 'race'[7] politics alone would never be enough to satisfy the demands for change that women of colour were making. Within the context of North American Black feminism, African-American women and women of colour[8] were among the first to insist on the interconnectedness and inseparableness of their 'Black'/female identity. They refused to ignore their double consciousness of ethnicity and gender.

This protest arose from their realization that mainstream feminism only viewed gender differences from a white perspective and that anti-racist dis-course was unrepentantly sexist. The intersections of gender, ethnicity, class and other complex diversities which form the everyday experiences and reali-ties of women of colour are not easily dissected and separated. Their ability to engage in life on multiple and conflicting levels – 'to look from the outside in and from the inside out' (hooks, 1984, p. 27) – is not generally addressed in theories on female subjectivity. For example, a lesbian, working-class woman of colour is not simply a woman of colour. Nor can she be considered as just another lesbian or working-class woman because all the components of her multilayered identity are inextricably intermeshed. Hence, instead of shying away from complexity, we should heed Maxine Hong Kingston who says: 'I learned to make my mind large, as the universe is large, so that there is room for paradoxes' (1981, p. 34).

The influence of post-modernism on post-colonial feminist scholarship has sparked significant contributions to the debates surrounding the social construction of multilayered female subjectivities. Through the deconstruction of Western literary texts, Gayatri C. Spivak's writings (1985, 1988, 1992) repeatedly explore the subject-positions of 'Third World' women caught within power structures that are not only patriarchal but also colonial and imperialistic. Similarly, Trinh T. Minh Ha (1989) sought to describe from her own perspective as a Vietnamese-American film-maker, the meanings of 'difference' for a woman who was both perceived as a woman and as an alien native. Unfortunately, social theorizing about what is 'real' and not simply imagined has been slow to incorporate their observations.

In addition to the parallel and dual oppressions of sexism and racism, the twin aspects of historical and geographical positioning have to be equally acknowledged and accounted for in a post-colonial context. Social explanations and theories of female subjectivity cannot neglect the vital dimensions of time and space because different cultural meanings reside in different combinations of historical time and geographical space. Chandra Mohanty (1991) particularly stressed the hybrid influences of culture, politics and history that stem from post-colonial conditions. For instance, the meanings of heterosexual 'marriage' may be experienced and interpreted differently by women who occupy different social locations in space and time. While 'marriage' in some cultures has no meaning outside the notions of 'love, romance and monogamy', 'marriage' in other cultures may represent purely economic and lifestyle arrangements. In the case of immigrant women, the condition of 'marriage' is often a crucially important component in their identities because it has significant implications for their national status and subsequent legal rights. Hence, within current debates about, say, lesbian identities or women's complicity in domestic violence, the ways in which a 'married' woman makes sense of her Self and her social negotiations are only meaningful if the framework of her material and cultural context is also acknowledged and included. The analysis of this complex and unique social positioning, where the meanings and experiences of diasporic women of colour reside, is insufficiently accounted for.

(Inappropriate) Woman-(Diasporic) Other

Trinh uses the term *Inappropriate Others* to refer to those who resist definitions of their Otherness by others and insist on defining difference from their own perspectives (1991, p. 74). Some forms of Otherness are recognized as appropriate and tolerated because they support and perpetuate unequal relationships of power. Yet when an inappropriate Otherness is articulated, it is perceived as a subversive threat to the order of dominance and rejected not by direct opposition (because this would admit the existence of a different perspective) but through a silent denial or distortion of such realities. In the particular case of ex-colonial women who have migrated to the West, not only do all of the above points apply but the very experiences of diaspora – for example, the conditions of dispersion and exile from a home culture and the resulting psychic griefs, losses and separations – become particularly cogent in the complexion of her social construction. Her physical (re)(dis)location and her polyphonous *oppositional consciousness*, as Chela Sandoval (1987, p. 187) puts it, challenge the appropriateness and adequacy of current ways of conceptualizing difference and diversity. Her Otherness and difference is paradoxically presented together with her likeness. Consequently, instead of a vague romanticized distant-difference permitted by colonial discourse, the diasporic woman's outsider-within status insists on four articulations: *I am like you, I am different, Look! This is me, I am here to stay*. First, *I am like you*: persisting in her difference. At the same time: *I am different* dispells cherished but imagined and fictionalized notions of Otherness. In its place she presents an *inappropriate Other* who not only says: *Look! This is me* to those 'who passively absorb white supremist thinking and therefore never notice or look . . . who render us invisible with their gaze' (hooks, 1991, p. 25) but also: *I am here to stay*, and therefore cannot be easily dismissed.

Now You See Me, Now You Don't: On Terminology and Stereotypes

The ways in which we try to see and understand each other are very much constrained by a deficiency of social and literal vocabulary. The idea that dominant language, in terms of text and visual images, mutes the experiences of women has been well debated.[9] One of the main problems I have encountered is in the use of available terminology. I have had to use permutations of words such as 'Black', diasporic, migrant, immigrant, visible minority, ethnic, women of colour, 'Third World' women, native (female) Other, all of which are individually wanting and inaccurate. There is an abundance of unsuitable terminology and vocabulary. It has been tempting to cut corners and simply revert to less verbose forms of description, using, for example, the more familiar British term 'Black' women or 'Third World' women, instead of adopting longer styles like diasporic women of colour. Yet, these terms are problematic and tinged with ambiguous meanings.

For example, the term 'Black' has different meanings when used in different academic and cultural contexts. In the USA this has a more specific reference to skin colour and peoples of African descent whereas in Britain it is used more loosely as a political category that includes all people who are not racialized as white. While I accept that in certain circumstances, like the anti-apartheid struggle in South Africa, the category 'Black' can provide us with a critical location from which to speak, the usage of the term 'Black', other than with specific reference to skin colour, falls into a binary dualism/opposition trap that artificially separates 'Blacks' from 'whites'. The processes of racialization are complex. They are not confined merely to skin colour but also include other social differences, such as language or religion. Other social divisions which may be more pertinent, such as gender, class and common culture, are obscured. Yet the political category 'Black' will present a different social division based solely on perceived primary identity. The popular images presented of 'Black' people resident in Britain are also dominated by peoples from the African and Indian subcontinents or of African descent from the West Indies. Although it is true that their populations are larger than other groups, these images distort and exclude peoples from other origins. Hence, the term 'Black' renders many women, who are often unpoliticized and cannot visibly identify as Black (or white), invisible. In such ways, women of colour – for example, Chinese, Filipina, Malay or Japanese – are denied spaces from which they can voice their own rights and concerns.

Similarly, the concept of one distinct 'Third World' is problematic. This term actually describes the regions and individual countries of Africa, Asia, the Carribbean, Latin America and the Middle East. Although these countries share a common predicament with respect to their economic status in a competitive world economy and in suffering the after-effects of colonization, the differences and variations between and within 'Third World' regions is enormous, such as in religion, political systems, culture and class structures. Like 'the West', the term 'Third World' is now used most often with a geographical and economic connotation and I use this term geographically to describe women of colour who originate from ex-colonies. 'Ethnic minority' is another difficult term, as it is often used as a blanket term for all peoples of colour inclusive of 'white ethnic minorities'. Apart from its Eurocentric imperialist overtones and the fact that, globally, Caucasians are distinctly in the minority, its usage also draws attention to a curious anomaly whereby 'we all know what we mean when we use the category minority to apply to an empirical majority' (Lippard, 1992, p. 168). More recently, in order to distinguish between 'white minorities' and 'non-white minorities', the term 'visible minority' is being used to mean Black peoples and peoples of colour.

In the context of my own study, I qualify ethnic descriptors by reference to place of origin or to country of settlement, for example, Hong Kong Chinese, Malaysian Chinese or Scots Chinese. This is because I am conscious that the term Chinese, when used as a unifying category, forces an unnatural unilateral homogeneity on Chinese peoples and fosters the myth of an 'authentic' ethnicity, whether manisfested as 'true native' or 'typical immigrant'. Notions of authenticity encourage the falsehood of a pure ethnic identity and support essentialist constructs of dominant stereotypes. In terms of Chineseness, a Chinese woman from Hong Kong has a completely different ethnic makeup from another Chinese woman from Singapore or mainland China. Their Chineseness alone cannot automatically be assumed to be a source of commonality. Similarly, in Britain the term Asian is used to describe peoples who originate from the Indian subcontinent (themselves widely varied culturally). There seems to be no distinction between Asians who are British subjects and those who are not. In the USA, the category Asian usually applies to peoples from the Indian subcontinents and from South-East and Pacific Asian countries such as Japan, Korea and the Philippines. On obtaining citizenship, these groups of peoples are then referred to as Asian-American, Chinese-American or Japanese-American. The status of 'immigrant' seems to be more transient in the USA than it is in Europe. In Britain, we have no words to reflect non-indigenous peoples who have decided to settled here. Subsequently, such peoples – whatever their length of stay or national status – are automatically viewed as permanent sojourners rather than as active citizens who participate fully in society.

Spivak (1988) claims that in Western literary texts, the native or 'Third World' woman is a gendered *subaltern*,[10] who is powerless to resist colonial definitions because such definitions do not require her to acknowledge the imaginary spaces and meanings that have been assigned to her occupation. She is strictly confined to a native-woman enclosure that is a product of the colonizer's imagination. Rana Kabbani (1988) has agreed that while the native (male) Other was negatively defined and demonized as barbaric, evil and dangerous, the native (female) Other was eroticized and seen to be exotic, desirable and available. Hence, whatever the material realities of that woman's experience – her educational level, professional status and financial situation – she is always viewed *under Western eyes*[11] and homogenized primarily as a sexualized being. Commenting on Chinese women, Amy Ling (1989) further pointed out that the stereotypes of 'lotus blossom' and 'dragon lady' were exotic versions of the more familiar madonna / whore dichotomy that has characterized Western stereotypes of women in general but both of these stereotypes were distinctly sexual in connotation. She identified the character Suzy Wong as a new permutation created for Western consumption, when Richard Mason in his novel *The World of Suzy Wong* combined the two into one – a prostitute with the heart of a child (Ling, 1989, pp. 310, 312).

The dynamics of poverty, the phenomenon of mail-order brides from the Far East and the socioeconomics of an international sex trade all continue to perpetuate these stereotypes and Eurocentric societies remain hostile to positive images of the diasporic immigrant woman. To illustrate, Kingston (1981) broke silences and started to dismantle the popular stereotypes of Chinese women when she addressed the experience of fractured identities and fragmented consciousness which were part of her own experiences as the American-born daughter of an immigrant Chinese woman. Her book *The Warrior Woman* became a bestseller several times over. Yet, although more and more women like Kingston have since begun to write of their own experiences of diaspora and about their specific social location and negotiation in the West, the fact still remains that such *inappropriate* pronouncements can only be tolerated in the form of fiction but not as part of the everyday recognized realities that inform policy-making processes. Nor are these reflected in social scientific work.

Unsaying the Already-said

Logically, when the *inappropriate* woman refuses the images imposed on her as exotic, erotic or authentic ethnic and resists the confines of her colonized pet-native-woman[12] enclosure, her articulations should challenge not only the inadequacy of social vocabulary but also expose the social practices that attempt to deny or distort her experienced reality. However, this simplistic standpoint fails to take account of the hierarchized power structures that are still in place which privilege the already-said as the 'truth'. From a sociological perspective, traditional analysis of multiple oppressions – gender, ethnicity, class – do not adequately reflect the modern realities of shifting boundaries that have arisen from post-colonial conditions. The phenomena of pluralistic hyphenated subjectivities, such as those sketched above, stay unaddressed. By exploring the effects of different social forces, including chronological sequence of time and physical (re)(dis)location that have shaped the outcome of immigrant identity, we can, in turn, start to understand the role that these identities have in either perpetuating or resisting those existing social forces.

When I asked S, my contact at a Glasgow-based Chinese centre, to put me in touch with some Chinese women who had immigrated to Scotland, she suggested that I joined a newly started aerobics class that was run by a group of Chinese women who regularly used the centre. The idea was that I get to meet potential interview participants in an everyday setting and establish my credibility first, rather than approach them as a stranger before inviting them to talk to me about their immigration experiences. Taking up her suggestion, I telephoned B who was responsible for this aerobics class and got myself enrolled. However, what transpired from that initial telephone conversation with B gave me plenty to think about concerning the very issues that I wanted to study: issues that dealt with notions of identity and belonging. After introducing myself as a friend of S's, I asked B if I could join the aerobics class. To my surprise, she sounded very hesitant and seemed reluctant to give me much more information about the class. Eventually, I realized what the 'problem' was. She asked me outright if I spoke Cantonese because the classes were run in that Chinese dialect. It dawned on me that B probably assumed that I was Caucasian, because of my Anglicized first name and because of my local Scottish accent. Meanwhile, she could not afford to offend me by declaring that it was a Chinese-women-only class. As expected, as soon as I explicitly identified myself as Malaysian Chinese and that I did speak Cantonese, her entire attitude to me changed. 'Oh! If you are Chinese, you are *most* welcome. I look forward to seeing you next Tuesday.'

Afterwards, I did wonder about the potentially 'racist' overtones that arose from that short conversation. Why was that space specifically reserved for Chinese women alone? Would I really be excluded from the class if I was a white woman? Was it not enough for me to have been a woman, whatever my colour or ethnicity? Was her attitude 'racist' or was it merely defensive? If defensive, why did B feel threatened by my perceived difference when she thought I was Caucasian? Do Malaysian Chinese and Hong Kong Chinese women really have so much in common? What were these unspoken rules that governed whether and who belonged? Previously, I have never really had to explain being Chinese because in everyday social interaction, I was always visibly oriental. However, in this instance, because B could not see me over the telephone, my 'race' or colour became an issue because it was perceived as a condition for belonging. What changed the difference in her perception of me as a white woman and then as a Chinese woman? Although I myself had not changed, in an instant my status changed from outsider to insider. With regards to 'belonging', there appeared to be a subtle distinction in this case between my identity and my eventual identification with B as Chinese. It was clear that while my material status as a Chinese woman gave me an immediate right of access to that group, I was actually not allowed to belong until I revealed my 'true' identity and identified myself as Chinese. In a sense, I had to come out to her as being Chinese.

It also struck me that all three of us involved in the episode above – S, B and myself – had non-Chinese Anglicized first names. It was clear that unless we literally saw each other, we were potentially invisible to each other as Chinese women. This phenomenon linking Western imperialism with British names and colonial identity is part of a neo-colonialism where the Western imperialism of past generations has filtered down to this one and lodged itself into the very personal names by which post-colonial diasporic women of colour – like S, B and myself – identify ourselves. The names we bear simultaneously give and rob us of an identity.[13] In the case of some Chinese women and Filipinas, who have married white men and adopted their surnames, this invisibility is even more insidious. These women are hidden behind names such as Tess MacDonald, Julie MacNabb, Michelle Lawson[14] and the lenses of Eurocentric naming practices render them invisible to each other.

Knowledge is not just a revelation of an objective 'truth': it also goes beyond perspectives of 'truth', it is more than simply a question of 'saying'. The 'truths' gathered in the course of my research are inevitably counter hegemonic and have arisen because I *know* (in the sense of the opening quotation by Trinh) what is to be unsaid. This is more than a case of privileging experience because such experiences do not yet enjoy the privileges of recognition and validation. Paradoxically, even if the language is not yet available, those of us who are familiar with the uncharted territories of unsayable knowledge already think and speak it among ourselves. We already recognize each other not by essentialist notions of diasporic identity but by a shared circumstance that is still imperfectly articulated. We are the ones who *try to keep on trying to unsay.*

So far, the problematics of terminology remain unresolved and one of the major concerns of post-colonial scholarship and Women's Studies is the whole area of 'language'. Available language is restricted – both in words and images – and yet the (re)naming processes must continue. It is not enough to use academically fashionable jargon. We have to move beyond merely politically correct forms of name-calling, reach deeply into the collective consciousness of everyday realities and dare to break the constricting moulds of existing meanings. Issues of identity, whether self-defined by women of colour as 'authentic' or imposed upon by others, only become meaningful when the structural forces that have a direct bearing on interpretations of authenticity and truth are scrutinized and deconstructed. The mere articulation of experience and apolitical versions of reality alone become dangerously simplistic in attempting to chart women's experiences of diaspora because the ways in which such articulations are permitted and the accompanying social practices that (dis)allow them remain unidentified and unchallenged. Unless we insist on moving beyond traditional knowledge production and adopt new forms of understanding that unshackle new meanings, the struggle for the space for self-definition is a fruitless one. For if the emphasis is on understanding how the construction of social identities severs or resists practices of dominance and oppression, then research into women's experiences of diaspora can contribute significantly towards a social dynamics which seeks to ensure that our daughters and sons will inherit modern identities and enter into a more egalitarian future.

A closing message to those of us who are Brave . . . *If you don't, they will not fail to fill in the blanks on your behalf and you will be said.*

Notes

1 Risking the danger of totalization, I have little choice but to use the term 'Western' before other terms introduced can have more precise meanings.
2 I prefer the term 'immigration' to 'migration' because the processes of arriving and settling in a new place not only encompass the present and future but also the past narratives of immigrant realities.
3 I use the term 'diasporic' to try and instil a sense of exile, (re)(dis)location and dynamic fluidity into the meanings intrinsic to immigrant experiences.
4 I use the term 'Black' in quotation marks exclusively within the context of anti-racist discourse and the term Black to refer specifically to peoples of African descent. The problematics of terminology is discussed in a later section.
5 For instance, the deconstruction of the category 'woman' has exposed what we now recognize as the homogenous stance that was previously adopted by Euro-American feminisms. The struggles and realities of women of colour, lesbians, working-class women, disabled women slowly moved out of the margins and into the centre of mainstream Women's Studies and

have in turn engendered new directions of study, such as Black Women's Studies, Lesbian Studies.

6 Such as Benedict Anderson (1983), Edward Said (1978), Homi Bhabha (1990). Nevertheless, the fact remains that within post-colonial discourse, the native Other is still a native (male) Other.

7 I use the term 'race' in quotation marks with the understanding that this is an historical rather than a biological and scientific construct.

8 See, for example, bell hooks (1981), Cherie Moraga and Gloria Anzaldua (1981), Audre Lorde (1984), Alice Walker (1984), Patricia Hill Collins (1989) and others too numerous to mention.

9 See, for example, Shirley Ardener (1975), Deborah Cameron (1990) and Dale Spender (1990).

10 Spivak's term for the colonized native.

11 This is also the title of a piece by Chandra Mohanty (1988) where she makes the same accusation of some Western feminist scholarship that categorizes 'Third World' women as a singular monolithic subject and refuses to confront the differences and diversity which are part of these women's lives.

12 Zora Neale Hurston (1979) compares white treatment of Blacks with that of pets: always within a relationship of ownership and dominance.

13 There is a fuller discussion of this in my M Litt dissertation *The Politics of Articulation* (1993).

14 Due to confidentiality, these names are fictitious but over 90 per cent of the women I have interviewed have European names, either given to them or self-adopted.

References

ANDERSON, BENEDICT (1983) *Imagined Communities*, London, Verso.

ANG-LYGATE, MAGDALENE (1993) 'Speaking subjects: A name of my own', in *The Politics of Articulation* unpublished. M Litt dissertation, University of Strathclyde.

ARDENER, SHIRLEY (Ed.) (1975) *Perceiving Women*, London, Malaby Press.

BHABHA, HOMI (Ed.) (1990) *Nation and Narration*, London, Routledge.

CAMERON, DEBORAH (Ed.) (1990) *The Feminist Critique of Language*, London, Routledge.

COLLINS, PATRICIA HILL (1989) *Black Feminist Thought: Knowledge, Consciousness and the Politics of Empowerment*, London, Routledge.

DERRIDA, JACQUES (1976) *Of Grammatology*, trans. G. C. SPIVAK, Baltimore, John Hopkins University Press.

HOOKS, BELL (1981) *Ain't I A Woman?*, Boston, South End Press.

HOOKS, BELL (1984) *Feminist Theory: From Margin to Centre*, Boston, South End Press.

HOOKS, BELL (1991) *Yearning: Race, Gender And Cultural Politics*, London, Turnabout.

HULL, GLORIA T., SCOTT, PATRICIA BELL and SMITH, BARBARA (1981) *All the Women Are White, All the Blacks are Men, But Some of Us Are Brave*, New York, The Feminist Press.

HURSTON, ZORA NEALE (1979) 'The pet negro system', in WALKER, A. (Ed.) (1979) *I Love Myself*, New York, The Feminist Press.

KABBANI, RANA (1988) *Europe's Myths of Orient: Devise And Rule*, London, Pandora Press.

KINGSTON, MAXINE HONG (1981) *The Woman Warrior: Memoirs of a Girlhood Amongst Ghosts*, London, Pan Books.

LING, AMY (1989) 'Chinamerican women writers: Four forerunners of Maxine Hong Kingston', in JAGGER, A. and BORDO, S. (Eds) (1989) *Gender/Body/Knowledge*, New Brunswick, Rutgers University Press.

LIPPARD, LUCY R. (1992) 'Mapping', in FRASCINA, F. and HARRIS, J. (Eds) (1992) *Art in Modern Culture: An Anthology of Critical Texts*, London, Phaidon Press.

LORDE, AUDRE (1984) *Sister Outsider: Essays and Speeches*, Freedom, CA, The Crossing Press.

MOHANTY, CHANDRA (1988) 'Under Western eyes', *Feminist Review*, 30.

MOHANTY, CHANDRA (1991) 'Cartographies of struggle', in MOHANTY, C. T., RUSSO, A. and TORRES, L. (Eds) (1991) *Third World Women and the Politics of Feminism*, Bloomington, Indiana University Press.

MOHANTY, CHANDRA, RUSSO, A. and TORRES, L. (Eds) (1991) *Third World Women and the Politics of Feminism*, Bloomington, Indiana University Press.

MORAGA, CHERIE and ANZALDUA, GLORIA (Eds) (1981) *This Bridge Called My Back: Writings by Radical Women of Color*, New York, Kitchen Table.

SAID, EDWARD (1978) *Orientalism*, London, RKP.

SANDOVAL, CHEVA, quoted in KAPLAN, CAREN (1987) 'Deterritorializations: The rewriting of home and exile in Western feminist discourse', *Cultural Critique*, 6, Spring.

SPENDER, DALE (1990) *Man Made Language*, London, Pandora Press.

SPIVAK, GAYATRI C. (1985) 'Three women's texts and a critique of imperialism', *Critical Inquiry*, 12, Autumn, 244–51.

SPIVAK, GAYATRI C. (1988) *In Other Worlds: Essays in Cultural Politics*, New York, Routledge.

SPIVAK, GAYATRI C. (1992) 'The politics of translation', in BARRETT, M. and PHILLIPS, A. (Eds) (1992) *Destabilising Theory*, London, Polity Press.

TRINH T. MINH-HA (1987) 'Difference: A special Third World Women issue', *Feminist Review*, 25, March, 5–22.

TRINH T. MINH-HA (1989) *Woman, Native, Other: Writing Postcoloniality and Feminism*, Bloomington, Indiana University Press.

TRINH T. MINH-HA (1991) 'Outside in inside out', in TRINH (1991) *When The*

Moon Waxes Red: Representation, Gender and Cultural Politics, London, Routledge.

WALKER, ALICE (1984) *In Search of Our Mother's Gardens*, London, The Women's Press.

Chapter 10

'The Home of Our Mothers and Our Birthright for Ages'? Nation, Diaspora and Irish Women

Breda Gray

We are a much dispersed nation and emigration looms large in the national consciousness. (Carruthers, 1991, p. 167)

In this chapter, I build on Carruthers' statement by suggesting that the Irish 'dispersed nation' is a gendered nation despite predominant representations of Irishness as either non-gendered or masculine by theorists of national identity and emigration. I focus on national identity and emigration from the Republic of Ireland only and explore how ideas of national identity and the transnational form of 'diaspora' might relate to Irish women migrants' national and migrant identities.

My initial assumptions are, first, that the experience of *colonialism* and its aftermath are important in any discussion of the gendered nature of Irish national identity and migration. The experience of colonialism, its economic, social and political legacies and its continuing constitutive impact on Irish-English identities and relations are central to understanding Irish identifications with culture, place and nationality. Gerardine Meaney (1991) draws on the work of Ashis Nandy, an Indian political philosopher, to highlight the ways in which colonialism is implicated in the gendering of national identity when she points out that:

a history of colonisation is a history of feminisation. Colonial powers identify their subject peoples as passive, in need of guidance, incapable of self-government, romantic, passionate, unruly, barbarous – all of those things for which the Irish and women have been traditionally praised and scorned. (Meaney, 1991, p. 6)

Second, I suggest that it is impossible to discuss Irish national identity without attending to the impact of *emigration* on how that identity has been constructed and experienced by migrants and non-migrants up to the present day. Emigration has been and continues to be a significant national phenomenon, because of its scale and the length of time over which it has taken place. The high levels of emigration for almost every generation of Irish women over the past two centuries makes leaving Ireland or coming to terms with the emigration of family members and friends an important aspect of Irish women's lives.

My third assumption is that Irish national identity and indeed all national identities are thoroughly *gendered*. For example, prominent icons and symbols of Irishness include images of suffering Mother Ireland (Meaney, 1991) and the idea of the national landscape as feminine (Nash, 1993). Similarly, the gendered institution of the family is represented in the Irish Constitution as the bedrock on which Irishness is built.[1] Although I refer to 'Irish women' throughout this chapter, I do not see Irish women as an undifferentiated group. I use the term 'Irish women' because, in the absence of empirical research, it is impossible to represent the diverse experiences of different groups of Irish women migrants.[2]

This chapter begins with a brief outline of the patterns of Irish women's emigration this century and the ways in which women's emigration was represented in relation to Irish national identity. This discussion covers three main waves of emigration from Ireland this century in the 1920s, the 1950s and the 1980s (O'Carroll, 1990).[3] I sketch some of the ways in which Irish national identity has been affected by emigration before moving on to examine how national identity is gendered. I then explore the potential of discourses of 'diaspora' as an alternative way of theorizing Irish women's identifications with Irishness which is more progressive than the predominantly masculine defined debates around national identity. Finally, I point to some of the difficulties in conceptualizing Irish women's identifications with nation, cultures, people and place.

Irish Women's Emigration in the Twentieth Century

Whatever the perspective taken in analysing Irish emigration[4] we know very little about the motivations and experiences of the Irish women who left and of those who stayed. Ann Rossiter's (1993) survey of the literature on Irish emigration identified 'collective amnesia' when it comes to the question of gender. She asserts that 'the lacunae in our knowledge of Irish female emigrants in the twentieth century are vast' (1993, p. 189). Jean Cross (1989, p. 6) suggests that 'Irish women's emigration is unique among European countries in that proportionately more women have left Ireland than any other country'.

In the 1920s, Irish women's emigration accounted for just over half of the total emigrants from Ireland in contrast to about one-third of the total in continental Europe (Lee, 1990).[5] The numbers of single women leaving Ireland has always been high and in some periods women have outnumbered men emigrants, making Irish women's emigration untypical of emigration in world terms (Cross, 1989). Emigration in the 1920s took place in the context of the establishment of the new Free State in Southern Ireland and the Northern Irish six counties as part of the United Kingdom. Following independence, a highly centralized State was established in the South 'modelled in every significant way on its colonial predecessor' (Coulter, 1993, p. 23). Restrictive legislation and policy initiatives were introduced in the 1920s and 1930s on issues of divorce, contraception, illegitimacy, barring women from jury service and restricting women's access to employment in the civil service (Coulter, 1993). Many of these policies were subsequently enshrined in the 1937 constitution, *Bunreacht na hEireann.*

Joe Lee (1990) suggests that official discourses in Ireland in the 1920s tended to emphasize psychological explanations for the high rates of emigration. He points out that the high numbers of women emigrating were explained by 'the impact of Hollywood, projecting images of lavish and romantic American lifestyles' which 'further unbalanced already flighty female minds' (1988, p. 34). The *Freeman's Journal* at the time lamented that:

> Irish girls, beguiled by hopes of fantastic wages abroad, give up more than they know, when instead of the simple neighbourly village life, or the friendly relations still existing in good Irish households, they choose at a distance the tawdry, uncertain splendours of a despised servant class, and take on themselves the terrible risk of utter failure far away from all home help. It is surely true that scarcely one Irish girl abroad is ever happy again at heart. (Lee, 1990, p. 34)

Lee analyses this quote by suggesting that the blame for emigrating was laid on the female character rather than on colonialism, economic or social factors in Irish society. Such an emphasis on Irish women making the wrong choices reflects, in my view, Irish patriarchal fears of the independence and agency of Irish women who, on emigrating, were outside the control of Irish men. As Yuval-Davis (1993) suggests, it is the control of women that underpins national social order, so that when women are seen to be acting on their own initiative, official (men's) anxiety levels are raised.

In contrast to 'official' constructions of Irish women emigrants as having 'flighty female minds', Janet Nolan (1989) suggests that the large-scale emigration of young single Irish women in the 1920s reflected these women's search for economic independence. Unlike many other emigrant groups, Irish women emigrated as single women and often joined sisters or female friends who had already left and who in some cases had sent the fares home. These women broke free of family ties. They emigrated 'as "sisters" to each other rather than daughters and wives' (Clear, 1992, p. 104).

While some of the above discussion might appear to suggest that emigration offered a liberation from conservative and patriarchal Irish life for Irish women, Janet Nolan (1989, p. 77) found that 'Irish born women in the United States chose jobs that were extensions of their traditional domestic skills' and were more likely to have more children and to remain at home than their American counterparts. It may be the case that the maintenance of these lifestyles enabled the preservation of an Irish identity in a foreign country.

However, these findings reflect the continuing patriarchal pressures within migrant Irish communities and the difficulties that Irish women experience with breaking free of Irish community norms even after emigration.

Emigration figures soared again in the *1950s*. In this decade emigration was explained more in terms of economics than the psychological deficits of those who left (Lee, 1990). According to the Commission on Emigration[6] which reported in 1954, the main cause of emigration was economic although social, political and psychological factors were also seen as influential. Pauric Travers' (1995) survey suggests that employment was a major determinant of Irish women's decisions to emigrate in the 1950s. He cites the low rate and the late age of marriage in Ireland at the time as another factor which cannot be overlooked.

> The Housewives' Association argued that the main causes of female emigration were the inferior status of women in Irish society, poor conditions on small farms and the fact that women were dismissed from public appointments on marriage. (Travers, 1995, p. 159)

Jenny Beale (1986, p. 35) puts women's emigration in the context of Irish politicians' vision of Ireland in the 1940s and 1950s:

> At a time when politicians were praising family life in rural Ireland, when de Valera was exalting the countryside, 'bright with cosy home-steads', the people of the west were streaming away, leaving the traditional way of life as fast as they could.

Beale suggests that many factors were involved in women's decision to emigrate in this period, including 'the lack of work and marriage prospects at home, the better pay and working conditions abroad and the higher status of women in Britain and America' (1986, p. 141).

Another commentator noted that emigration was 'sex-selective' and points out that:

> rural areas in particular have been affected by the greater propensity of females to leave, producing distorted sex ratios which have impor-tant implications for the maintenance of community cohesion and marriage rates. (Coward, 1989, p. 66)

According to Pauric Travers, women's emigration in the 1940s and 1950s received regular public comment. He quotes from Daniel Morrissey's (TD) 1948 public letter to his constituents in which Morrissey links women's emigra-tion to the needs of the nation. Morrissey pointed out that Ireland had 'failed to retain any percentage of the cream of young Ireland to build up the nation' (in Travers, 1995, p. 154). Dr T. F. O'Higgins is also quoted in Travers (1995, p. 154) as asking 'Could anybody contemplate a more serious national situation . . . [with] a steady outflow of young women so that many parishes have not a single young girl left.' Women's decisions to emigrate are, therefore, only included in public discourses of emigration in relation to the balancing of sex ratios, the reproduction of the nation and the maintenance of community cohesion.

Between 1971 and 1981 there was a net backflow of over 100,000 Irish migrants from Britain to Ireland (Garvey, 1985). These were mostly families and couples; single women did not return. Travers (1995) suggests that economic improvements in Ireland in the 1960s benefited men more than women. He points out that a study of Irish emigrants leaving in the 1970s found that Irish women were more dissatisfied 'with their life and status in Ireland' than Irish men and a larger proportion of women indicated that they did not intend to return to Ireland. This may reflect, among other things, single Irish women's perceptions of Irish society and its emphasis on family life.

The 1970s generation was the one that did not have to emigrate. Fintan O'Toole, in an article in the *Irish Times*, comments on this generation in which he includes himself:

> There was a real sense, then, that we were the terminus of a whole era of Irish history, that we were the reward for which all those sacrifices had been made. At last the struggles of history had borne fruit in a generation of young Irish people who didn't have to go, who were free to stay and build a life in their own country. (1989, p. 10)

Yet within a few years, things had changed. O'Toole continues:

> I keep turning over that basic question of why it is that emigration, which was virtually unthinkable for the people with whom I grew up, had become, for people only three or four years younger, something that you don't have to think twice about. (1989, p. 10)

Even if young Irish people of the 1970s and early-1980s grew up with the expectation that they would make a life for themselves in Ireland – and many did so – the option of emigration was never far from the surface. Indeed, emigration was easily reinstated as an acceptable option for dealing with the recession and consequent unemployment of the 1980s.

However, emigration is not always only about employment prospects. In her discussion of Irish women's emigration to the USA in the 1980s, Ide O'Carroll (1990) suggests that women emigrating in this decade 'seem to be seeking to escape from repressive legislation and economic hardship in Ireland'. This repressive legislation includes the 1980s Abortion and Divorce amendments to the constitution prohibiting abortion and divorce in the Republic of Ireland and the continuing criminalizing of homosexuality which was only decriminalized in 1993. In a later article, O'Carroll (1995, p. 192) discusses the specific cases of three women who left in the 1980s in which sexual abuse may have acted as 'a conscious/unconscious push factor in their decision to emigrate to America'. O'Carroll found that many of the women she interviewed would like to return to Ireland to live 'but only if it changed in terms of its attitudes to women' (1995, p. 198). O'Carroll is hopeful that what she calls the 'Robinson Ireland'[7] of the 1990s offers a more positive environment for women than the Ireland of the 1980s.

In the next section I explore the other side of emigration: that is, the experiences of women in their nation of destination. Although most Irish emigration in the twentieth century was to Britain (Ryan, 1990), I locate this discussion specifically in the context of England.

Dominant Stereotypes of Irishness and Irish Women in England

Irish migrant women in England are affected by dominant English stereotypes of Irishness and by stereotypes of Irish women within Irish communities in England. Jean Cross (1989, p. 6) suggests that within Irish communities in Britain, Irish women are predominantly represented as inhabiting Irish Catholic mothering roles and as 'smiling decorations happy to remain on the sidelines of events'. While this stereotype may not pervade all Irish communities in England, it is one that many Irish women will encounter. Jean Cross continues:

> just as the Irish community cannot rely on British society to represent it, so too the Irish women's community cannot rely on the wider Irish community for representation. (Cross, 1989, p. 6)

These stereotypes have contributed to the cumulative processes of editing out and silencing which have implications for Irish women migrants in England today.

> Our sisters, mothers, aunts and grandmothers have been coming to work, live and die in Britain for centuries, yet we remain without a popular image or concept of their achievements. We know little of their concerns and aims and less still of how they express the realities and aspirations of their lives. (Cross, 1989, p. 6)

Although 'Irish women have made up the largest female migrant workforce in Britain for the last 100 years' (Wall, 1991, p. 9), Bronwen Walter (1995) suggests that 'there is no clear stereotype of Irish women' in Britain. She contrasts this with the United States of America:

> where 'Bridgets' and 'colleens' have distinctive images as independent and outspoken single women and as strong mothers. (1995, p. 10)

In Britain, Walter (1995) points out that Irish people are collectively known as 'Paddies' or 'Micks' which imply male images of drunkenness, violence and stupidity. Despite the masculine nature of these stereotypes, Walter (1995) suggests that Irish women are not shielded from their impact.

Rita Wall (1991) paints a different picture when she refers to a range of stereotypes of Irish women in England. She suggests that the dominant stereotypes of Irish women in England include the 'mystical *Mother Ireland* – a quite, gentle, caring figure'. This stereotype puts Irish women in the position of symbolizing a passive Ireland in opposition to the more active and progressive England. Another stereotype of Irish women in England, according to Wall, is that of *Irish Mother* who 'is seen as having a large number of children, Catholic, poor, uneducated and married to an alcoholic labourer' (1991, p. 9). The profession of nursing in which many Irish women emigrants are employed compliments both of the above stereotypes in that they are seen as caring, capable and physically strong. They were regarded as 'kind and considerate, but were mostly valued for their strength and good health' (Tilki, 1994, p. 910). These stereotypes may have contributed to the discrimination that many Irish nurses experienced when it came to promotion (Tilki, 1994). Wall's final stereotype is that of the nun, 'who occupies the convent, school, hospital or nursing home but is dominated by a male hierarchical church' (1991, p. 9). In the case of each of these stereotypes, Irish women are largely invisible and contained by various institutions and/or the demands of others.

A recent Dove soap advertisement shown on British television has a fresh-faced, gentle young Irish woman extolling the virtues of Dove soap in a soft Irish accent. She has a pleasant smile and a complexion that might be associated with the fresh air of the West of Ireland far away from the industry and busyness of English cities, but reinforcing the stereotype of Irish women as rural, fresh-faced and gentle.

While there has been some suggestion that there has been a revival of Irish ethnic identity in Britain in the 1980s, it may not be a revival, as Ann Holohan (1995, p. 8) suggests, but merely that Irish people are more willing to make their Irishness visible. Irish cultural and social events have taken place in Britain for a long time. However, many of these events have taken place mainly *within* Irish communities rather than as part of wider British society. Holohan suggests that many of the recent emigrants and second-generation Irish people she interviewed 'act more publicly as Irish people, than Irish people did in the past' (Holohan, 1995, p. 8). However, one of her interviewees, Avril MacRory, Head of Music Programmes at BBC television pointed out:

> I can be as Irish as I want, because the world I live in is very tolerant
> of people from all sorts of different backgrounds and cultures be-
> cause television, the media generally, is made up of a huge diversity
> of people . . . I think it's a lot more difficult if you're coming off the

boat, maybe without qualifications, without the security of a job. Then, I think, being Irish in Britain is a whole different kettle of fish. (in Holohan, 1995, p. 19)

This quote draws attention to class as just one of the variables differentiating Irish women's experiences of being Irish in England in the 1990s. The invisibility and misrepresentation of Irish women within constructions of Irishness at home, within Irish communities in England and among English people have been challenged by women's groups throughout this century (Coulter, 1993). It is only more recently that Irish feminist activities have achieved more visible results, such as the election of Mary Robinson in 1990 as President of Ireland and the establishment of the London Irish Women's Centre in the 1980s. These developments have begun to problematize dominant misrepresentations of the links between women and nation and women and Irishness.

Emigration and Irish National Identity

In recent years some writers have begun to explore the view that emigration, because of the large numbers of emigrants in the past and present, is constitutive of what it means to be Irish. David Lloyd (1994, p. 3) describes the Irish as 'a population scattered by transportation, exile and emigration throughout the world, though mostly throughout the "English speaking world" of the formerly British settler colonies'. According to Mary Corcoran (1994, p. 6) emigration has 'come to be seen as an inevitable aspect of Irish life, *across all social classes*'. Emigration is integrated into Irish 'national consciousness as acceptable, unremarkable, inevitable and often even a positive development' (McAdam, 1994, p. 12). A central part of one's imagining from an early age is the view that to be Irish may mean living outside Ireland.

> The 'image elsewhere' . . . is part and parcel of growing up with the experience and consciousness of emigrant aunts and cousins, of other destinies and possibilities than those on offer at home. (Jackson, 1991, p. 93)

Irish people live their lives with many of their closest family and friends living thousands of miles away.

Benedict Anderson (1983, 1991) developed the idea of the nation as an imagined political community existing within the territorial boundaries of the nation-state. However, emigration and diaspora may have the effect of extending or fragmenting the national imagined community and the potential to destabilize national identity. Ireland may be imagined, therefore, in a less boundaried way than Benedict Anderson suggests. Leopold Bloom in James Joyce's *Ulysses* defines a nation as 'people living in the same place . . . and also in different places'. Here we see another version of Anderson's imagined

community which extends this community to places beyond the boundaries of the nation. According to Leo Chavez (1994, p. 54) the internalization of images of the imagined community and a sense of connectedness to the national community is 'as important as actual physical presence in the community'. Yet it is unclear in the case of Ireland (as in many other cases) what that connectedness means. How is such connectedness fostered and enabled? While President Mary Robinson has made the fostering of communication between emigrants and non-emigrants an important goal for her presidency, it is not clear how emigrants and non-emigrants might form one imagined community. Although Mary Robinson speaks of 'cherishing the Irish Diaspora'[8] there appears to be little popular support in the Republic of Ireland for extending voting rights to emigrants[9]. If emigrants were to be included in the national political imagined community it would be much more difficult to pin-down the boundaries of the imagined Irish community.

As I noted earlier, women's presence in the imagined national community or as emigrants is only acknowledged in relation to the preservation of the Irish 'race'. Catherine Nash (1993) points to the ways in which Irish women are constructed purely in terms of the reproduction and continuation of the Irish 'race':

> Concern over emigration fused issues of gender and race, as it was felt that loss of those who 'would have made the best mothers and wives' leaves 'at home the timid, the stupid, and the dull to help in the deterioration of the race and to breed sons as sluggish as themselves'. (Russell, 1912, pp. 67–8, in Nash, 1993, p. 49) Both ideas of racial pride and racial fears were thus projected on to the body of the woman. (Nash, 1993, p. 49)

An Irish woman's duty was to stay in Ireland, where her main role is the reproduction of the 'race', the maintenance of Irish culture. However, the high levels of women's emigration suggests that many Irish women felt a need to escape the expectations and restrictions of Irish society and sought wider opportunities and lifestyle possibilities elsewhere. Mary Kells (1995) in her study of Irishness among young Irish middle-class migrants in the London of the 1980s found great diversity among Irish women in the ways in which they relate to Irishness. The most basic consensus in relation to Irish identity among the twenty- to thirty-year-olds in her study was that of a 'shared cultural heritage and early, formative experiences in Ireland' (1995, p. 7). They saw their experiences of growing up in Ireland as an important part of their sense of self and their relationship to Irishness. It is not clear what second and third generation Irish women might identify as central to their Irishness. Indeed, Irish women's (and men's) relationships to Irishness may be so diverse and fragmented that any notion of a unified Irishness or Irish diaspora has to be challenged.

Discourses of National Identity and Irish Migrant Women's Identifications with People, Place or Nation

> In many societies being feminine has been defined as sticking close to home. (Enloe, 1989, p. 21)

When Ailbhe Smyth (1991) sets out to reflect on the problem of national identity for women in Ireland by trying to find a way of writing about it, she suggests that:

> In the end, I couldn't get a fix on identity. But identity is not an end. Only a beginning.
> (*What, after all, do you do when you find it?*)
> In the end, I couldn't speak for Irish women. Can barely speak of myself. Can barely speak. (Smyth, 1991, p. 22)

Although it might be possible to locate identifications, it may never be possible to find identity. However, it may be that women's voices are so excluded from discourses of national identity that it is difficult for women even to identify with, or declare themselves, Irish, English or Indian, without at the same time being conscious that to speak of national identity is not the whole story.

The nation-state and associated discourses about national identity achieve the status of a macro discourse because the nation-state is the main repository of legitimate power in the world. These discourses of national identity, based on the primacy of the nation-state as a category of identification, highlight the continual obliteration of difference in order to construct a unity within a bounded space. Gender and other inequalities are institutionalized and perpetuated within the macro discourse of national identity. Anne McClintock (1993, p. 61) suggests that:

> nations have historically amounted to the sanctioned institutionalization of gender *difference*. No nation in the world gives women and men the same access to the rights and resources of the nation-state.

Discourses of nationalism and national identity are, therefore, an important area of investigation for feminists. National identity is said to give us a sense of 'place', continuity and connectedness (Anderson, 1991; Game, 1990). It makes it possible to place ourselves within the narrative of the nation (Game, 1990). However, the price of this belonging may be both invisibility and subordination for women. The material implications for women of living and working within a nation-state cannot be underestimated. For example, women living in Ireland do not have access to abortion services and divorce was unavailable until 1995.

Our national identity is generally one of the first questions asked of us by strangers. But what does the answer English, Irish or Indian mean to us and how does the meaning of our national identity change in different contexts? The large numbers of Irish women emigrants might be seen as indicating that they reject the restrictive aspects of what it means to be Irish by emigrating. Yet the stereotypes of Irishness experienced by Irish women following emigration may lead to a greater identification with nation. Carole Boyce Davies (1994, p. 3) points out that 're-negotiating of identities is fundamental to migration'.

Irish migrants are usually first identified as Irish by their accent which then leads to some discussion of national identity. It is in response to comments about one's origins that Irish emigrants find themselves drawing on discourses of Irish national identity. The experience of migration often 'helps you to understand just how very Irish you are . . . you almost have to get out of Ireland to be Irish at all' (O'Conner, 1993, p. 18). However, the available discourses of Irish national identity are limited and Irish women may find that these do not adequately reflect their experiences or identities. In the process of defending their sense of national identity there is a danger that Irish feminists in England might find themselves subordinating their feminist identities. Kate Kelly and Triona Nic Giolla Choille (1990, p. 25) point out that '[m]any aspects of Irish community life in Britain are male-dominated and women have remarked on how difficult it is for them to participate'. It is difficult, therefore, for Irish women to find discourses of Irishness that recognize their agency and contributions to Irish national identity.

Identity for Irish women, as for other women, is experienced and constructed on many levels, in different practices and in a variety of contexts. It is negotiated at the levels of citizenship, culture, legislation and State policies. For migrant women the parameters of identity are even harder to pin down. It is constructed in everyday practices between Irish women and men, between Irish migrants and non-migrants, among Irish women and between Irish women migrants and those in the country to which they migrate. Although we now know of the many problems with how discourses of national identity construct women, we know very little about the ways in which women identify or dis-identify with these discourses.

'Diaspora' – a More Fruitful Source of Identification for Women?

Discourses of national identity position women as the symbols of the unity of the nation, as the transmitters and maintainers of the national culture and the reproducers of the nation (Anthias and Yuval-Davis, 1993). However, little is known about how women migrants engage with these representations. Because migratory subjectivities exist simultaneously within multiple locations, migrant women often find themselves questioning their identifications with their nation of origin.

In this section of the chapter I look to recent post-colonial theories of diaspora for help with my attempts to develop theories of Irish migrant women's identifications with nation or place. To what extent do Irish women living in England identify with a 'homeland'-Ireland, and/or with their land of destination, England? While there are some possibilities for mixing and intermixings of cultures and identities for second-generation Irish women migrants, I see first-generation Irish migrants as having to negotiate racialized perceptions of Irishness based on their accents. Before discussing these questions further, I explore what is meant by the concept of diaspora[10] as it is used by recent post-colonial theorists.

James Clifford (1994, p. 308) sees diasporas as being defined against both the norms of nation-state and the notion of indigenous peoples:

> Diaspora discourse articulates, blends together, both roots *and* routes to construct what Gilroy calls 'alternate public spheres', forms of community consciousness and solidarity that maintain identifications outside the national time/space in order to live inside, with a difference.

Clifford sees diaspora identities as reaching outside the geographic territory and temporality (myth/history) of the nation-state. The view that place and nation can no longer straightforwardly support identity has led to what Judith Squires sees as post-colonial theorists' preoccupation with displacement and identity formation. She suggests that '[a]s the old order gives way, identities (of both colonized and colonizer) are rendered insecure' (Squires, 1993, p. v).

James Clifford (1994) suggests that due to decolonization, increased migration and globalization, diaspora discourse today is being used to describe the experiences of many communities of dispersed peoples. He concludes that it is not possible to sharply define the meanings of diaspora as used in post-colonial writing. Instead, he offers a description of diaspora as 'a loosely coherent, adaptive constellation of responses to dwelling in displacement' (1994, p. 14).

Michael Keith and Steve Pile (1993) describe diaspora as:

> an invocation of communal space which is simultaneously *both inside and outside the West*. The outcome of such positioning is a form of cultural fusion; such syncretism produces diaspora-specific resources of resistance. (Keith and Pile, 1993, p. 18, my emphasis)

Irish people are excluded from this definition of diaspora by their location within the West whether within Ireland or as emigrants to mainly Western countries. Keith and Pile (1993) go on to suggest that diaspora represents the space in which lines of insider and outsider are drawn. These lines, they believe, stress interconnection as much as distinction (1993, p. 18). However, distinction can actually be *based upon* interconnection, as in the case of Irishness which is defined in opposition to masculine middle-class Englishness (Walter, 1995). While these identities are interdependent, because they rely so much on the dichotomy Irish/English, it is difficult to identify the spaces 'in-between'. Yet this notion of being in-between cultures is according to Bhabha a central aspect of post-colonial identity (Bhabha, 1994; Puranik, 1994). Stuart Hall (1993) emphasizes the diversity, hybridity and difference of diaspora identities. By hybridity he means 'a conception of "identity" which lives with and through, not despite, difference' and which is constantly being reproduced and transformed (1993, p. 402).

Colonialism meant that Black cultures were defined, bounded and knowable. As the first systematically colonized territory of the English Empire (Bell, 1993a) it is also true to say that white Irish culture was defined, bounded and made knowable by the colonizer. The activities of mapping and naming in colonized Ireland represented colonial attempts to control what they defined as a 'feminine' race. This colonial construction of the Irish landscape and culture:

> became part of the collective imagining of the Irish themselves. Irish
> nationalism in many ways internalised elements of the very colonial
> culture it struggled to free itself from. (Bell, 1993b, p. 19)

Catherine Nash (1993, p. 40) in her discussion of the possibility of a feminist and post-colonial identification with place for Irish women, suggests that:

> the shift from colony to independence did not entail the redundancy
> of discourses of male power; rather, these were transposed and trans-
> lated into new forms within nationalist discourse.

Emigration since independence and the consequent interconnectedness with other cultures may have brought about some hybridity of Irish identities and highlighted the abilities to live through and with difference. However, aspects of the colonial fixed and knowable Irishness remain. While post-colonial theorists may draw on metaphors of mobility to destabilize the fixed and the ethnocentric, I suggest that strong elements of colonial constructions of Irish national identity continue to powerfully influence everyday cultural practices and identities in Ireland, in England and in Irish emigrant communities in England. Some Irish immigrants to England, although aware of multiple Irish identities, are subject to a fixing of Irish identity via stereotyping and anti-Irish racism.

Because most Irish migrants are white, there is sometimes a blurring of the continuing existence of Irish and English colonial stereotypes and relations. This may contribute to many Irish migrants' wish to maintain a distinct Irish identity. The idea of hybrid identities may be more attractive to Black people whose difference is signified by colour. It is often difficult for Irish

migrants in England to assert their different national/cultural identities because to do so would disrupt 'the myth of a cohesive white identity' (Puar,
1994, p. 40). This 'dominant white gaze' relies on the definition and upholding
of oppositional boundaries (Puar, 1994) which are based on colour. As Mary
Hickman and Bronwen Walter (1995) point out, '"colour" has become a
marker of national belonging and being of the same "colour" can be equated
with "same nation" implying "no problem" of discrimination' (1995, p. 8).

While Black diaspora culture in post-colonial Britain may involve the
expansion of ways of being British to incorporate Black and allow for Black
British identities, many Irish communities continue to define themselves in
opposition to English – to be Irish is *not* to be English. Seamus Deane (1984)
argues that 'Irishness is the quality by which we want to display our non-
Britishness . . . The idea of what is British continues to govern the idea of what
is Irish.'[11] Yet President Mary Robinson in her recent visit to England highlighted the hybrid nature of Irishness no matter where it is located:

> Irishness is not simply territorial. Therefore it can reach out to every-
> one on the island and show itself capable of honouring and listening
> to those whose sense of identity, and whose cultural values, may be
> more British than Irish (John Galway Foster Lecture, London,
> 1995b).

President Robinson goes on to emphasize the hybridity of Irishness when she
suggests that 'the Irish today . . . are both Irish and European. It is as though
it were a seamless web – the European dimension simply being an extension of
modern Irishness.' While President Robinson is keen to construct an inclusive
and pluralist sense of Irishness which includes the diaspora and those who
identify as British in Northern Ireland, such fluid constructions of Irishness
tend to overlook the differential political and economic locatedness of Irish
people and particularly Irish migrants.

While the term 'diaspora' tends to celebrate the cultural aspects of migrations, the term 'emigration' has, according to David Lloyd, political and economic undertones (1994, p. 4). The term emigration evokes memories of the:

> famine, of eviction, of dispossession and of economic depression and
> failure. The term itself bears for us the reminder of the political and
> economic legacies of colonialism.

Lloyd emphasizes the necessity of recalling this history as the political work
of emigrant communities. However, like most other commentators, he
ignores the gendered nature of colonialism, diaspora, national identity and
emigration.

James Clifford (1994, p. 313) points to the tendency in theories of
diaspora to discuss 'travel and displacement in unmarked ways, thus normal-
ising male experiences'. He asks whether 'diaspora experiences reinforce or

Breda Gray

loosen gender subordination?' (p. 313). In response, he posits two possibilities. First, he suggests that women migrants may experience new political spaces and opportunities as a result of migration which are conducive to the development of more positive gender relations. Second, women in diaspora may, he suggests, selectively draw on a 'home' culture and tradition to gain empowerment. Although he alludes to the complex positive and negative potentials of diaspora for women, these raise more complex questions that are not addressed by Clifford. Migrant women may be *subject-ed* by the double articulation of cultural difference and patriarchy' (Ganguly, 1992, p. 38). For example, the tasks of maintaining community and cultural ties in England and with family and friends in Ireland often falls to Irish migrant women rather than men. Connections with family and friends in Ireland and England can be simultaneously empowering and oppressive. Opportunities for new political spaces and identities may not be as readily available to migrant women depending on their position in the labour market, family commitments and the policies and attitudes towards immigrants in their country of destination.

Janet Wolff (1993) suggests that the discourses and metaphors of travel are so heavily compromised by their traditionally androcentric usage that it is necessary to modify our vocabulary to include women's experiences of the social structures and processes associated with movement. Wolff (1993, p. 234) raises many questions about the connections between the constructions of 'women's place' and the rendering 'invisible, problematic and in some cases impossible' of women 'out of place'. Wolff's analysis raised important questions in relation to Irish migrant women. Are Irish migrant women seen in terms of being 'out of place'? Is it possible for them to construct a non-oppressive place for themselves within national and diasporic formations? Is it possible to make visible the kinwork that Irish women do which is so necessary to the maintenance of Irish national identity? Is it through Irish migrant women's work in maintaining connections between communities in Ireland and England that the possibilities of more hybrid or in-between identities emerge? How might hybrid identities be any more liberatory to Irish women than national identity? These questions have the potential to uncover many more layers of migrant women's experiences and their complex identifications with movement and place.

To date, issues of gender and women's experiences remain absent from discourses of national identity, emigration or diaspora. In fact, all of these discourses in different ways reinscribe dominant patriarchal gender relations. Race, gender and other inequalities tend to be maintained within discourses of post-colonial subject positions just as much as more traditional discourses of national identity. Eagleton, Jameson and Said (1990, p. 30) warn that:

> to attempt to bypass the specificity of one's identity in the name of freedom will always be perilously abstract, even once one has recognized that such an identity is as much a construct of the oppressor as

one's 'authentic' sense of oneself. Any emancipatory politics must begin with the specific, then must in the same gesture leave it behind.

Concluding Thoughts

The shift in academic and some political analyses from a focus on the nation-state and processes of assimilation for immigrants, towards the idea of the transnational diaspora may help to expand our understanding of complex identifications with nation and place in the context of an increasingly mobile labour force. However, the constraints of both the idea of nation and diaspora as sources of identification become evident when examined from a feminist point of view. Women's activities and contributions to the development and maintenance of both forms of community and identity are rendered invisible in the accounts of nation and diaspora available in the literature to date.

Towards the end of the twentieth century we still know little about the subjectivities of the millions of Irish women who emigrated during this century. It is only in the past decade that some of these women's experiences have begun to receive attention (London Irish Women's Centre, 1993; Wall, 1991; O'Carroll, 1990; Kelly and Nic Giolla Choille, 1990; Lennon, McAdam and O'Brien, 1988; Jackson, 1987). While many Irish women migrants identify with their Irish nationality, they have also been excluded, constructed in limited and passive roles and made invisible by that very identity. National identity represents a complex mix of capitalist and patriarchal interests as well as meeting individual and collective needs to belong, to be part of a larger community and to be located in a particular place, space and time.

For Irish women in England, traditional constructions of Irishness in opposition to Englishness may make identification with Irishness even more intense. Bronwen Walter (1995, p. 46) concludes that:

> the unifying tendencies of Irishness both internally as ethnicity and externally as racism work to deny gender differences, whilst simultaneously embedding these differences into their structures.

Alongside an identification with nationality, there is a recognition of differences among Irish women as Mary Kells' (1995) study revealed. However, first-generation Irish women's identities in particular, despite the many ways in which their lives intersect with English and other cultures, do not, in my view, fit easily within current formulations of hybridity and diaspora identities. These identities may more closely reflect the identifications and experiences of some second-generation Irish women.

Although Irish national identity is profoundly affected by the experience of colonization, the location of Ireland within the West, as a member of the European Union (one of the major world trading blocs), makes 'white' 'post-colonial' Irishness difficult to locate in the 1990s. Discussion of Irish identities cannot be separated from the continuing colonial conflict over Irishness and Britishness of Northern Ireland. In view of this, any detailed analysis of the usefulness of 'post-colonial' theorizing of Irish identities would have to address current events in Northern Ireland, Anglo–Irish relations and the roles being played by the Republic of Ireland in the development of European Union policies on trade and immigration.

Irish women migrants are caught in the middle of the many contradictions of Irishness in the 1990s. To date, it has been the women of Northern Ireland who have had to deal with nationality as an integral aspect of their identities and everyday practices. The Northern Irish conflict has not been high on the agendas of many women in the Republic. Women migrants to England from the Republic have had to address national identity in relation to Englishness and other national/ethnic identities in England. However, with the exception of the work of the London Irish Women's Centre, these women's experiences are frequently individualized and go unrecorded. It seems important at this time of change in Ireland, north and south, that there is more acknowledgement of the power of existing categories of identity such as nationality, to affect women's sense of themselves. By questioning these categories, women may be able to better imagine ways of addressing ongoing colonial power dynamics, articulating women's identifications with people and places and ways of belonging that undermine the patriarchal discourses of national identity and diaspora.

Notes

1 See Anne McClintock (1993) 'Family Feuds: Gender, Nationalism and the Family' *Feminist Review*, No, 44, Summer, pp. 61–80.
2 This chapter discusses some of the theoretical issues raised in the early stages of my research on Irish national identity in the 1980s and 1990s. I am doing empirical work which involves group discussions and individual interviews with Irish women in London and in Ireland. However, I am at too early a stage in my research to introduce the views of the Irish women participating in my study to the discussion in this chapter.
3 *Some facts and figures on Irish emigration in the twentieth century*

- *1920s*: Between 1884 and 1926, the population of the twenty-six counties that constitute the Irish Republic fell from more than 6.5 million to 2.97 million, 'a unique demographic experience for the world of the time' (Lee, 1993, p. 117). Average net emigration between 1926 and 1936 was about 16,700 per annum (Drudy, 1985).
- *1950s*: The 1948 British Nationality Act included a provision for the 'special position' of Irish immigrants from the Republic of Ireland giving them official parity with British citizens. Between 1951 and 1961 the population of the Republic of Ireland decreased from 2.96 million to 2.82

million (Lee, 1993). Emigration in the 1950s was at the highest level this century at 14.1 per 1000 (Lee, 1993). Between 1946 and 1961, 75 per cent of those who left were below 34 years of age (Drudy, 1985).

- Between 1971 and 1979 there was a net inflow of 13,600 immigrants to the Republic of Ireland per annum (Drudy, 1985).
- *1980s*: Between 1987 and 1990 the population of the Republic of Ireland decreased from a peak in the twentieth century of 3.54 million in 1987 to 3.50 in 1990 (Lee, 1993). The rate of emigration between 1981 and 1986 was 4.1 per 1000 and increased to 9.6 per 1000 between 1986 and 1990 (Lee, 1993). An average of 34,000 people emigrated a year between 1986 and 1990, 'the highest for any five-year period this century except during the 1950s' (Lee, 1993, p. 118). About 200,000 people emigrated in the 1980s, about 150,000 of them in the second half of the decade (Lee, 1990). The majority of emigrants in the 1980s were between 15 and 24 years old (NESRC, 1991). In her study of Irish immigrants to England in the 1980s, Ellen Hazelcorn (1989) found that Irish immigrants after 1980 have higher rates of unemployment than recorded for any other wave of Irish immigrants, reaching a peak of 19.6 per cent in the period 1980 to 1983, and 16.2 per cent post-1984.
- Manufacturing employment dropped in the Republic of Ireland from 243,000 in 1980 to 201,000 in 1986 (Mac Laughlin, 1994).
- *1988*: About 70 per cent of all those who left in the year ending 1988 went to Britain (O Cinneide, 1991). Nearly 14 per cent of those who left in the same year went to the US (NESRC, 1991).
- 'In Ireland alone in 1988, probably unique among the nations of the earth, did the numbers leaving the state (45,000 approx.) come close to the annual numbers being born (54,000) (Ryan, 1990, p. 45).

4 *Explanations of Irish emigration this century*

- *Nationalist explanations*: A consequence of colonialism and consequent underdevelopment (see Miller, 1990). Following on from this explanation emigration was seen as 'exile'-'involuntary expatriation' (Miller, 1990).
- *Psychological inadequacy*: Following the establishment of the Free State in the 1920s some of the middle classes began to explain emigration in terms of psychological inadequacies of the emigrants (Lee, 1990).
- *Inheritance patterns*: The higher proportion of Irish women leaving prior to 1940 was explained by Kennedy (1973) as resulting from inheritance patterns which favoured sons.
- *Behaviourism*: By the 1960s there was a shift away from nationalist explanations towards a focus on behaviourism which emphasized the 'social psychological attributes and aspirations of young Irish adults' (Mac Laughlin, 1994, p. 245).

- *Modernization*: Irish emigration 'central to the Irish experience of being modern' (Ryan, 1990, p. 45).
- *Economic developments in destination countries and globalization of capital and labour markets* (Hazelcorn, 1989).
- *World systems perspective*: Currently being put forward by Jim Mac Laughlin who sees Irish emigration as 'a response to restructuring processes operating at the level of the national and global economy' (Mac Laughlin, 1994, p. 269).
- *Insupportable population pressure*: In 1987 Ireland's Minister for Foreign Affairs stated:

> We regard emigrants as part of our global generation of Irish people. We should be proud of them. The more they hone their skills and talents in another environment, the more they develop a work ethic in a country like Germany or the UD, the better it can be applied in Ireland when they return (Whelan, 1987).

The State sought in the 1980s to represent emigration as a blessing rather than in terms of national failure (Lee, 1993).

5 Twentieth-century Irish emigration has been mainly to Britain. 'Since 1900 two out of every three Irish emigrants settled in Britain', amounting to over two million in all (Ryan, 1990, p. 46).

6 This commission was established by the government in 1948 to investigate the roots of emigration. Travers (1995, p. 158) notes that despite the fact that the majority of emigrants at the time were women, the Commission contained only two women, a fact simply condemned by the Irish Housewives Association.

7 She is referring here to the impact of Mary Robinson's presidency on attitudes towards women in Ireland.

8 The President's second speech to a joint session of the Houses of the Oireachtas in February 1995 was on the subject of the Irish diaspora and entitled 'Cherishing the Irish Diaspora'. In this speech she points to the potential for the diaspora to inform, even challenge, politics within the Republic of Ireland.

> [O]ur relation with the diaspora beyond our shores is one which can instruct our society in the values of diversity, tolerance, and fair-mindedness . . . The men and women of our diaspora represent not simply a series of departures and loss. They remain even while absent, a precious reflection of our growth and change, a precious reminder of the many strands of identity which compose our story . . . We need to accept that in their new perspectives may well be a critique of our old ones (Robinson, 1995a).

9 Ireland is one of the few countries in Europe which does not provide voting rights to emigrants.

10 The term diaspora has traditionally been associated with the Jews. David Lloyd (1994, p. 3) suggests that the Jewish sense of diaspora meant 'not simply a scattering, but the survival of a culture, a religion and an ethos through the many forms and disguises which exile historically demanded'.
11 Although Northern Irish Unionists identify with a British identity, my discussion in this chapter relates to emigrants from the Republic of Ireland.

References

ANDERSON, BENEDICT (1983) *Imagined Communities: Reflections on the Origins and Spread of Nationalism*, London, New Left Books.
ANDERSON, BENEDICT (1991) *Imagined Communities: Reflections on the Origins and Spread of Nationalism*, London and New York, Verso.
ANTHIAS, FLOYA and YUVAL-DAVIS, NIRA in association with HARRIET CAIN (1993) *Racialized Boundaries: Race, Nation, Gender, Colour and Class and the Anti-racist Struggle*, London, Routledge.
BEALE, JENNY (1986) *Women in Ireland: Voices of Change*, Basingstoke, Macmillan.
BELL, DESMOND (1993a) 'Culture and politics in Ireland: Postmodern revisions', *History of European Ideas*, 16 (1–3), pp. 141–6.
BELL, DESMOND (1993b) 'Framing nature: First steps into the wilderness for a sociology of the landscape', *Irish Journal of Sociology*, 3, 1–22.
BHABHA, HOMI, K. (1994) *The Location of Culture*, London and New York, Routledge.
CARRUTHERS, LEO (1991) 'Book review of *Migrations: The Irish at Home and Abroad* edited by Richard Kearney (1990)', *Irish University Review*, 21, (1), 166–9.
CHAVEZ, LEO, R. (1994) 'The power of the imagined community: The settlement of undocumented Mexicans and Central Americans in the United States', *American Anthropologist*, 96 (1), 52–73.
CLEAR, CATRIONA (1992) 'Book review: *Ourselves Alone: Women's Emigration From Ireland, 1885–1920*', *Irish Historical Studies*, 28 (109), 104–6.
CLIFFORD, JAMES (1994) 'Diasporas', *Cultural Anthropology*, 9 (3), 302–38.
CORCORAN, MARY (1994) 'Of emigrants "Eirepreneurs" and opportunities', *Irish Reporter*, 13 (1), 5–7.
COULTER, CAROL (1993) *The Hidden Tradition: Feminism, Women and Nationalism in Ireland*, Cork, Cork University Press.
COWARD, JOHN (1989) 'Irish population problems', in CARTER, R. W. G. and PARKER A. J. (Eds) *Ireland: Contemporary Perspectives on a Land and its People*, London and New York, Routledge.
CROSS, JEAN (1989) 'Irishwomen arts and media', *Fan*, 3 (3), 6–7.
DAVIES, CAROLE BOYCE (1994) *Black Women, Writing and Identity: Migrations of the Subject*, London and New York, Routledge.

Breda Gray

DEANE, SEAMUS (1984) 'Remembering the Irish future', *The Crane Bag*, 8 (1), 81–6.

DRUDY, P. J. (1985) 'Irish population change and emigration since Independence', in DRUDY, P. J. (Ed.) *The Irish in America: Emigration Assimilation and Impact*, Cambridge, Cambridge University Press.

EAGLETON, TERRY, JAMESON, FREDERIC and SAID, EDWARD, W. (1990) *Nationalism, Colonialism and Literature*, Minneapolis, University of Minnesota Press.

ENLOE, CYNTHIA (1989) *Bananas, Beaches and Bases: Making Feminist Sense of International Politics*, London, Pandora Press.

GAME, ANN (1990) 'Nation and identity: Bond', *New Formations*, 11, 105–21.

GANGULY, KEYA (1992) 'Migrant identities: Personal memory and the construction of selfhood', *Cultural Studies*, 6 (1), 27–50.

GARVEY, D. (1985) 'The history of migration flows in the Republic of Ireland', *Population Trends*, 39, 22–30.

HALL, STUART (1993) 'Cultural identity and diaspora', in WILLIAMS, PATRICK and CHRISMAN, LAURA (Eds) (1993) *Colonial Discourse and Post-colonial Theory: A Reader*, New York, London, Harvester Wheatsheaf.

HAZELCORN, ELLEN (1989) *Irish Immigrants Today: A Socioeconomic Profile of Contemporary Irish Emigrants and Immigrants in the UK*, occasional paper, No. 1. London, Polytechnic of North London.

HICKMAN, MARY and WALTER, BRONWEN (1995) 'Deconstructing whiteness: Irish women in Britain', *Feminist Review*, 50, 5–19.

HOLOHAN, ANNE (1995) *Working Lives: The Irish in Britain*, London, The Irish Post.

JACKSON, JOHN (1991) 'Review symposium', *Irish Journal of Sociology*, 1, 69–73.

JACKSON, PAULINE (1987) *Migrant Women: The Republic of Ireland*, Dublin, Commission of European Communities.

KEITH, MICHAEL and PILE, STEVE (1993) (Eds) *Place and the Politics of Identity*, London and New York, Routledge.

KELLY, KATE and NIC GIOLLA CHOILLE, TRIONA (1990) *Emigration Matters for Women*, Dublin, Attic Press.

KELLS, MARY (1995) *Ethnic Identity Amongst Young Irish Middle-Class Migrants in London*, Irish Studies Centre Occasional Paper No. 6, London, University of North London Press.

KENNEDY, ROBERT (1973) *The Irish: Emigration, Marriage and Fertility*, Berkeley, California, University of California Press.

LEE, JOE, J. (1990) 'Emigration: A contemporary perspective', in RICHARD KEARNEY (Ed.) *Migrations: The Irish at Home and Abroad*, Dublin, Wolfhound.

LEE, JOE, J. (1993) 'Dynamics of social and political change in the Irish Republic', in KEOGH, DERMOT and HALTZEL, MICHAEL H. (Eds) *Northern Ireland and the Politics of Reconciliation*, Cambridge, Cambridge University Press.

LENNON, MARY, MC ADAM, MARIE and O'BRIEN, JOANNE (Eds) (1988) *Across the Water: Irish Women's Lives in Britain*, London, Virago.

LLOYD, DAVID (1994) 'Making sense of the dispersal', *Irish Reporter*, 13 (1), 3–4.

LONDON IRISH WOMEN'S CENTRE (1993) *Roots and Realities: A Profile of Irish Women in London 1993*, London, London Irish Women's Centre.

MAC LAUGHLIN, JIM (1994) 'Emigration and the peripheralization of Ireland in the global economy', *Review*, XVII (2), Spring, 243–73.

MCADAM, MARIE (1994) 'Hidden from history: Women's experience in emigration', *Irish Reporter*, 13 (1), 12–13.

MCCLINTOCK, ANNE (1993) 'Family feuds: Gender, nationalism and the family', *Feminist Review*, 44, 61–80.

MEANEY, GERARDINE (1991) *Sex and Nation: Women in Irish Culture and Politics*, Dublin, Attic Press.

MILLER, KERBY A. (1990) 'Emigration, capitalism, and ideology in post-famine Ireland', in KEARNEY, RICHARD (Ed.) *Migrations: The Irish at Home and Abroad*, Dublin, Wolfhound.

NASH, CATHERINE (1993) 'Remapping and renaming: New cartographies of identity, gender and landscape in Ireland', *Feminist Review*, 44, 39–57.

NATIONAL, ECONOMIC and SOCIAL RESEARCH COUNCIL (1991) *The Economic and Social Implications of Emigration*, Dublin, NESRC.

NOLAN, JANET (1989) *Ourselves Alone: Women's Emigration From Ireland, 1885–1920*, Lexington, Kentucky University Press.

O'CARROLL, IDE (1990) *Models for Movers: Irish Women's Emigration to America*, Dublin, Attic Press.

O'CARROLL, IDE (1995) 'Breaking the silence from a distance: Irish women speak on sexual abuse', in O'SULLIVAN, PATRICK (Ed.) *Irish Women and Irish Migration*, Leicester, Leicester University Press.

O CINNEIDE, SEAMUS (1991) 'Review symposium', *Irish Journal of Sociology*, 1, 66–9.

O'CONNER, JOSEPH (1993) 'Introduction', in BOLGER, DERMOT (Ed.) *Ireland in Exile: Irish Writers Abroad*, Dublin, New Island Books.

O'TOOLE, FINTAN (1989) 'Strangers in their own country', *Irish Times*, Thursday, 28 September, 10.

PUAR, JASBIR K. (1994) 'Rethinking identity: Racism, "whiteness", and the South Asian Other', *Diatribe*, 3, 39–59.

PURANIK, ALLISON (1994) 'Post-colonials from the edge', *The Times Higher Education Supplement*, 11 February, 17.

ROBINSON, MARY (1995a) Speech to both Houses of the Oireachtas (Dublin) 'Cherishing the diaspora', 2 February.

ROBINSON, MARY (1995b) John Galway Foster Lecture, (London) 'Imaginative possessions', 26 October.

ROSSITER, ANN (1993) 'Bringing the margins into the centre: a review of aspects of Irish women's emigration', in SMYTH, AILBHE (Ed.) *Irish Women's Studies Reader*, Dublin, Attic Press.

RYAN, LIAM (1990) 'Irish emigration to Britain since World War II', in KEARNEY, RICHARD (Ed.) *Migrations: The Irish at Home and Abroad*, Dublin, Wolfhound.

SMYTH, AILBHE (1991) 'The floozie in the jacuzzi', *Feminist Studies*, 17 (1), 8–28.

SQUIRES, JUDITH (1993) 'Editorial', *New Formations*, 21, Winter, v–vi.

TILKI, MARY (1994) 'Ethnic Irish older people', *British Journal of Nursing*, 3 (17), 909–13.

TRAVERS, PAURIC (1995) ' "There was nothing for me there": Irish female emigration, 1952–1971', in O'SULLIVAN, PATRICK (Ed.) *Irish Women and Irish Migration*, Leicester, Leicester University Press.

WALL, RITA (1991) *Leading Lives: Irish Women in Britain*, Dublin, Attic Press.

WALTER, BRONWEN (1995) 'Irishness, gender and place', *Environment and Planning D: Society and Space*, 13, 35–50.

WHELAN, TOM (1987) 'The new emigrants', *Newsweek*, 10 October.

WOLFF, JANET (1993) 'On the road again: Metaphors of travel in cultural criticism', *Cultural Studies*, 7 (2), 224–39.

YUVAL-DAVIS, NIRA (1993) 'Gender and Nation', *Ethnic and Racial Studies*, 16 (4), 621–32.

Further Reading

BOLGER, DERMOT (Ed.) (1993) *Ireland in Exile: Irish Writers Abroad*, Dublin, New Island Books.

CARTER, ERICA, DONALD, JAMES and SQUIRES, JUDITH (Eds) (1993) *Space and Place: Theories of Identity and Location*, London, Lawrence & Wishart.

GILROY, PAUL (1987) *'There Ain't No Black in the Union Jack': The Cultural Politics of Race and Nation*, London, Hutchinson.

HOLMES, MICHAEL (1994) 'Symbols of national identity and sport: The case of the Irish football team', *Irish Political Studies*, 9, 81–98.

JACKSON, PETER and PENROSE, JAN. (Eds) (1993) *Constructions of Race, Place and Nation*, London, UCL Press.

KEARNEY, RICHARD (Ed.) (1990) *Migrations: The Irish at Home and Abroad*, Dublin, Wolfhound Press.

O CONNER, KEVIN (1972) *The Irish in Britain*, London, Sidgwick and Jackson.

O'DOWD, LIAM (1993) 'Strengthening the border on the road to Maastricht', *Irish Reporter*, 9 (1), 12–16.

O'SULLIVAN, PATRICK (Ed.) (1995) *Irish Women and Irish Migration*, Leicester, Leicester University Press.

WILLIAMS, PATRICK and CHRISMAN, LAURA (1993) (Eds) *Colonial Discourse and Post-colonial Theory: A Reader*, New York, London, Harvester Wheatsheaf.

Chapter 11

Boundary Politics: Women, Nationalism and Danger

Jan Jindy Pettman

All nationalisms are gendered, all are invented and all are dangerous . . . (McClintock, 1993, p. 61)

This chapter[1] explores a politics of nationalism and danger in which women's bodies figure prominently, both symbolically and materially. Despite the very different kinds of nationalisms, and individual women's different views on and actions within each nationalism, there is remarkable similarity in the ways in which nationalisms construct women. The chapter begins with the gendered language of nation and goes on to examine the uses made of women in constructing national boundaries and difference. It looks at women's roles as reproducers or mothers of the nation and at the symbolic uses made of women as boundary-markers of political identities – roles that make them vulnerable to body-policing and to sexual violence. It concludes by tracing some implications of national/ist differences among women for attempts to build an international feminism – or for coalitions across national and State boundaries.

Woman/Nation/Sex

Women are the symbol of the nation, men its agents, regardless of the role women actually play in the nation. (*Feminist Review*, Editorial, 1993, p. 1)

There is a complex gender politics of nation and nationalism, including both the gendering of the nation as female and the construction of women as mothers of the nation, responsible for its physical, cultural and social reproduction. The gendered and often sexualized language of nation and nationalism makes for dangers for women, especially at times of heightened national mobilization or international conflict and war.

The nation is called up in familial language – motherland, kin, blood, home. Love of nation or country eroticizes political associations. In a complex play, the State is often gendered male and the nation gendered female, the mother country. The citizen/children become kin. Catherine Hall suggests that the common theme of the nation as female 'implies the gendering of the citizen as male' and relatedly we often think of the state as masculine (Hall, 1993, p. 100; see also Elshtain, 1992; Pettman, 1993).[2]

The nation is frequently represented as a woman under threat of penetration or domination, so her sons must sacrifice for her safety, and for her – or for their fathers? – honour. This can take different forms. The defence of Egyptian honour against colonial power was represented as defence of female purity (Baron, 1993) and early-twentieth century Iranian nationalists represented the nation as a beautiful woman raped by foreigners (de Groot, 1993). Here the association of indigenous and colonized nations with the female body leads to construing imperial power as 'male heterosexual rape' (Parker, Russo, Sommer and Yaeger, 1992, p. 9). Foreign occupation is similarly depicted, for example, by the French against German occupation in the First World War, the Greek Cypriots after the Turkish invasion and recently the 'rape of Kuwait'. The metaphor of rape to represent national or State humiliation reveals 'how deeply ingrained has been the depiction of the homeland as a female body whose violation by foreigners requires its citizens and allies to rush to her defence' (Parker, Russo, Sommer and Yaeger, 1992, p. 9). It also confuses the rapes of actual women with the outrage of political attack or defeat, and in the process appropriates women's pain into a masculinist power politics.

Eroticizing the nation/country as a loved woman's body leads to associating sexual danger with boundary transgressions and boundary defence. It can materialize in competition between different men for control of women (Lerner, 1991). Indeed, a triangle, a love story, a fairy tale is often constructed, necessitating a villain, a victim and a hero. The sexual subtext and gendered politics of nationalism are further complicated through the feminizing – and hypermasculinizing – of 'other' men.

The language of nationalism and war also calls up affective relations, bonding, familial loyalty, self-sacrificing behaviour – quite different from the free, competitive individual of the rational market/polis. Ross Poole (1985) argues, in a problematic formulation, that the language of war is not, as we might expect, of violence and death, but of caring, courage and self-sacrifice – in Australian parlance, mateship. 'War is not so much the construction of a new and virulent form of masculinity, as the recovery, for masculine identity, of that relational form of identity constituted within the family. It is, in this sense, the return of the feminine' (1985, p. 78; see also Jean Elshtain's (1987) drawing of parallels between the good soldier and the good mother).

In a further (related?) move, men appropriate giving birth, women's power, to themselves. Nationalism, war, sacrifice and death are associated with the birth of the nation – through the killing and maiming of young men on territory where women aren't supposed or aren't allowed to be. Thus the birth of the Australian nation is frequently sited on the killing fields of Gallipoli in Turkey, where Australian and New Zealand troops landed under British command in 1915. This is a masculinist birth, a 'mission impossible'

(Lake, 1992). Men are the agents and what they birth – the nation – is feminized.

'The trope of the nation-as-woman of course depends for its representational efficacy on a particular image of women as chaste, dutiful, daughterly or maternal' (Parker, 1992). Jean Elshtain (1987) pursues these images in terms of the gender of war and war's production of gendered as well as national civic identities. Here, the nation's men are Brave Warriors, the defenders and protectors; and its women are virtuous, the Beautiful Souls, the protected ones. Women are passive, non-political and domestic, underlining women's dependent status and men's roles as national actors.

But only the national women are the Beautiful Ones. Other men's/nation's/state's women, especially those who have been racialized or otherwise othered, may be exotic, licentious, tempting, dangerous, inferior, but they are not Beautiful like the home/national woman is. (Though home/national women may place themselves outside the bounds of protection by unruly, ungrateful behaviour, or by dishonouring themselves/their men/nation by associating with 'other men'.) Here we are not talking only about discourse, about ideology, but also about the material effects of category and collectivity politics. Who you are seen to be may cost you your life.

Women/Nation/Rape

'Woman-as-nation' 'contains the tacit agreement that men who cannot defend their woman/nation against rape have lost their claim to that body, that land' (Peterson, 1994, p. 80).

The difficult and dangerous protector/protected relationship constructs the male citizen-warrior, and women (and children) as needing protection. In a slide from protected through possession to control, women become vulnerable to violence from their own-group men if they appear rebellious or if the burden of protection becomes threatening to the men. Women are also terribly vulnerable to rape in war, both as spoils of war and as ways of getting at 'other men's women' (Roberts, 1984; Runyan, 1990). Those men who are unable to protect their women can be feminized as not real men. In this context, conflict can become competition over control of and access to women. Violence against women becomes an assault of men's and national honour (Gibson, 1993).

Rape has long been a weapon of war and nationalist conflict (though usually of 'theirs' and not 'ours', apparently).

In France in the months following German occupation in the First World War, the actual rape of French women was rapidly translated through to a feminized France whose national honour had been violated. Consternation about the 'child of the barbarian' and fierce arguments about whether French women then pregnant with 'enemy' babies should abort was reflected in an official commission of inquiry into the happenings. These debates were soon thereafter subjected to 'virtual amnesia' (Harris, 1993).

German women were raped by occupying Russian troops in the closing moments of the Second World War (Bernard, 1994). Greek women raped by Turkish soldiers in Cyprus were again cruelly dealt with when their rape was judged grounds for their husbands to divorce them and their fiancés to be released from their marriage promise, while abortion was allowed in the case of rape pregnancies (Anthias in Yuval-Davis and Anthias, 1989; Callaway, 1987). Many thousands of women were raped in Bangladesh during its violent separation out from Pakistan and some women were not taken back into their homes. Indeed, attention to women's experiences in nationalist conflicts and wars reveal similar stories of rape, sexually directed violence and shame and distress in their wake (Nordstrom, 1993).

Reports from Bosnia and Herzegovina estimated the numbers of women subjected to organized sexual violence as between 20,000 and 35,000 (Balen, 1993). The Report of the Commission of Experts appointed by the United Nations Security Council to investigate reported war crimes in ex-Yugoslavia found systematic and pervasive use of rape and other forms of sexual assault. While there were victims and perpetrators on all sides, the overwhelming experience was of attacks on Bosnian Muslims by those engaged in a Greater Serbia nationalist project. Rape was closely associated with a policy of 'ethnic cleansing', which was 'designed to instil terror . . . in order to cause them to flee and never return' (United Nations, 1994, p. 34). Here, rape funtions as a strategy to deliver 'a blow against the collective enemy by striking at a group of high symbolic value' (Bernard, 1994, p. 39). The strategy included forced pregnancies and holding women prisoners to prevent abortion, 'to make Bosnia a Serbian State by implanting Serbian babies in Muslim mothers' (Robson, 1993, p. 14).[3] Although the Commission found the magnitude of victimization 'extraordinary' and established systematic support or at least complicity of Serbian Bosnian authorities, it also recorded a pattern familiar in war rapes elsewhere (Amnesty International, 1991a; Nordstrom, 1993). Many rapes were committed in public, in front of family and community. They aimed to terrorize and intimidate individuals and their communities. They were often multiple and included other forms of humiliation and torture and in some cases victims were forced to assault other family or community members. But a 'new category of rape emerged – "international rape with political conse-quences"' (Meznaric, 1994, p. 93).

While most of those raped were women and girls, some Bosnian Muslim men were also raped or sexually mutilated. Some were forced to rape or bite off the penis of other Muslim men. Such feminization and castration of the enemy pushes us back to connections between proving manhood and nation-hood, between masculinity, militarism and violence, that have been much attended to in feminist peace research and women's peace writings. It is a reminder that all politics is gendered and that much dangerous politics is sexualized. Here, too, bodies, boundaries, violence and power come together in lethal combination.

Writing Rape

How then may we speak of horror? (Gibson, 1993, p. 251)

There are complex questions about how 'items' enter the public international agenda, and in what language/with what associations. Feminism has a brave record in terms of struggles to name, publicize and politicalize 'family secrets' (*Feminist Review*, 1988). Feminism makes a strategic claim that the personal is political and that sex is political. So too feminists in political theory and international relations attempt to reclaim both women and sex, in disciplines where sex has long been projected on to women (but not men: Brown, 1987; Pettman, 1993). Women have in turn been doubly relegated away from the international, disappearing (along with most men) within State borders and therefore within the confines of other disciplines and then relegated within the State away from the public and into the private, the family.

It is only recently that feminists and other women organizing have made rape visible as a crime against women's bodies and rights. Feminists argue that rape is about power, and nationalist war rapes are about collectivity power and domination strategies. War rape has come even more recently to international attention, especially in the context of systematic militarized rape and rape camps in Bosnia and the witnessing of women survivors of Japanese military rape, those called the comfort women (though the word rape is rarely used in mainstream media on them, while 'sex slavery' sometimes is: Seidel, 1993).

Women face particular difficulties in becoming subjects in nationalist politics (Natarajan, 1994, p. 85). Given the long history of associating actual women's rape with national, communal and male dishonour, Suzanne Gibson argues 'to respond to war rape with outrage and anger is not enough. We must make absolutely clear the terms in which we object to these atrocities. Our objections must be unambiguously founded upon women's right to physical autonomy' (1993, p. 258).

Attempts to document war rape come up against some women's denial or silence, as a survival strategy and also as an attempt to keep the 'shame' secret to protect relatives and self. This may involve the researcher in what Martha McIntyre calls 'collaborative silences' (1993). So feminists seeking to help break the silence, but not wishing to speak for or dangerously expose other women, struggle to find ways of writing that do not appropriate other women's experiences and pain in ways that those women may not recognize, or in interpretations they themselves might reject. There are more dangers in writing, for fear that the endless repetition of the appalling is ultimately numbing and will 'turn off' the reader. Worse, it may turn some of them on, as women's pain becomes 'warnography' (Gibson, 1993, p. 254). This is an issue in drama or film re-enactments of terror where, for example, a play condemning sexual torture can become complicit with that which it critiques and the audience become voyeurs (Taylor, 1993). There are difficulties too in finding ways to write that do not feed into and so reproduce 'the woman as victim' as the primary image of women in circulation.[4] While feminists and activists speak of torture not shame, and of survivors not victims, not all those so terrorized do survive.

Women as Territory

> Women become the subjected territory across which the boundaries of nationhood are marked. (*Gender and History*, Editorial, 1993, p. 159)

There is a complex relationship between actual women's bodies and the dangers women face and nationalist discourse using representations of women's bodies to mark national or communal boundaries. Here policing the boundaries too easily becomes the policing of women's bodies and relations with 'other' men and women.

Tessie Lui's analysis of race also applies to nation when she argues that 'race is a *gendered* social category that rests on regulating sexuality and particularly on controlling the behaviour of women' (1991, p. 163). Distinctions between legitimate and illegitimate children and rules and sanctions condoning or prohibiting certain kinds of marriages and sexual relations become part of body/boundary policing (Yuval-Davis and Anthias, 1989; Stoler, 1991; Baustad, 1994). Sex is often seen as the vulnerable link in maintaining raced and nationalized boundaries. So it becomes especially important for nationalist men to control their own group women's sexual behaviour and domestic lives. Sex, gender and women's bodies become part of the material for the construction of group boundaries. 'Women's bodies [are] the contested terrain on which men buil[d] their political regimes' (Lui, 1991, p. 163).

Constructing women as mothers of the race/nation has 'the effect of placing their reproductive capacities at the centre of their service to the nation' (Hall, 1993, p. 100). Different nationalisms have pursued different reproductive politics at different times, but always by distinguishing between own and other group women and between good and bad mothers. The sterilization and forced abortion policies of Nazi Germany offer horrific evidence of women's bodies becoming, literally, part of nation-building (Bock, 1992). Historically and at times still, dominant women were subjected to systematic control in terms of marriages, sexuality and children through reproductive politics which sought to boost the maternal health and family support of the 'right' women (de Lepervanche, 1989; Lake, 1992). Women in nationalist projects are often exhorted to have children for the State/nation, in Ceausescu's Romania (Kligman, 1992) and Israel and Palestine for example (Yuval-Davis, 1989;

Sharoni, 1993). Other State policies reflect particular natalist nationalisms, for example the Malaysian State urging Malay women to have more children. State 'population' policies frequently differentiate between desirable and undesirable children and between those who can claim legal citizenship and not (Yuval-Davis, 1991). The different meanings given to maternity and category membership and to women's roles as literal reproducers are evident too in Western Europe and in settler States like Australia, in the lack of care and the institutional racism which effectively deny minority and racialized women equal health and reproductive rights.

This means that, while all women experience their bodies being sexualized and associated with the maternal, the meanings made in these associations differ considerably in terms of the nationality, 'race'/ethnicity of particular women. Some are urged to have more children while others, including racialized and ethnic minority women, face assaults on their mothering and family in, for example, forced sterilization or inadequate or unsafe contraception. There is a complex politics of reproduction here, as the category 'woman' fractures along lines of power, identity and difference. These fractures have implications for feminist politicing across the lines and for finding a language and alliances to support all women's reproductive rights.[5] These rights need asserting against the long historical and continuing appropriation of women's bodies as a kind of national resource, or national threat, rather than as rights bearers and subjects.

Woman/Nation/Culture

In the new script for the past, the women's question holds a key place. (Chakravati in Sangari and Vaid, 1990, p. 27)

Women's bodies also become the material for the symbolic construction of the nation and its boundaries. Culture as 'tradition' is mobilized in anticolonial, postcolonial and communalist movements defining difference against the predatory West. This difference is most often located within the cultural, the family, and marked especially by 'women' (Chatterjee in Sangari and Vaid, 1990).

In the process of developing a new nationalist consciousness, tradition is reinvented and women are constructed as the bearers of the authentic/ated culture. So 'the women question' often appeared on the public agenda in association with the rise of anti-colonial nationalism and in response to political, economic and cultural encroachments by the West (Jayawardena, 1986; Kandiyoti, 1991b). In this politics, women's bodies, relations and roles become the battleground for different idealized versions of the past and constructions of nationalist projects for the future. Here we find particular contests around notions of cultural difference, in which women's roles become a key marker.

This was dramatically demonstrated in one of the most sustained operations to salvage women and through them national honour. Partition and the creation of Pakistan was accompanied by horrific violence and massive displacement and migration. In the process, an estimated 50,000 Muslim women in India and 33,000 non-Muslim women in Pakistan were abducted, abandoned or separated from their families. This led to an extraordinary Central Recovery Project of the government of India and a similar but less vigorous project by Pakistan, during which some 30,000 women were 'recovered' by their respective State agencies (Menon and Bhasin, 1993).

These recoveries were often forced, as many women were married and absorbed into the 'abducting' community and often feared rejection if they returned home. Ritu Menon and Kamla Bhasin observe of the Hindu women:

> abducted as Hindus, converted and married as Muslims, recovered as Hindus but required to relinquish their children because they were born of Muslim fathers, and disowned as 'unpure' and ineligible for marriage within their erstwhile family and community, their identities were in a continuous state of construction and reconstruction, making of them . . . 'permanent refugees'. (1993, p. 13)

They ask: 'Why should the matter of national honour have been so bound up with the bodies of women and with the children born of "wrong" unions?' and point again to the significance of women as markers of difference and as reproducers of both members and boundaries of nation and community.

Here again women appear as objects of male discourse, in contests about women's bodies and roles, as part of other people's agendas. So, too, Lata Mani argues in her work on sati in India that '(t)radition was thus not the ground on which women's status was being contested. Rather the reverse was true: women in fact became the site on which tradition was debated and reformulated' (in Sangari and Vaid, 1990, p. 118). Colonial authorities, nationalists and traditionalists frequently ignored women's resistance and agency, using 'women' to pursue other objectives and agendas. In a masculinist debate, 'Indian women were not conceived as agents but rather formed the enabling ground or "site" of the discourse' (C. and S. Mohanty, 1990, p. 21). Given the frequency with which women do become the site of nationalist discourse and the symbolic bearers of tradition, we need to resist pressures to abandon 'other' women to an essentialized 'culture' in contemporary debates about women's rights in different nationalist politics (Bannerji, 1987; Chow, 1990; Ram, 1993; Spivak, 1989).

Nationalizing Women

Nationalism is gendered – women's bodies are the boundary of the nation, and the bearers of its future. (*Feminist Review*, Editorial, 1993, p. 1)

The use of women as boundary-markers suggests why the control of women and especially their sexuality is strategic in the maintenance and reproduction of identity and difference and so of 'the community'. In this context, some men give particular ideological weight to the community, women's appearance and sexual purity. They see women, in Cynthia Enloe's (1990) formulation, as the community's, or the nation's, most valuable possessions; as those responsible for transmitting the nation's values and through this its political identity; as the bearers of the community's future generations, as 'nationalist wombs'; and as the members of the community most vulnerable to abuse, violation or seduction by 'other men' (1990, p. 54; see also Yuval-Davis and Anthias, 1989).

These concerns remain pertinent in much post-colonial and post-migratory identity politics in, for example, post-revolutionary Iran and more recently in Afghanistan, where women's dress and mobility are fiercely regulated, for women are seen as 'the most dangerous bearers of moral decay' (Kandiyoti, 1991b, p. 8). Contemporary nationalist and minority struggles, communal and fundamentalist revivals materialize in contests and demands over women's dress, movements, rights and relations (Sahgal and Yuval-Davis, 1992; Moghadam, 1994). In situations of deterritorialization, where a post-migratory identity is being constructed, women themselves can become the territory (Bloum, 1993).

Given their investments in 'women', nationalist movements and communal identities pose particular problems for feminists and suggest a difficult relationship between nationalism, women's rights and feminist struggles; though these will be negotiated in different ways over time and place. We are left observing that nationalism is a contradictory relation for women. Nationalist movements often mobilize women's support and labour, while simultaneously seeking to reinforce women's female roles and femininity. In their turn, many women are activists and many more support nationalist movements, often as women and particularly as mothers (West and Blumberg, 1990; Cock, 1992). Their involvement may unsettle gender roles and relations and may politicize and radicalize those women who join, initially, in defense of their maternal and family responsibilities. But they remain trapped in the symbolic uses made of them and by the tendency of mobilized or beseiged nationalisms to underline and reassert women's roles as mothers and bearers of the nation's traditions (Kandiyoti, 1991a). As a consequence, they are often sent 'back home' after the fighting or campaigning is over and their contributions are 'forgotten' and removed from the national stories.

Despite this forgetting, feminist recovery projects and women's own remembering enable us to challenge women's symbolic entrapment within the nation. Since 1993 especially there has been a remarkable outpouring of writings on women/gender/sex/nationalisms to help us in this task (for example, special issues of *Gender and History*, 1993 and *Feminist Review*, 1993). We can see, too, that for all the differences between nationalisms, and women's changing relations with any one nationalism, their particular rights and claims are often contained and domesticated. They remain a category or occasionally a political constituency (Sangari and Vaid, 1990). Gender relations and the gender power of dominating practices are kept beyond scrutiny. In this way, the role of gender difference as both structuring and structured by national and other political identities is obscured.

The very power of the nation and its articulation of gender rules and gender power make feminist theorizing about and politics towards nationalism extremely difficult. We can ask, then, how have different feminisms engaged with and understood different nationalist projects? 'Othered' women are endangered by their national/ethnic/racialized identity membership, though always in gendered forms. Dominant group women may share interests in maintaining privilege with men of their group, which may lead them to support forms of political action which deny other women's rights or even cost them their lives. But feminist analyses find it difficult to address the powerful appeal of nationalism, communalism and other identity politics to some – many? – women; and also to respond to Parker, Russo, Sommer and Yaeger's provocative question whether 'the notion of a Feminist Nation is a contradiction in terms' (1992, p. 8).

Woman/Nation/Inter-nation

[I]t is not the resolution of identity that is necessary for political action, but oppositional mobilisation and coalitional, transnational feminist practices. (Grewal and Kaplan 1994, p. 251)

Despite differences over time and place, women generally do experience the sexualization of their bodies and their treatment as sexed beings. They also frequently experience construction as bearers of identity and difference as, for example, community members, boundary-markers and transmitters of culture, in ways that undermine their individual rights claims as citizens and that may endanger them as women (or as men's property?). And while not all women experience violence at the hands of their own or other group men, many women, everywhere, do (Hanmer, Radford and Stanko, 1989). Many experience violence across national, racialized and other identity boundaries, especially in times of conflict or mobilization around these boundaries.

Nationalism is one of the most powerful forces in the contemporary world and currently judged as in resurgence. It simultaneously constructs us and them, the insider and the other, the citizen and the foreigner, migrant, exile (Lerner, 1991). Nationalist discourses use women to mark the boundaries and especially where those boundaries are contested or fought over, they are urged to reproduce, socialize, love and labour for its good. But the identity politics which locate them inside or outside the boundary of belonging also disguise shared experiences. They pressure women to place loyalty to their particular group above connections with other women. It is especially difficult for women to reach out across warring lines (Mladjenovic and Litricin, 1993). In times of crisis or seige, making women's or feminist demands are frequently met with accusations of disloyalty or worse.

At the same time, identity politics mean that difference – as usual – signals unequal power relations. Differences are not only ideological or symbolic, but are part of the construction of relations of domination and subordination, of inclusion and exclusion, with severe and at times deadly material effects. Nationality, 'race' and culture all construct women as members (albeit usually as second-class members) of political collectivities that are located in unequal relations to each other and to the State and which systematically penalize or privilege those marked as different.

Political identities, boundaries and relations between them are not fixed, uncontested or unproblematic. Much ideological work goes into the reproduction and naturalizing of differences; and people's own multiple identities can rarely be reduced to a simple belonging or exclusion on the grounds focused on in this chapter. But at the same time, nation, race and culture are markers of difference that structure power relations between women, too. Dominant group feminists' meetings with non-dominant group women resonate with the making of difference. Attending to colonial and nationalist (hi)stories challenges dominant group women to attend to their/our own nationalized identities and take responsibility for the ways in which those identities are spoken and privileged in contemporary politics (Mohanty, Russo and Torres, 1991; Pettman, 1992; Sharoni, 1993; Frankenburg, 1993).

Differences don't mean that feminist alliances and friendships are not possible across the identity divides – but they do mean that such connections cannot be presumed and must be worked for. A politics of location (Rich, 1986; Grewal and Kaplan, 1994) historically and in terms of contemporary social relations is one way to expose the power relations between different women, including feminists, as a way towards changing those relations.

Another way is building links and alliances across national and other boundaries for feminist political goals, while respecting specificity and difference. Working towards more international feminisms is never easy, but it has gained momentum since the 1985 End of Women's Decade non-governmental forum at Nairobi and especially since 1991 through the preparatory politics towards the Vienna conference, which saw women's rights as human rights emerge strongly on to the international agenda for the first time. The 1993 Universal Declaration against Violence against Women and current moves to have war rape treated as a war crime reveal the strength of women's politicing across the borders and encourage the growth of transnational feminist analyses and practices (Grewal and Kaplan, 1994).

Notes

1 This chapter draws on my writing for my forthcoming book *Worlding Women: a feminist international politics*. An earlier version was given at the International Studies Association conference, Washington, March 1994.
2 Within the State there may be a gendering of its different functions or aspects, such that the Welfare State is characterized by some as a 'nanny state', which both feminizes and weakens the nation through undermining independence and rewarding dependence; or alternately as a shift from private patriarchy to public patriarchy, subverting the male role as bread-winner and protector by generating a large number of women and children who are State dependants.
3 See the Pope's appeal to raped women in ex-Yugoslavia to spurn abortion and to birth and love their 'enemy babies'. In this and much local nationalist language, national identity appears literally 'in the blood' and following the biological father's heritage.
4 Here my own focus on boundaries/bodies/sex/danger may unwittingly rein-force representations of women as victims, though in these sites many women are dreadfully victimized. There is now much written and a lot more known among women about women warriors, women as activists, for war causes and for peace (Sylvester, 1989; West and Blumberg, 1990; Cock, 1992; Radcliffe and Westwood, 1993). The substantial literatures on women in State militaries and women in national liberation and other struggles confront many feminists with other kinds of challenges, especially where those women may act violently or condone or encourage such action against others, or where women's fighting (or men's) is seen as exciting or liberating by them.
5 Hence the very different responses to abortion and pro-choice campaigns, as for example the European Network for Women's Right to Abortion and Contraception (ENWRAC) negotiates across differences between old East and West in transition and transnational feminist alliances mobilized for the Cairo population conference (Sen and Germain, 1994).

References

AMNESTY INTERNATIONAL (1991a) *Rape and Sexual Abuse: Torture and Ill-treatment of Women in Detention*, London.
AMNESTY INTERNATIONAL (1991b) *Women in the Front Line: Human Rights Violations Against Women*, London.
BALEN, IVANA (1993) 'Using women for war propaganda: Responding to war-time rapes', reprinted in *Women's Studies International Forum*, 16 (5), x–xiii.
BANNERJI, HIMANI (1987) 'Introducing racism: Notes towards an anti-racist feminism', *Resources for Feminist Research*, 16, 10–12.

BARON, BETH (1993) 'The Construction of National Honour in Egypt', *Gender and History*, 5 (2), 244–55.

BAUSTAD, SUZANNE (1994) 'Sex and empire building: Prostitution in the making and resisting of global orders', paper for the Citizenship, Identity, Community: Feminists (Re)Present the Political conference, York University, Ontario.

BERNARD, CHERYL (1994) 'Rape as terror: The Case of Bosnia', *Terrorism and Political Violence*, 6 (1), 29–43.

BLOUM, RACHAEL (1993) 'Engendering Muslim identities: De-territorialization and the ethnicization process in France', Gender Relations Project Seminar Paper, Canberra, ANU.

BOCK, GISELA (1992) 'Equality and difference in national socialist racism', in BOCK, G. and JAMES, S. (Eds) *Beyond Equality and Difference*, London, Routledge, 98–109.

BROWN, WENDY (1987) 'Where is the sex in political theory?' *Women and Politics*, 7 (1), 3–23.

CALLAWAY, HELEN (1987) 'Survival and support: Women's forms of political action', in RIDD, H. and CALLAWAY, H. (Eds) *Women and Political Conflict*, University Press, New York.

CHOW, REY (1990) *Women and Chinese Modernity: the Politics of Reading Between East and West*, University of Minnesota Press, Minneapolis.

COCK, JACKLYN (1992) *Women and War in South Africa*, London, Open Letters.

DE GROOT, JOANNA (1993) 'The dialectics of gender: Women, men and political discourses in Iran', *Gender and History*, 5 (2), 256–68.

DE LEPERVANCHE, MARIE (1989) 'Breeders for Australia: A national identity for women?', *Australian Journal of Social Issues*, 24 (3), 163–81.

ENLOE, CYNTHIA (1990) *Bananas, Beaches and Bases: Making Feminist Sense of International Politics*, London, Pandora Press.

ELSHTAIN, JEAN BETHKE (1987) *Women and War*, New York, Basic Books.

ELSHTAIN, JEAN BETHKE (1992) in PETERSON, S. (Ed.) *Gendered States: Feminist (Re)Visions of International Relations*, Boulder, Lynne Reinner.

Feminist Review (1988) Special Issue on 'Family Secrets', 28.

Feminist Review (1993) Special issue on Nationalisms and National Identities, 44.

FRANKENBERG, RUTH (1993) *White Women, Race Matters*, Mineapolis, University of Minnesota Press.

Gender and History (1993) Special issue on Gender, Nationalisms and National Identities, 5 (2).

GIBSON, SUZANNE (1993) 'On sex, horror and human rights', *Women: a cultural review*, 4 (3), 250–61.

GREWAL, INDERPAL and KAPLAN, CAREN (1994) *Scattered Hegemonies*, Minneapolis, University of Minnesota Press.

HALL, CATHERINE (1993) 'Gender, nationalisms and national identities', *Feminist Review*, 44, 97–103.

HANMER, JALNA, RADFORD, JILL and STANKO, ELIZABETH, A. (Eds) (1989) *Women, Policing and Male Violence: International Perspectives*, London, Routledge.

HARRIS, RUTH (1993) 'The "child of the barbarian": Rape, race and nationalism in France during the First World War', *Past and Present*, 141, 170–206.

JAYAWARDENA, KUMARI (1986) *Feminism and Nationalism in the Third World* London, Zed Books.

KANDIYOTI, DENIZ (1991a) 'Identity and its discontents: Women and the nation', *Millennium*, 20 (3), 429–43.

KANDIYOTI, DENIZ (Ed.) (1991b) *Women, Islam and the State*, London, Macmillan.

KLIGMAN, GAIL (1992) 'The politics of reproduction: Ceausescu's Romania', *East European Politics and Societies*, 6 (3), 364–419.

LAKE, MARILYN (1992) 'Mission impossible: How men gave birth to the Australian nation', *Gender and History*, 4 (3), 305–22.

LERNER, ADAM (1991) 'Transcendence of the ImagiNATION', International Studies Association conference paper.

LUI, TESSIE (1991) 'Race and gender in the politics of group formation', *Frontiers*, 12 (2), 155–65.

McCLINTOCK, ANNE (1993) 'Family feuds: Gender, nationalism and the family', *Feminist Review*, 44, 61–80.

McINTYRE, MARTHA (1993) 'Virtuous women and violent men: Salvadorian women and the sexual politics of machismo', Canberra, Humanities Research Centre, Australian National University.

MANI, LATA (1990) 'Multiple mediations: Feminist scholarship in the age of multination reception', *Feminist Review*, 35, 24–41.

MENON, RITU and BHASIN, KAMLA (1993) 'Abducted women, the State and questions of honour', Gender Relations Project Paper, 1, Canberra, ANU.

MEZNARIC, SILVA (1994) 'Gender as an ethno-marker: Rape, war and identity politics in the former Yugoslavia', in MOGHADAM, VALENTINE (Ed.) *Identity Politics and Women: Cultural Reassertions and Feminism in International Perspective*, Oxford, Westview Press.

MLADJENOVIC, LEPA and LITRICIN, VERA (1993) 'Belgrade feminists 1992: Separation, guilt and identity crisis', *Feminist Review*, 45, 112–19.

MOGHADAM, VALENTINE (Ed.) (1994) *Gender and National Identity*, London, Zed Books.

MOHANTY, CHANDRA and MOHANTY, SATYA (1990) 'Contradictions of colonialism', *Women's Review of Books*, 7 (6), 19–21.

MOHANTY, CHANDRA, TALPADE, RUSSO, ANN and TORRES, LOURDES (Eds) (1991) *Third World Women and the Politics of Feminism*, Bloomington, Indiana University Press.

NATARAJAN, NALINI (1994) 'Woman, Nation and *Midnight's Children*', in GREWAL, INDERPAL and KAPLAN, CAREN, *Scattered Hegemonies*, Minneapolis, University of Minnesota Press.

NORDSTROM, CAROLYN (1993) 'Rape: Politics and theory in war and peace', Canberra, ANU Peace Research Centre Paper.

PARKER, ANDREW, RUSSO, MARY, SOMMER, DORIS and YAEGER, PATRICIA (1992) *Nationalisms and Sexualities*, New York, Routledge.

PETERSON, V. SPIKE (1994) 'Gendered nationalism', *Peace Review*, 6 (1), 77–83.

PETTMAN, JAN (1992) *Living in the margins: Racism, Sexism and Feminism in Australia*, Sydney, Allen & Unwin.

PETTMAN, JAN JINDY (1993) 'Gendering international relations', *Australian Journal of International Affairs*, 47 (1), 47–62.

PETTMAN, JAN JINDY (forthcoming) *Worlding Women: A Feminist Interntional Politics*, Sydney, Allen & Unwin.

POOLE, ROSS (1985) 'Structures of identity', *Intervention*, 19, 71–9.

RADCLIFFE, SARAH and WESTWOOD, SALLIE (Eds) (1993) *'Viva': Women and Popular Protest in Latin America*, London, Routledge.

RAM, KALPANA (1993) 'Too "traditional" once again: Some poststructuralists on the aspirations of the immigrant/Third World female subject', *Australian Feminist Studies*, 17, 5–28.

RICH, ADRIENNE (1986) 'Notes towards a politics of location', in RICH, ADRIENNE, *On Lies, Secrets and Silence*, London, Virago.

ROBERTS, BARBARA (1984) 'The death of machothink: Feminist research and the transformation of peace studies', *Women's Studies International Forum*, 7 (4), 195–200.

ROBSON, ANGELA (1993) 'Rape: Weapon of war', *New Internationalist and Amnesty*, June, 13–14.

RUNYAN, ANN S. (1990) 'Gender relations and the politics of protection', *Peace Review*, Fall, 28–31.

SANGARI, KUMKUM and VAID, SUDESH (Eds) (1990) *Recasting Women in India: Essays in Colonial History*, New Brunswick, N.J., Rutgers University Press.

SAHGAL, GITA and YUVAL-DAVIS, NIRA (Eds) (1992) *Refusing Holy Orders: Women and Fundamentalism*, London, Virago.

SEIDEL, HELEN (1993) 'The comfort women challenge realism', Honours' thesis, Political Science, Canberra, ANU.

SEN, GITA and GERMAIN, ADRIENNE (Eds) (1994) *Population Policies Reconsidered: Health, Empowerment and Rights*, Boston, Harvard University Press.

SHARONI, SIMONA (1993) 'Middle East struggles through feminist lenses', *Alternatives*, 18 (1), 5–28.

SPIVAK, GAYATRI (1989) 'In a word: Interview', *Differences* 1 (2), 124–56.

Stoler, Ann (1991) 'Carnal knowledge and imperial power: Gender, race and morality in colonial Asia', in DI LEONARDO, M. (Ed.) *Gender at the Crossroads of Knowledge*, Berkeley, University of California Press, pp. 51–101.

SYLVESTER, CHRISTINE (1989) 'Patriarchy, peace and women warriors', in FORCEY, LINDA (Ed.) *Peace, Meanings, Politics, Strategies*, New York, Praeger/Greenwood.

TAYLOR, DIANA (1993) 'Spectacular bodies: Gender, terror, and Argentina's "dirty war"', in COOKE, M. and WOOLLACOTT, A. (Eds) *Gendering War Talk*, Princeton NJ, Princeton University Press.

UNITED NATIONS (1994) *Final Report* of the Commission of Experts Established Pursuant to the Security Council Resolution 780 (1992).

WEST, GUIDA and BLUMBERG, RHODA (Eds) (1990) *Women and Social Protest*, New York, Oxford University Press.

YUVAL-DAVIS, NIRA (1991) 'The Citizenship Debate: Women, the State and Ethnic Processes', *Feminist Review*, 39, 58–68.

YUVAL-DAVIS, NIRA and ANTHIAS, FLOYA (Eds) (1989) *Woman-Nation-State*, London, Macmillan.

Chapter 12

Gender, Colonialism and Nationali~~sm~~: Activists in Uttar Pradesh, India

Suruchi Thapar-Björkert

Introduction

This paper explores the relationship between gender, colonialism and nationalism in India. The central theme of the paper is to throw light on the ways in which gender relations intersected with and shaped the wider social and political relations in colonial India. The historical period from the early-twentieth century until India's independence in 1947 witnessed the development of social reform activities by men and women, the formation of national women's organizations, the proliferation of nationalist writings by men and women and, finally, the participation of the nation in the anticolonial struggle. This study focuses on the development of the nationalist movement in Uttar Pradesh, a regional state of North India. Uttar Pradesh was an important political site for the participation of women in large numbers and it is to women's activities in this State that I draw attention.

I will argue that middle-class women and the nationalist movement shared a symbiotic relationship, where both the women and the nationalist leaders required mutual support and benefited by their involvement in the movement. The nationalist leaders required the participation of women in the nationalist movement because the movement's importance and success was dependent on women's contribution to and involvement in it. For the middle-class women, the nationalist movement served as an important vehicle for encouraging them to engage in activities and to adopt new role models, not only in the public sphere but also in the domestic. In this chapter, I discuss the representations of women constructed by the nationalist project. While these representations were crucial for the progress of the movement, they also enabled women to play a political role through the avenues they opened, in both the public and private domains. These representations were also popularized by women in the vernacular literature. The representations of women have been studied separately for the domestic and the public domains.

This study draws on oral life accounts of middle-class women activists. All the activists had been involved, at some point, in the Nationalist Movement, from the Civil-Disobedience (1930s) to the Quit-India movements (1940s). I have explored the ideas generated in the Hindi literature by men and women during the first decades of the twentieth century. Newspapers and scribed literature have been additional sources of information.

Historical Background

Women's issues were at the centre of both colonial and nationalist discourses from the nineteenth century onwards. The primary concern of the early Indian nationalists and reformers was with the status of Indian women. Social reform activities in the nineteenth century were greatly stimulated by the attacks made by British officials, missionaries and reformers on what they took to be the 'degraded' position of women in Indian society. The British reformers considered the status of Indian women to be one measure of the progress the nation had made. Omvedt (1975, p. 46) states that:

> any serious cultural revolt required an attack on the subordination of women (and) that any serious nationalist struggle required concessions to and linkages with movements of cultural revolt, including that for women's emancipation.

Women's subordinate position in Indian society provided a justification for British rule and, as Liddle and Joshi have argued, British interest lay 'both in maintaining women's subordinate position and in liberalising it', thus contradicting itself in its approach towards women (Liddle and Joshi, 1985a, p. 524). While through the former the British argued for India's unfitness for self-rule, the latter proved British advanced thinking on relations between the sexes. In both these aspects British interests were being served. However, what is significant is that women, by their participation in the national movement, could dispel certain stereotypes created by the colonial rulers on women's subordinate and degenerate conditions:

> Their participation exposed British contradictions in their approach to and treatment of women. The effect was to demolish 'moral' justifications for foreign rule based on Indian men's oppression of women. (Liddle and Joshi, 1985b, p. 77)

Within the nationalist discourse, women's rights were also aligned with the movement in an ambiguous and contradictory way. It was argued by nationalist leaders that women's emancipation could be achieved by the political emancipation of India from colonial rule. A crucial feature of this political liberation was women's contribution and involvement in the national movement.

The process through which women's involvement was facilitated was by different representations of women constructed by nationalist leaders. Assigning women to certain role-models through these representations was essential for the strategic development of the movement. However, these representations, while soliciting nationalist contributions from women, opened both the public and domestic domains from where women could contribute to the nationalist movement. Not only were the public/private, material/spiritual, domestic/worldly boundaries diffused but the domestic arena also underwent steady politicization. As a consequence of this diffusion, the public sphere was not at all times seen as the centre of political activity. Women could also engage in nationalist activities within the domestic sphere, which enabled them to establish political links with the public domain. For example, while representations like, 'defender of civilization' enabled women to step out 'on the streets', the representations of 'nurturer' and 'good mother' facilitated women's alignment to the nationalist movement from within the household. For some women, the domestic sphere gave as much satisfaction and was as much a centre of active involvement as going out in the public sphere.

Women accommodated themselves to these representations and role-models and encouraged other women to do the same. The literature, both prose and poetry, is rich in examples of women's perceptions of these representations and both men and women were propagating these ideas through their writings. The life histories of women activists also reiterate the qualities inherent in these representations.

In the following section I discuss the representations made available to women in the domestic sphere and how women articulated their ideas about these representations both through their life accounts and the vernacular literature.

Representations in the Domestic Sphere

During the early phase of the Nationalist Movement, the need to construct a model of the 'new woman' for middle-class women was realized by the nationalist leaders. Partha Chatterjee's analysis discusses the dichotomy of the 'outer' (public) and the 'inner' (domestic) domains and the need for the nationalist project to maintain a consistent balance between the two. The construct of the 'new woman' was essential for the maintenance of the inner domain (Chatterjee, 1989, p. 238) which was the representative of the unchallenged identity and culture of the Indian nation. On the other hand, it was in the outer domain where the Indian nation had been challenged by the colonial power.

The nationalist leaders also realized that the 'new woman' was to adapt to the changing external situation and the contradictory pulls of modern ideas, while still retaining her spiritual role in the family (Chatterjee, 1989, p. 245). For the success of this 'new woman' construct, women had to be given not only formal education but also made more responsible towards their familial duties (Chatterjee, 1989, pp. 238–46). The formal education that middle-class women received inculcated 'feminine' virtues of cleanliness, discipline, restraint and domestic responsibility. Her dress and eating habits underwent changes too. What is important is that the 'new woman' construct was used by those women who wanted to acquire limited education, but still maintain the harmony of the household.

Meredith Borthwick (1984) in her study of middle-class women (Bhadramahila) in Bengal has raised similar points. She argues that changes were brought in the domestic lives of women in Bengal to construct a role model of the Bhadramahila which was similar to the Victorian woman model (Borthwick, 1984, p. 358). Similarly, Jayawardena (1986, p. 12) has also pointed out:

> how the new bourgeois man, himself a product of Western education . . . needed as his partner a 'new woman', educated in the relevant foreign language . . . attuned to Western ways – a woman who was 'presentable' in colonial society yet whose role was primarily in the home.

The issues around the role of the new woman, women's education and representations of these women as good mothers and nurturers are raised in the literature of the period. These issues are raised in debates around the conflicting ideas of modernity versus tradition to which both the women readers and writers were exposed in the changing political situation.

Representations in the Literature

In the twentieth century, women's literature in the Hindi belt burgeoned. Some of the popular magazines were *Stree Darpan*, *Grihalaksmi* and *Chand*, published from Allahabad. Issues of widow-remarriage, women's education and women's role in the nationalist movement were discussed in these tracts (Talwar, 1989, p. 210). The literature is rich in expressions of nationalist sentiments and a theme emphasized is the idea of a 'healthy nation' and women's duties towards defending it. Women's role in the nationalist movement was appreciated in this literature but constant worries expressed by women writers were the lack of feminine virtues associated with women's new role in the public arena, emerging ideas on Western modernity and the nature of women's education. In an article in *Usha*, the author describes the contribution of the woman to the nation through her roles as mother and wife:

> Because religious and domestic subjects are completely sidelined women have been led astray. They have forgotten their true national role of being an able mother and a successful housewife and moved towards unbridled freedom and conversation. (Sushma, 1943, pp. 94–5)

Sushma argues that women, through education, possess a consciousness of acquiring equal relations with men within the household and it is from the household that women could contribute to the political movement. By maintaining a conducive atmosphere in the domestic space, women were politically assisting the nation.

Women's roles in the 'inner domain' are reflected in another article in *Kamala* 'We women' by Meenadevi Bhuradia. She states, 'Any nation's progress or backwardness is dependent on its womankind' (Bhuradia, 1940, p. 57), which reiterates the point that women were the upholders of the nation's culture. Bhuradia also suggests some reforms in the domestic sphere in the article. First, women should not indulge in unnecessary expenses. Second, they should not wear expensive clothes and jewels and third, they should not be negligent towards their children. 'If we reform our children then the future will be a creation of our minds' (ibid., p. 57). The qualities that the 'new woman' was encouraged to inculcate, like good housekeeping, avoidance of unnecessary expenditure and care and attention towards children, are emphasized by the author and the title of the article 'We women' refers to all Indian women.

Similar developments were experienced in Irish homes. It was the mother who enforced the necessary moral discipline. It was 'she . . . who persuaded her children to emigrate, postpone marriage or not to marry at all. It was she who, through the changes she helped introduce in Irish lifestyles, became the impetus behind the creation of homes' (Inglis, 1987, p. 188).

Through writings in the literature, women were encouraged to develop a consciousness towards social and political issues which could be achieved from the confines of the domestic sphere. Women could draw links with the political situation from the domestic domain which was being steadily politicized. Through the role models of 'nurturers' and 'good' mothers, women could politically assist the nation as well as maintain the sanctity of Indian culture.

Closely associated with the construct of the 'new woman' were the constructs of 'femininity' and 'motherhood'. Both these constructs and the qualities they encouraged further enabled women to make nationalist contributions from within the confines of their homes.

The concept of 'femininity' in the new woman construct which emerged was based on mythology, literature and history. The mythical figures of *Sita* and *Savitri* were representatives of an ideal Indian womanhood. Both these mythical figures had qualities of steadfastness, courage and determination. The woman was projected as her husband's '*Ardhangini*' (complementary half) and '*Sahadharmini*' (helpmate). She possessed the virtues of benevolence and self-sacrifice, as well practical knowledge of raising a family. In relation to the Indian state, the construct was identified with the 'motherland' where women were seen as agents of national progress and esteem, in the same way as their mythical counterparts.

The literature also emphasized the qualities of an ideal womanhood. A poem titled 'Strength', in a monthly magazine, *Maharathi*, particularly ad-

dresses women. It refers to the notion of the sacrosanct image of the mother and wife, through the role models of *Sita* and *Savitri*, symbolizing deference to the god-like husband. The political role of women is indicated through images of Joan of Arc and Laksmi Bai. Laksmi Bai was a woman fighter from Uttar Pradesh who fought the British in the 1857 revolt.

> Hey mother!
> It was only you in the role of Lakshmi Bai who had moved the
>   grounds of the enemy,
> In the role of Sita and Savitri you taught how to worship the
>   husband,
> In the incarnation of Joan of Arc, for the welfare of the nation,
>   you burned your body. (Devi, 1927, p. 600)

An article in the same magazine, *Maharathi* refers to other ideas of the woman being the helpmate and the complementary half of the husband. The article called 'The position of women in different spheres' states that the:

> woman of the house should have the ability to work hard, keep her husband happy, look after his welfare. A woman is a man's real friend and for a man searching for heavenly bliss a well-matched wife is his greatest companion. (Devi, 1927, p. 602)

In the same article the author, Devi, addresses women in a poem:

> A wife is half the man (*ardhangini*), his truest friend,
> A living wife is a perpetual spring of virtue, pleasure and wealth,
> A faithful wife is his best aid in seeking heavenly bliss,
> A sweet speaking wife is companion (helpmate),
> In solitude she is a father in advice and a mother in all seasons of
>   distress. (Devi, 1927, p. 604)

Another poem called 'Swaraj for women' instructs women in their household duties and suggests it as the best support to the nationalist cause. This poem was written anonymously by a Hindu woman in purdah in Lucknow. It was recovered from proscribed literature (Hin.B.3121, 1922, Lucknow). In this poem domestic duties are emphasized as the woman's '*Stri dharm*' (woman's religion):

> Womankind, its time to look around,
> Try to be economical,
> Do not spend your time in laziness,
> Call Swaraj yourself in your homes,
> When you have spare time, spin the charkha,
> Make the cloth yourself in the home,

Grind the grain in the house,
Make the bread yourself on the fire,
It is because of your determination and willpower,
That your men have got the strength now.

(Anonymous, 1922)

Two themes can be located in this poem. First, the successful management of the house is important and essentially required of a good housewife. Second, qualities of determination, will-power and the woman being a source of strength to her husband are tied to the concepts of *Ardhangini* and *Sahadharmini*. All these aspects complemented the requirements of the construct of 'femininity' and were important to the nationalist movement as it gained momentum in the early decades of the twentieth century.

Most poems written during the nationalist period had the special feature of 'exhorting' other women. The poetry during the nationalist period is rife with the images of 'motherhood' 'nationhood' and 'femininity' and reflects women conforming to these images and representations. The images in the poetry and prose written both by men and women continuously reminded women of their duties towards the nation. Role-models of 'good companions' and 'helpmates' assigned women to specific activities. By adopting these role-models and the qualities associated with them, women were pillars of support to their menfolk who were fighting the colonial power in the public sphere.

Thus two simultaneous processes can be understood to be taking place in the domestic sphere. The representations of women which were being articulated through the literature and by the nationalist leaders, while facilitating the nationalist cause, also enabled women to be politically aligned to the movement from the domestic sphere. On the other hand, the new ideas around women's changing role and the idea of women acquiring education, even though limited, contributed towards the steady politicization of the domestic sphere.

The representation of 'motherhood' further enabled women to align their domestic roles to the nationalist cause. This representation is best understood in the light of the criticism it was subjected to by the British. Early motherhood, a result of child-marriages, was seen by the British as both a cause and result of the depraved nature of Indian men. Katherine Mayo's book *Mother India* (Mayo, 1927, p. 24) questioned the adequacy of Indian masculinity. To counter these attacks a sanctified image of the mother was projected to convey the idea of a strong civilization to the British. Motherhood was projected as a woman not only loving or caring for her children, but also producing healthy progeny. It entailed the idea of the mother as the 'race nourisher'. She had also to undertake the task of educating her progeny to be the future enlightened citizens of India. This representation is expressed in the literature of the twentieth century.

In a poem by Vaidnath Misra in *Stree Darpan*, motherhood and the associated qualities are described. Literally translated, the magazine means 'women's mirror'. The magazine was edited by Rameshwari Nehru and received articles both from men and women (Misra, 1922, p. 177).

> Only those mothers will be forever happy in the society,
> Who will fight illiteracy and show the light of knowledge,
> Who will remove unhappiness and jealousy,
> And lay the grounds for a peaceful existence with their holy arrow.

This poem outlines the responsibility of the mother towards the general populace and the next two quotes emphasize the implications of a 'healthy progeny', an idea related not only to the physical aspects of bringing up children but also to their mental development. In an article in *Chand*, it is stated by Mahadevi Verma that the:

> issue of motherhood is as important as other issues. This issue is related to the progress of the human race. When the mothers are ignorant of the correct way to bring up children, then how can the persons of that society reach the pinnacle of perfection, vanquish their opponents and gain victory? It is important to give training and lessons to girl children in motherhood. It would be of utmost advantage to their unborn children. There is a necessity for training in mothercraft because it is only through this that mothers will be able to provide us with ideal citizens. (Verma, 1937, pp. 160–1)

In an article in *Stree Darpan* called 'The dharma of women in the current political upheaval' (Devi, 1921, p. 46) it is emphasized that a crucial question is the extent to which women can take part in the 'Dharma-war'. Devi then goes on to say:

> That mother is not a good mother who does not give the correct advice to her son and who is not anxious to sacrifice her son for the nation. To remove cowardliness from his heart and instil it with brave thoughts is the duty of the mother. That woman cannot be considered as consort of the man if she does not, through her kind soul make her god-like husband do his duties according to his dharma and to make his weak heart into a strong one. A lot of brave women have asked their husbands to take part in the struggle and if the husbands have turned back from the 'battleground' then on certain occasions the doors of the house have been closed to them. It is our duty to fill our sons, husbands and brothers with all possible enthusiasm and to change their thinking towards the nationalist cause.

These examples from poetry and prose relate to the qualities of good motherhood and wifehood, traits that are highlighted in the life history of an activist,

Sushila Devi, discussed in the next section. The mother was not only responsible for healthy progeny but also for educating her children to be enlightened citizens of the nation. The same mother was required to instil patriotic feelings in her children. The significance of these activities is that women were responsible to the nation and served the nationalist cause by producing and training ideal citizens. These citizens were the future sons of the nation and would serve their nation in the anti-imperialist struggle.

The preceding section has analysed representations of women as articulated in the literature. In the next section, I discuss how representations of 'nurturer' and 'good mother' were articulated by women activists.

Women Activists Speak

Sushila Devi was married to the late Brahmdutt Misra in 1926 at the age of fourteen. She is a Hindu middle-class woman. Feelings about the importance and the responsibilities of the 'mother', both towards the nation as well towards the domestic sphere (towards the husband and children), were expressed strongly by her. What makes this study more striking is that, while the respondent emphasized the importance of the home and children, she did not hesitate to question the political integrity of her husband. Sushila Devi was confined to the 'domestic sphere' but expressed no displeasure about it. She utilized her educational qualifications as a teacher once her husband started his jail sentence. However, her services were terminated because of the revolutionary activities of her husband. She said, 'I never went to jail, I never led a procession. I was actually a housewife and would prefer to serve my husband.' By this statement she meant that being a good housewife would not only give her personal satisfaction but would be of political support to her husband, who was active in the public sphere.

When I asked her about the best thing her husband had said to her, she replied, 'Because of you my life has become successful. You are managing the house and my children.' Her activities were hiding revolutionary material for her husband and his friends. In Kanpur she says she often used to hide pistols under the mud and bring them out when it was required. As to other activities, such as taking part in processions, she said, 'Only if I had spare time from my household duties.'

Up to this point in the interview, it was implied that political activity did not interest Sushila Devi. Then she narrated the following incident, suggesting that political duties towards the nation can be fulfilled through the domestic sphere; having a sense of moral duty towards the nation, a belief in right and wrong, in itself constituted involvement in the nationalist movement.

Her husband was arrested in 1929 in the Lahore Conspiracy Case, along with other associates. However, he turned approver and gave evidence to seek pardon from the British government. When I interviewed another associate of Brahmdutt Misra (Shiv Verma) he said that the reason for the former's actions was 'moh' (lust) for his wife. However, I think it was more just to be close to his newly married wife. The wife told her mother-in-law that she did not want to see her husband again, implying that he was not worthy enough if he sought a pardon from the British government. This statement can also be interpreted as a form of moral power exercised by the woman in the household. The mother of Brahmdutt Misra went to the prison and said,' Your wife prefers to be called a widow and I without an issue. You have put a blot on my name.' Such was the impact that the approver tore the pages off the register and refused to say anything about his associates in front of the government prosecutor.

In Indian households the woman's power and influence over male members of the house increases with her age. The above story is an example of how good wifehood and good motherhood were constituted in the early nationalist period. For the respondent, Sushila Devi, the role models of a 'good mother' or 'good wife', together with the support she provided to her husband within the domestic sphere, were indirectly supporting the nationalist cause. Her husband was a participant in the public sphere and she supported his nationalist goals from within the domestic sphere.

The representations of the 'nurturer', 'good mother', 'helpmate', 'good wife' and the qualities associated with these were encouraged throughout the nationalist movement. However, some additional representations and qualities were emphasized by the nationalist leaders in conjunction with the changing momentum of the movement. These are discussed in the next section.

Representations Modified

Symbolic representations were fairly flexible and were modified to meet the requirements of a changing political atmosphere. Different representations were constructed as the Nationalist movement progressed during the 1930s. However, certain features were carried over to later in the twentieth century and the constructs of femininity and motherhood had to be modified accordingly (Thapar, 1993a, p. 87). The nationalist movement now emphasized qualities like strength of will, steadfastness of purpose and fortitude in the face of adversity. The woman was expected stoically to bear long separations from her husband and patiently bear the mental and physical trauma of his imprisonments and his disappearance for days on end. Yet when the need arose this same woman was exhorted to come out of the home and undertake leadership roles in the absence of her husband (Thapar, 1993a, p. 87). Women were given the choice of being both publicly visible, by taking leadership roles, and also of contributing to the nationalist cause from within their homes by bearing the mental traumas. On the latter point, most of the respondents I interviewed expressed the view that the period of the Nationalist Movement was a stressful time for their families and one of great transition and upheaval in their personal lives (Thapar, 1993b, pp. 14–16). Nationalist activities were not a matter of a particular individual getting involved in the movement, for the significant feature is that the whole household was equally affected and became the centre of political activity.

Some of these modified representations can be demonstrated through the personal narratives of women activists. Some of the respondents never felt the necessity to cross the boundaries of the domestic sphere to be political. Maintaining traditional virtues like purdah, yet giving support to the husband's activities, managing the household and the children during an economic crisis, giving moral support to a woman activist and looking after her children while she was away at her nationalist activities were ways of identifying with the movement (as suggested in the interviews).

Uma Dixit, an activist, expressed the usefulness of some of the representations in her life. She said she saw involvement in nationalist activities more as a way of supporting and encouraging the male members in jail, while facilitating, at the same time, the respondent's desire to stay close to her husband. The mental trauma of long separations from her husband, facing adversities, yet never complaining, facilitated the nationalist project and its demands.

Uma Dixit, a Hindu woman, is the daughter of a famous poet, the late Chail Bihari Cuntak. Chail Cuntak was a member of the Congress Committee. He married Kishori Devi (Uma's mother) at the age of fourteen, before the Civil Disobedience movement started. Disagreements with his father, because of his involvement with the Congress party, forced Chail Cuntak and his family to migrate from Itawah to Kanpur. In Kanpur, there was no family income and the financial condition of the household deteriorated. Chail 'would barely come out of the jail for a few months before going back again'. Kishori Devi, however, was too scared to object to her husband's activities because she feared that he would send her back to her in-laws in Itawah. She said, 'You could do something that will at least give food to the children.' Her children and their upbringing worried her more than the political situation. The respondent, Uma Dixit, said, 'My mother may have had very little money but still she never objected to our education.' Kishori Devi's desire to maintain a good domestic environment is reflected when she used to tell her daughter (the respondent), who was thirteen years old at the time of the Quit India Movement (1942), 'You don't have to come out in the movement so openly. You have a younger brother and sister to look after.'

The Nationalist Movement called for upheavals and readjustments in Kishori Devi's life. While strictly observing purdah, which she did out of choice and not wanting to discard it, she wanted to give as much support as she could to her husband. She once said to him, 'I will bear all hardships but will not leave you alone.' Kishori Devi used to hide her husband's books and pamphlets or keep proscribed literature in her women friends' houses. Sometimes the menfolk of these women objected and would ask their wives to return the books.

Uma Dixit narrates, 'Near about the Quit India Movement my twelve-year-old brother died. My father was in the prison. When he was informed he sent a message: "The whole of India is full of boys. So what happens if one does not exist anymore?"' Uma carries on, 'It was my mother's courage that she faced it bravely. She often used to cry silently but never in front of us.'

It was the anguish, the sadness of a wrecked domestic life, a husband always in jail, that affected Kishori Devi more than the colonial crisis. What is remarkable is her ability and courage to conceal this, and still be of moral support to her husband. On this issue the respondent remarked, 'Was not so much support itself a contribution to the Movement?' She tried to explain, through personal experiences, that it was possible to contribute to the nationalist movement without making activities public. For the respondent, activities like looking after the children of another activist's family, facing economic adversities and long separations while the husband (serving a political cause) was in prison, or offering support and assurance to those involved in public activities served the nationalist movement. At no point did the respondent see this as a form of women's oppression or subordination.

I have discussed representations of women in the domestic sphere and how they facilitated the alignment of women's activities within the domestic sphere with the nationalist movement. The alignment could be through the roles of mother, supportive wife, nurturer or by bearing the mental and physical trauma of separations from their menfolk. Representations were also essential to facilitate women's entry into the public sphere. In the next section I discuss the representations that enabled women to come out on the streets. Women's entry into the public sphere was also important for the success and progress of the nationalist movement.

Representations in the Public Sphere

Representations which encouraged women's entry into the public sphere were popularized through the vernacular literature written by both men and women. The writings in the vernacular reflected the authors' perceptions of the political situation. Women activists also associated with the representations in their own lives.

Qualities of self-sacrifice, benevolence and patience, discussed in the preceding sections, were essential for both the public and private domains. However, if women were to be encouraged to come out on the streets then representations which suggested the defence of the nation or motherland were required. While earlier images of the 'nurturer of the civilization' were maintained, new models of the mother as the 'defender of civilization' were popularized by the nationalist leaders. With specific reference to colonial Bengal, Dagmar Engels (1989) has pointed out certain changes to the image of women. She notes that, 'Bengal gender ideology which marked women as incarnations of the motherland, now had to adapt to women as being among the protagonists of the movement' (Engels, 1989, p. 433). I now demonstrate how the representations were articulated in Hindi literature.

Images in Literature

Women wrote poetry and prose, emphasizing nationalist sentiments and instilling patriotic feelings in both men and women. The poetry reflected the responsibilities women had to take up to 'save the nation'. The literature also reflected the importance of ideas, such as Indian womanhood and motherhood, to the nationalist ideology.

A poem called 'The agitated voice of brave women', written from jail by Satyavati Devi, expresses:

> Listen hey! youth of India we go forwards in the battlefield,
> If you are scared of dying then we will go forward,
> We will fight for our rights (independence) and our faith,
> Listen youth we do not now need the veil of shyness. (Devi, 1931)

Another poem by Satyavati brings up not only issues of 'Dharma' but the phrase, 'Put your head first for sacrifice', has implications of 'defending the nation':

> Your sister from the jail says
> You should not slacken in your work,
> Jump in the fire of independence,
> And fight for our Dharma with no hesitation,
> Die before the men in the battleground,
> Do not be scared of the bullet or the sword,
> Put your head first for sacrifice,
> Do not let the embers of the movement die out,
> Lose your head but do not lose faith. (Devi, 1931)

Ideas around the representation of women were seen to be formulating as early as the pre-mutiny period. Percival Spear, talking in terms of the burgeoning nationalist sentiments, notes: 'Mother India had become a necessity and so she was created. Freedom was an interesting idea but patriotism was a warm emotion' (Spear, 1965, p. 166). And again, Spear reiterates his point that, 'The government's use of Indian troops for imperial purposes, manipulation of tariffs, and handling of the press, were all thought to be attacks on the dignity of the new conception of Mother India.'

The 'mother' role-model, mentioned earlier, was now identified with the 'motherland' or 'Bharatmata' (Mother India). The duties and responsibilities of the mother were aligned with the duties of a woman towards her nation. Some of the activists used the word *Mata* which means mother, when referring to the 'soil' of India. The idea of the 'Bharatmata', while being important for the nationalist project, enabled women to contribute politically towards the movement, by their participation on the streets. The responsibility of women as mothers to their nation also prevented them from showing resentment and anger when their sons/fathers/brothers were hauled into jails. The image of a 'single' mother of the whole nation who was 'pure' and 'untouched', and whose honour had to be protected, also aroused the national sentiments and emotions of the population as a whole. The symbolic representation of the 'Bharatmata' effectively controlled the feelings of resentment and disappointment felt by women towards the nationalist leaders for encouraging their menfolk to fight the British. However, it enabled women to receive respect and appreciation as 'wives' and 'mothers'. In the Indian context, women continuously strived for this exalted status.

The idea of the 'Bharatmata' was propagated through poetry, literature and the media. A poem in the newspaper, *Dainik Jagron*, called 'The never-dying soldiers of the freedom movement', invokes imagery of 'tears' in the 'eyes of Bharatmata'. The last few lines suggest notions of 'honour' and 'pride' of the symbolic mother, which had to be protected.

> Not faltering on the rugged path,
> The freedom-fighters said with pride,
> 'Let us tie ourselves in one thread now'
> When the tears fell from the eyes of Bharat-mata,
> Then the hearts of her sons were touched,
> They became anxious to save her pride and womanhood.
>   (Dubey, 1972, p. 147)

The symbolic representation of the 'Bharatmata' gave a choice and opened up the possibility for women to come out on the streets. This also served the nationalist project, whose success was dependent on women's contribution and involvement in it.

While symbolic representations of 'mother India' encouraged and aroused the nationalist sentiments of the populace in general, it also brought up the issue of 'masculinity'. Protecting women, being assured of their safety while they picketed, being responsible 'guardians', all enabled men to bring into sharper focus their 'masculine' virtues. The British government, on the other hand, saw the 'safety' of women as a conscious strategy of the Congress members. They were specially critical of Gandhi for involving women in the movement and saw it as a 'direct attempt to complicate the situation by bringing in the possibility of a clash between women and police'.

> Every nation is jealous of its womankind and no Indian could regard complacently the rough handling of his mother, sister or wife by the representatives of law and order. (*The Indian Mail*, April 1930)

Women in various writings, in fact, played on this idea of 'masculinity' by referring to the 'loss of their pride', if the menfolk chose not to be involved in the nationalist movement.

However, guardianship (father, father-in-law, husband) did not always mean that women were allowed to come out on the streets. Some of the activists pointed out that their freedom to participate in the nationalist movement was curtailed when the 'guardian' shifted from father to husband after their marriage. Sridevi Tewari, a Hindu activist from Kanpur, was encouraged by her father to participate in 'dharnas' and burn foreign cloth (*holi*). As a twelve-year-old girl she was well informed on the political situation and attended meetings, spun *charkha* (the spinning wheel) and picketed. When married at the age of sixteen, she explained when interviewed how her husband, G. L. Tewari, an inter-college teacher, asked her to 'stay in the house with the kids'. He also showed no interest in Sridevi's previous political activities. What is interesting is that Sridevi, after marriage, could not complain to her father because she had to comply with the wishes of her new 'guardian': her husband. However, she kept in close touch with the movement by reading nationalist literature.

Women engaged in various public activities during the Civil Disobedience and Quit India movements. They broke the salt laws, picketed foreign cloth and liquor shops, led demonstrations and organized meetings. The representations of 'mother of the nation' and 'defender of the nation' both served the nationalist movement as well as enabling women to come out in the public sphere.

Conclusion

This chapter argues for an independent place for women, rather than an accommodation of them, within the prevailing frameworks of historical interpretation. Although women's activities in the Indian nationalist movement are discussed in various historical accounts, the interaction between gender and nationalism has not been previously sufficiently explored.

Using representations which were articulated and propagated in the vernacular literature, together with life histories of women activists emphasizing the adoption of these representations, I have focused on the relationship between women and the nationalist movement, a relationship based on mutual support. The nationalist movement was dependent on the participation of women in it and constructed women in specific role-models. The women used these role-models to contribute to the movement from both the domestic and public domains. Through alignment with the political movement from within the domestic sphere, women also helped in the steady politicization of it. For example, representations of 'nurturer', 'good mother', 'helpmate' and 'companion' enabled women to make political contributions to the nationalist cause from within the domestic domain. On the other hand, representations of 'mother of India' and 'defender of civilization' facilitated women's entry into the public sphere and the diffusion of the boundaries between the public and private domains helped women to associate with the nationalist cause.

Note

I am grateful to Joanna Liddle and Carol Walkowitz for their useful comments. My special thanks to Stefan Bjorkert and Rita Thapar. An earlier version of this paper was presented at the Women's Studies Network (UK) Association Conference, July 1994.

Proscribed Literature

Agra District Congress Committee: Agra Satyagraha Sangrama, PP.Hin.B.33, 1931, India Office Library, London.
Hin.B.3121:1922, Lucknow, India Office Library, London.
Devi, Satyavati (1931) 'Jail Sandesh', Delhi: PP Hin B146, published by Babu Rama Sharma.

Newspapers

The Leader, Allahabad.
Dainik Jagron, Kanpur.

References

BHURADIA, MEENADEVI (1940) 'We Women', *Kamala*, Benares, Uttar Pradesh, Babu Rao Vishnu Paradkar.
BORTHWICK, MEREDITH (1984) *The Changing Role of Women in Bengal 1849–1905*, Princeton, Princeton University Press.
CHATTERJEE, PARTHA (1989) 'The Nationalist resolution of the women's question', in SANGHARI, KUM KUM and VAID, SUDESH (Eds) (1989) *Recasting Women: Essays in Colonial History*, New Delhi, Kali for Women.
DEVI, CHANDRA (1927) 'Striyon ka Sansar Me Bhin Bhin Shatryon Me, Sthan', *Maharathi*, Delhi, Maharathi Karyalaya.
DEVI, TARAVATI (1921) 'Vartman Rashtriya Halchal Me Striyon ka dharma', *Stree Darpan*, Prayag, Kamala Nehru.
DUBEY, MANORMA (1972) *Dainik Jagron*, Special Independence Issue, Kanpur Uttar Prodesh.

ENGELS, DAGMAR (1989) 'The limits of gender ideology: Bengali women, the colonial state, and the private sphere', *Women's Studies International Forum*, 12(4).

INGLIS, TOM (1987) *Moral Monopoly: The Catholic Church in Modern Irish Society*, Dublin, Gill and Macmillan.

JAYAWARDENA, KUMARI (1986) *Feminism and Nationalism in the Third World*, London, Zed Press.

LIDDLE, J. and JOSHI, R. (1985a) 'Gender and colonialism: Women's organisation under the Raj', *Women's Studies International Forum*, 8 (5).

LIDDLE, J. and JOSHI, R. (1985b) 'Gender and Imperialism in British India', *Economic and Political Weekly*, XX (43).

MAYO, KATHERINE (1927) *Mother India*, London, Howard Baker.

MISRA, VAIDNATH (1922) 'Adarsh Mata', *Stree Darpan*, Allahabad, Journal Press.

OMVEDT, GAIL (1975) 'Caste, class, and women's liberation in India', *Bulletin of Concerned Asian Scholars*, 7 (1) January – March.

SANGHARI, KUM KUM and VAID, SUDESH (Eds) (1989) *Recasting Women: Essays in Colonial History*, New Delhi, Kali for Women.

SPEAR, PERCIVAL (1965) *A History of India*, Vol. 2, Harmondsworth, Penguin Books.

SHUSHMA, KUMARI (1943) 'Women's Education', *Usha*, Shakuntla Sethand Ayodhya Nathvir Jammu.

TALWAR, V. (1989) 'Women's journals in Hindi, 1910–20', in SANGARI, KUM KUM and VAID, SUDESH (Eds) *Recasting Women: Essays in Colonial history*, New Delhi, Kali for Women.

THAPAR, SURUCHI (1993a) 'Women as activists, women as symbols: A study of the Indian nationalist movement', in *Feminist Review*, 44, 81–96.

THAPAR, SURUCHI (1993b) 'The Nehru women: Conflicts and stresses during the Freedom Movement', in *Manushi: A Journal about Women and Society*, 77, 13–21.

VERMA, MAHADEVI (1937) 'Matarv Shiksha', *Chand*, Allahabad, Fine Printing College.

Further Reading

DEVI, SHAKUNTLA (1927) 'Shakti', *Maharathi*, Delhi: Maharathi Karyalaya.

Chapter 13

East German Women Five Years after the *Wende*

Hanna Behrend

East German Women's Special Bonus

Different from their sisters in the West, most of whose lives continued as before, East German women were profoundly affected by the tremendously fast political changes in 1989–1990, which completely altered their living conditions, their prospects and their ways of thinking. In certain respects, the transformation East German women were subjected to was shared by the women in Eastern Europe; in other respects, however, the East German experience was unique because of the 'Anschluß' character of German unification. East Germany was de-industrialized, the countryside was transformed when many agricultural co-operatives were dissolved or reorganized, private farms re-established, and the heirs of the former big landowners bought up State farms and forests. GDR foreign trade collapsed, its home trade was taken over by West German chains. Mass unemployment deprived women, in particular, of their previously guaranteed right to gainful employment. The East Germans' collective achievements, their individual records of qualifications and competence were devalued, their entire culture set at nought by the authorities and the dominant media.

Far from bewailing the passing away of the hierarchical, patriarchally constructed State socialism which deserved its downfall or, on the other hand, from turning to right-wing extremism, the overwhelming majority of East Germans profited from experience in two social systems which taught them critically to evaluate the changes in the light of gains and losses. Indeed, this new awareness must be considered their special bonus. It benefited women in particular, whose situation changed even more than the men's.

East German women's individual experience of the period from 1989 to the present varied considerably, as did their personal response. Statistics reveal that while no more than 10 per cent of the women and 14 per cent of the men in East Germany are downright dissatisfied with their lives, just over 80 per cent being either satisfied or more or less so, their satisfaction rests chiefly in their partnership, home and neighbourhood (Winkler, 1993a, pp. 20–9). Growing dissatisfaction is registered in the areas of gainful employment, social security, public safety, compatibility of gainful employment and having a family. They also resent being *second-class citizens* compared with the West Germans in rates of pay, career prospects and in many other ways.

Despite the fact that two-thirds of those out of work were women, East German women continued to insist (even five years after the *Wende* only between 1 and 4 per cent of them considered the status of a housewife desirable) on gainful employment even under conditions of dequalification, insecure and temporary jobs (Schröter, 1994, p. 4). Investigations in most of the East German Federal States show that for about 90 per cent of the women of working age, irrespective of whether they have children or not, of their social background and particular age group, gainful employment continues to mean more than just an independent income. Work, trade and professional skills and the family ranked equal in these women's catalogue of values and still have a high priority. Women stated that, next to the material advantages of gainful employment, granting them economic independence and a higher standard of living, there were and still are also social (for example, contacts, being needed, acknowledgement of one's own value), professional (for example, making full use of one's skills) and psychological (for example, acquiring self-confidence, overcoming isolation) issues which are important. In January 1990, 97 per cent of the men interviewed for a project were in favour of equal opportunities in gainful employment for both genders (Bertram, 1992, pp. 1–9). Most East German women still make every effort to find a job and keep it. For any foreseeable period, then, most East German women will clearly remain unwilling to return to the kitchen sink. Instead, they will forgo marriage and motherhood.

The importance of gainful employment to women has, in fact, risen in proportion to their decreasing chances of finding a job. An opinion poll revealed that, whereas in 1990 93 per cent of the women interviewed considered employment to be very important or important, in 1992 the relevant figure was 98 per cent (Institut für Soziologie und Sozialpolitik/Empirische Studien zur Sozialen Lage in der DDR. bzw in den neuen Bundesländern ISS/Leben) 1990; 1991 Ostdeutschland; 1992 nbl; in Winkler, 1993a, p. 85). Many, particularly academically trained women, would rather continue their meaningful work without remuneration and live on the dole or social security than give it up altogether. Only 19 per cent of the women (against 27 per cent of the men) approved of the changes in respect of the labour market, social services,

Table 13.1 East Germans who were less satisfied with social and employment issues than before the Wende.*

Public and personal safety	77
Social security	71
Wage/price relation	45

* Figures in percentages. *Source*: 'sfz/Leben 1992 nbl' in Winkler, 1993a, p. 24.

housing and prices. Those dissatisfied with the present situation in this respect ranged between 68 per cent and 81 per cent of the East German population, depending on gender, age and education (Winkler, 1993a, p. 24). Table 13.1 shows the issues with which East Germans were less satisfied than before the *Wende*, in percentages.

Although the majority of both men and women in East Germany still desire children, the number of women who want to have two children sank slightly (from 69 per cent in 1990 to 64 per cent in 1992) whereas, significantly, the number of men rose (63 per cent in 1990 as against 71 per cent in 1992) (Winkler, 1993a, p. 51). However, their long-term wishes and their immediate intentions do not tally. For instance, women in the twenty to twenty-five age bracket who were interviewed in the Leipzig district in 1991 gave their professional career priority over having a family. In this research a young woman intending to have a baby in the near future was an exception. The women realized that the new option was children or profession (Bertram, 1992, p. 8). Thus the number of children born in East Germany sank from 198,922 in 1989 to 107,021 in 1991; the number of marriages dropped from 130,989 to 50,683 during the same period and this trend is continuing (Winkler, 1993a, p. 47).

The spectacular rise in women undergoing sterilization operations, very much frowned on under the GDR regime, is due in part to women's unwillingness to pay for contraceptives, formerly free of charge. It is, however, also their response to some employers' demands to see evidence from a medical practitioner or hospital that this operation was performed on them as a prerequisite to being employed. Although this stipulation is incompatible with the law, it has not been stopped. Rostock's biggest women's hospital registers 300 sterilizations each year as against nil before 1989 (*Berliner Zeitung*, 7 February 1991).

This insistence of women on being entitled to a job must be seen as their most clearly articulated form of resistance against being deprived of their indigenous culture, of which gainful employment and having a family were values which ranked highest. Seventy-eight per cent of the East German women (as against 81 per cent of the men) were in favour of the political and social changes in May 1990 but this figure had dropped to 39 per cent by May 1993 (as against 51 per cent of the men) (Schröter, 1994, p. 27). The 39 per cent who still approve of the changes reflect the fact that women in work have a higher income than they had before (but not compared to what men earn), that they enjoy the availability of commodities and services, among them the travelling and leisure-time facilities outside their orbit before, and the altogether greater variety and choice of options. While many women rejoice in these new freedoms, they are also, often at the same time, fully aware of the deficits of the present system. The bulk of East German women are more critical of present conditions than their menfolk and less optimistic about their job prospects. The trust they set in political liberty in 1989 has waned considerably.[1] Many young women did not go to the polls in 1994. While most East German women's response to the new system is ambivalent this, however, does not mean that they are indifferent to what is happening around them or are generally retiring and inactive.

Yet about one-third of East German women cope badly with the new conditions. They consider themselves to be losers, feel discriminated against and helpless, are often depressed and withdraw from all public activities. They are to be found especially among the unemployed or in precarious jobs, undergoing retraining or employed under job-creation schemes. Their incomes average less than 1500 Deutschmark and they tend to come from a working-class or agricultural background, are below averagely qualified and live in small and middle-size towns or in the countryside. Academically trained and elderly women of over pensionable age, who were above the average represented in this group of 'losers' in 1991, have been found less often in this category since 1993.

At the other end of the scale, about 20 per cent of East German women in 1991 and 12 per cent in 1993 stated that they were leading a more active and enjoyable life than before the *Wende*. They are, on average, under 40 years of age, single or divorced, and in jobs which allow them a considerable degree of independence. Fifty-eight per cent of this group feel fully integrated and fully approve of the social changes that have taken place. More than half the women in this category are optimistic about their prospects (as against 28 per cent of all East German women). They tend to come from an intellectual and highly educated background, with their pre-*Wende* jobs relating to administrative, trade or planning work.

The Storm Clouds of Change

Although the experiences of different generations of women in the GDR varied considerably, as did their appreciation of the social benefits with which the State provided them, the vast majority felt the need for profound changes long before the exciting October days of 1989. Most people's growing resentment was directed at the poor supply of everyday commodities, at not being able to travel freely to the West and, last but not least, at the regimentation of people's lives by those 'above'. Most women did not consider their grievances to be gender-specific. However, even before the *Wende*, undercover, semi-legal and legal groups of independent feminists had met more or less regularly and critically assessed the deficits of woman's role under the system. Both the feminist-minded minority and the gender-indifferent masses of women enthusiastically welcomed what came to be called the *velvet revolution* in East Germany in October 1989, which swept away an ineffectual and repressive political system.

Social Benefits Conferred on Women under Patriarchal Structures

Previously, the social benefits available to East German women were much superior to those available to women in West Germany. Among the privileges which GDR women enjoyed – all of which have since been lost or severely curtailed – were one year's paid maternity leave for the first child and one-and-a-half year's leave for each subsequent child; free contraception and free abortion on demand during the first twelve weeks of pregnancy since 1972; adequate paid leave to attend to sick children; cheap and accessible childcare provision; one paid household day per month; reduced working hours and other privileges for single parents of young children; cheap housing for large families; job training and other training facilities during working hours.

In the 1950s and 1960s women were encouraged to take over jobs which, up until then, had been purely male domains. All the same, the inequality in respect of family duties and household chores burdening women in the GDR remained more or less unchanged. The social benefits were increasingly geared to underwriting women's domestic responsibilities. This produced a gender-specific segmentation of the labour market and reproduced a different pattern of socialization for girls and boys.

Even though the over 90 per cent of gainfully employed women made up just under 50 per cent of all the gainfully employed, their proportion in the different branches of employment differed greatly.[2] Most of the women in the GDR worked in typical women's jobs such as the retail trade and other services, where they made up nearly three-quarters of all employees (*IAB Kurzbericht*, 28 May 1991, Table 1). In healthcare and education, women's share was even higher with 83 per cent and 77 per cent being employed in each respectively (Gensior *et al.*, 1990, 11, p. 20). As a result, there was a clear gender differentiation in the various training courses at all levels of education.[3]

There was also a strong polarization of the genders in university courses in the GDR. Before the *Wende*, the relatively low proportion of women in the technical field was rarely a topic of public discussion, whereas their disproportionately high attendance at medical schools and teachers' training courses was considered a problem.[4] Even so, women were much better represented on these courses in GDR times than ever in the West or post-unification East Germany.

The gender-segmentation of the labour market in the GDR resulted from and reproduced the considerable difference in income between typical men's and typical women's jobs. In 1988 the net income of fully employed women was only 76 per cent of men's (Deutsches Institut für Wirtschaftsforschung (DIW) 1990, p. 263ff). Even in GDR days, women accepted, more often than men, work below their original qualifications and their chances of promotion were poorer than men's since, due to their family obligations, they were not as generally available. Gender inequality also varied according to the different professional or workplace hierarchies, although GDR women both in industry, agriculture and the services were very highly qualified.[5]

Women's Enthusiastic Response to the *Velvet Revolution*

The events in the autumn of 1989 made many hitherto gender-indifferent women join, if transitorily, the ranks of the new women's movement in East Germany founded by committed East German feminists. For a time, it looked as if the women of the GDR would shake off, once and for all, the paternalistic tutelage they had been subjected to under the State socialist system. Among the newly established civil rights organizations and reformed political parties, the Independent Women's Association (UFV) took pride of place in respect of a fast-growing membership and outstanding activism. After the implosion of the gerontocratic regime, thousands of women from all parts of the GDR and from all walks of life euphorically welcomed their new democratic liberties. They wanted to exploit these to the full, not just to travel extensively to those parts of the world that had been closed to them. They flocked to the meetings of the UFV, eager to bring about the much-needed political, economic and social reforms.

Women served on the different committees attached to the *Round Tables* at local, regional and national levels. They stood for parliament at the first free general elections in March 1990 and the subsequent local and regional elections. They were appointed as equal opportunity officers, UFV public relations officers and election organizers.[6] Backing-up the political spokeswomen of the UFV were the many women's groups which had snowballed into existence. They met regularly, organized women's clubs and cafés, established battered women's shelters, discussed feminist theory and formulated their demands. UFV women naturally never wished to forgo the social benefits they had taken for granted under the former system. The desired reforms were to do away with the patriarchal character of these social privileges which burdened chiefly the women with the task of raising children and looking after their homes. To achieve truly equal opportunities for both genders, GDR feminists wanted the unpaid labour of love to be shared by mothers *and* fathers. They wanted *all* privileges to be available to men and women alike, no matter whether they related to professional promotion, training and employment in prestigious and well-paid trades and professions which had, as a rule, been afforded to men, or the *privilege* of staying at home with full pay to look after the baby, generally allotted to women. Women also wanted improved and less-uniform childcare and health facilities, less rigidly regimented school and university education and social acknowledgement of other than heterosexual lifestyles.

Exchanging More Merciful for Merciless Masters

When the first democratically elected GDR government, which was also to be that country's last one, took office in March 1990, all these grand reform plans were gradually eclipsed by the ill-fated struggle to retain as many as possible of the former social privileges. After unification on 3 October 1990, the established West German political parties took over the reins of power with a handful of particularly adaptable East Germans allowed to deputize for them. The political influence of the civil rights movements – and therefore of the women's movements – waned. The media began to pay them less and less attention. Funds for projects were harder to get. Above all, the social and economic situation of East German women deteriorated with spectacular speed.

Even before unification, the GDR retail trade was completely ousted by West German chains which refused to list East German products and thereby started the avalanche by which more than half the jobs available in 1989 were destroyed. Redundancy, a phenomenon utterly alien to East Germany, swept over the country like a hurricane. Those able to stay in work were confronted with the harsh realities of gainful employment under capitalist conditions, with employers, at best, completely indifferent to women's domestic liabilities. Gradually, therefore, the previous solidarity among staff turned into distrusting competitiveness, particularly in academic and professional workplaces. Redundant women were shocked to find themselves discriminated against by the labour offices and enterprises because they were the mothers of small children, or considered too old to be given a job at fifty-plus.

Women were worse hit by this development than men for three main reasons. First, in contrast to GDR times, women no longer enjoyed full legal independence. For example, unmarried mothers were subjected to an official guardianship on behalf of their children. Another humiliating step backward for East German women was the eventual repeal of the 1972 law permitting free abortion and contraceptives on demand. Other retrogressive aspects of the family, labour and social legislation imposed on East Germany, more subtle but no less effective, were the loss of social benefits with regard to child birth and the care of children. Paid maternity leave (the baby year) gave way to much less generous provisions. Paid leave for the care of sick children was sharply reduced to no more than ten days for each parent or twenty days for single parents. The Federal German social constitution thus reduced the pronounced economic independence of GDR women to the 'marginal Federal German level' (Steffen, 1991, p. 41).

Another example of legal discrimination was the *de facto*, and in some instances also *de jure*, non-recognition of women's professional qualifications acquired in the GDR by the present authorities. These qualifications were also often disregarded by labour offices in offering the women re-employment and in retraining schemes, resulting in massive de-skilling. The system of joint annual tax statements for both spouses privileges the non-gainfully employed wife *vis-à-vis* the gainfully employed. The State thereby subsidizes unwaged married women at the expense of those who go out to work.

Under the 1992 Law on Pensions Adjustment (for East Germany) claims to maintenance and dependants' pensions discriminate against women who have been in gainful employment and single or divorced women as against the married or widowed (Steffen, 1991, p. 41). The claimants are also no longer granted acknowledged periods for bringing up children if they were fully employed at that time.[7] The additional bonus of five years towards their pension, which had been granted to women who could retire at the age of 60 (men at 65) in recognition of their work of family care in addition to gainful employment, was scrapped. The family-supporting principle was introduced, making an unemployed or needy person's partner, parents or children responsible for financial assistance prior to such person being able to claim social benefit.

A second way in which women were affected by the political changes was by the fact that their rate of unemployment was much higher than men's and they were more often and longer unemployed. Even though in GDR times women's independence was on a modest scale, it gave them freedom of action which today they sorely miss. Unemployment is the chief agency by which East German women are massively robbed of a continuous working career and driven into economic dependence on the husband or a State welfare institution.

Third, women are affected by a higher degree of discrimination than men. Single parents with young children, those 'too old' at forty–forty-five years, foreigners or people with health problems are labelled 'hard to place' by the labour exchanges. Firms that want to fill vacancies prefer men. Such discrimination devalues the applicant's qualifications and professional competence. So far only the Federal State of Brandenburg has offered enterprise tax reductions and other incentives to encourage employers to take on women.

Gender-specific training facilities depriviledging girls, which are offered to school-leavers, go back to the last decade of the GDR period. After the *Wende*, the trend towards offering training for the more attractive trades preferably to boys not only increased considerably but, also, most of those who were unable to find any vacant apprenticeship were girls (Jasper, 1992, p. 7). Young women are confronted with training opportunities inferior both to men in East Germany and to West German girls (see Bertram, 1993, p. 195). The training dilemma is threatening to become a gender dilemma.[8]

The Social Backlash in East German Women's Situation

With average incomes amounting to less than 50 per cent of those in West Germany, developments in pricing indicate that the nominal rise of wages (which in 1993–4 either slowed down or were frozen altogether), which brought the average net household income a rise of 33.2 per cent from 1990 to 1992, was inadequate in lower-income-bracket households to balance the rising cost of living (Winkler, 1993a, p. 134).[9] Average household spending has risen by 72.1 per cent.[10]

At the end of 1989 some 4.7 million women and 5 million men were gainfully employed in the GDR. Three years later, at the end of 1992, only 2.8 million women were in regular employment in the primary labour market (Engelbrech, 1993, p. 1995). The proportion of women among the gainfully employed dropped from 49 per cent at the end of 1989 to 43 per cent at the end of 1992 (Engelbrech, 1993). The officially quoted unemployment rate of 21.2 per cent among women in East Germany was nearly double that of men (12.6 per cent), while the actual unemployment rate among women, comprising women in further training or retraining, in work under job-creation schemes or in early retirement, stood at 35 per cent. More women than men were forced into early retirement. Unemployment figures in January 1994 soared to over 4 million, an increase of 340,000 compared with the December 1993 figures. The cuts in social benefits and in the job-creation schemes, which came into force in 1994, further decreased the chances for women to re-enter gainful employment. Already, from 1989 to 1990, the number of people living on social assistance rose from 5535 to 129,526, the number of adult women (excluding children, young adults and pensioners) rising from 2905 to 66,293.[11]

Under the present process of displacement and polarization in East Germany, men are displacing women, academics are displacing skilled workers, women without children are displacing those with children, the young are displacing the old and so on.[12] Women are worse off in the labour market than men. This is because they still or once again carry the chief burden of family care; typical women's jobs in the textile and clothing, leather and shoe-making industries have been lost to a considerable degree; former areas of employment for women, for example, banks, the postal service and insurance have been (re)conquered more and more by men. Moreover, the dismantling of the GDR social infrastructure, above all of the cheap childcare, has had negative effects. For nearly a third of all women, the lack of affordable childcare facilities has become a problem. Below school-age East German children, formerly almost 100 per cent cared for in kindergardens, are less likely to be sent there than in West Germany if their mothers are unemployed (Engelbrech, 11 June 1993).

As a rule, in the new scheme of things the West German legal system has prevailed over former GDR legislation, except where the new rulers found their intentions better served by the former laws, for example in respect of divorce rulings. Thus, in contravention of the West German law, East German women with children who were divorced before unification cannot claim maintenance for themselves. As most of these women are out of work, this spells a considerable loss of income. Their ex-husbands, more likely than they are to be in work, need only continue to pay the relatively small maintenance provisions for the children.

Almost an entire generation has been forced to take some form of early retirement. The proportion of gainfully employed women in the fifty-five-plus age bracket dropped to 5 per cent by the end of 1992, whereas in 1989 it was still 13 per cent. Eight per cent of unemployed women belonged to this age bracket, many of them living on the brink of poverty or facing poverty in old age.[13] GDR wages were generally low but subsidized rents, services, children's clothing and so on, called the second wage packet, also gave those in the lower-income brackets, among them large sections of women, the chance of an independent existence. Previously, labour shortages made jobs available to old age pensioners who wanted to carry on working in order to add to their meagre pensions. They often continued in full or part-time gainful employment. The *Wende* almost immediately put an end to pensioners' employment, as it also did to that of many disabled workers. Although some women got the benefit of a widow's pension, which they did not before, this was granted in full only to women with no other means of subsistance.

Many of the early retirees suffered from not being needed any more, from the abrupt termination of decades of communicative relations and from a loss in social status as much as from material insecurity (Winkler, 1993b, p. 26). The incomes of the fifty- to sixty-year-olds in part-time jobs, early retirement or in receipt of unemployment benefit or social security are already below that of old age pensioners and much lower than the earnings of the under-fifties who have a job (Engelbrech, 11 June 1993, p. 27). East German pensions stand at 70 per cent of the West German level, added to which a West German pensioner has, as a rule, additional sources of unearned income not available to East Germans.[14] The gap between men's and women's pensions continues to widen as men's wages differ more from women's than ever before (Helwig and Nickel, 1993, p. 107). Those who were eligible for pensions from their previous employment in the civil service, in local government, at universities and colleges, in health or school education, as lawyers, in the army, police or security services saw, after unification, their value cut to a level far below that of their Western colleagues because they were considered to have been too close to the GDR State. Some categories of pension were actually down to social security level. Many women are in the forefront of organizations fighting for equal treatment in respect of pensions, going to court or petitioning for fair treatment.

Women who were Particularly Hard Hit

Among the worst afflicted sections in respect of gainful employment were East German academic women. However, they were also the section least likely to give up the struggle for meaningful work and withdraw into the home. Of the 140,000 men and women in academic posts in the GDR period, only a little over 40,000 had remained in permanent employment by the end of 1992. The largest section of academically trained personnel in East Germany – almost 80 per cent – was in permanent middle-strata employment at the universities and colleges, with research teams in the institutes attached to the Academy of Sciences, other academies, independent institutions and, last but not least, to the major industrial and agricultural enterprises. The professorships (20 per cent in the GDR as against 30 per cent held by academics in West Germany) were largely a man's domain (5 per cent of professors were women (Geißler, 1991, p. 17)). In the GDR, however, 37 per cent of the middle strata in higher education and research were women in permanent appointments. The closure of many academic institutions, the almost total disappearance of industrial research teams and the rigid cuts in permanent middle-strata posts to adapt this area of employment to the miserly West German practice, contributed considerably to the imbalance of gender-specific redundancy. In the age bracket fifty-five to fifty-nine, 50 per cent of academic women, as against 27 per cent of men, lost their jobs (Felber, 1993, p. 59).

The restructuring of the education system below universities, to adapt it to the West German system, also meant considerable cuts in the number of teaching staff, 80 per cent of whom were women. GDR schools had been day schools providing, as a rule, a twelve-hour child-minding service and, in the rural areas, adequate boarding facilities for children too far away from school to travel to and fro. The West German school and higher educational system provided for a higher student/teacher ratio, except at grammar schools. The ruthless adaptation of the East to the West German system made thousands of school and university teachers redundant. Teachers were politically screened and many dismissed for their closeness to the State.[15]

Most big enterprises had provided childcare services which they gave up almost immediately after the *Wende* when State funding for the firms' social services ceased. Charges for childcare facilities run in the community were raised, so that many unemployed, particularly single parents (most of them women), could no longer afford them and kept their children at home. This, together with the sharp drop in the birthrate, led to fewer of these services being required. All the same, childcare facilities in East Germany are still far more plentiful than in the West. Parents, particularly mothers, join forces with the kindergarten teachers to keep their institutions alive. Though many kindergarten teachers had to give up their profession and retrain, those who were able to keep their jobs frequently availed themselves of the new post-graduate training facilities, improving the standard of childcare in their kindergarten.

Under conditions of co-operative farming in the GDR, more than 90 per cent of the 350,000 women in the countryside had undergone some professional training.[16] Subsequent to the changes in 1989, much co-operative farming was boycotted by the West German retail chains' refusal to list their produce and they became bankrupt. The co-operatives that survived were discriminated against by the authorities. Mass unemployment ensued on a scale exceeding even urban redundancy. In the Province of Brandenburg, for instance, 120,000 of the 180,000 agricultural jobs were lost. Former co-operative farmers' net household incomes dropped to 84.3 per cent within the first six months after the *Wende* (Winkler, 1993a, p. 133). Most of the social services were cut back when the large agricultural enterprises were either closed, divided up into smaller new style co-operatives or even smaller private family farms with much reduced production, or when the arable land was either laid to waste or used for non-agricultural purposes. The proportion of redundant women was even higher than female redundancy rates in the towns. Highly qualified women were unable to find even unskilled work because they lost their mobility through the closure of childcare facilities and the cutting-down of public transport. The men often got what suitable jobs were available. Many young people left the country for the West.

Women in rural communities also had fewer opportunities than urban women to become involved in self-help and other projects. It is, therefore, not surprising that the proportion of women without much hope for the future is higher in rural than in urban areas. Yet, even in the countryside, many women began new careers, establishing themselves in market-gardening businesses, embarking on ecological farming, or opening catering establishments. They organized self-help groups and funds for women's projects to make up for the deficiencies in public transport or shopping facilities.

East German Feminism in Retreat

Recent opinion polls confirm that 58 per cent of the East Germans approached felt excluded from political decision-making and 72.9 per cent wanted a new constitution (Ident-Projekt, PF345, 13003, Berlin). Only 10 per cent claimed common interests with the West Germans, whereas 85 per cent considered their interests to be incompatible (*Freitag*, 28 May 1994). This mood was mirrored in the recent election results which revealed a steep rise in the vote for the PDS, the reformed formerly ruling socialist party. Increasingly, people put their trust in this opposition party, which the government coalition, as well as the established opposition parties, berate and malign. This mood, while it also gives rise to a great many and diverse protest actions which are supported by women has not, as yet, produced any massive alignment of women in respect of their gender-specific grievances. On the contrary, both the feminist UFV and the reformed DFD, the GDR's officially acknowledged women's organization, have gradually dwindled to political insignificance. The latter have kept their clientèle of mostly elderly countrywomen. The former, also a mere shadow of its immediate post-*Wende* glory, has failed, despite some committed efforts, to merge with West German feminists in one united German feminist movement.

Five years of a united Germany have not united the women's movements or closed their ranks. Far from it. The deficits in mutual understanding between East and West German women are only rarely and with much effort overcome. However, quite a sizeable faction among East and West German feminists continues in its efforts towards closer mutual understanding and co-operation. Although some West German women's organizations and the odd trade union branch did support the women's strike called for 8 March 1994 by the UFV, the venerable, originally West German, Frauenrat (Women's

Council) did not. The event did get a certain amount of publicity in the media. But although attention was thereby drawn to some of the major problems confronting women, no lasting effects were achieved, largely because of the German women's movement's divisiveness. This, in turn, stems from their inability to rise above the level of those former GDR dissidents who fought ancient battles with long-deceased enemies, thus playing into the hands of those in favour of the *status quo* instead of rallying people to oppose the present injustices and tackle the currently vital issues. Thus they failed to approach women across party barriers in support of a joint minimum anti-backlash programme. Neither did they encourage women from feminist groups or projects, also on an anti-backlash ticket, to accept nomination by any party that puts independent candidates on their lists. So far, such a mini-mum programme has not even been drafted.

How Do East German Women Cope with the Backlash?

While the post-*Wende* women's groups gradually shifted the focus of their work away from politics, which to many of them appeared to be nothing but futile and time-consuming bickering, this did not mean that women lost inter-est in what was going on in the world. It merely meant that a great many lost their former trust in the government, the civil service and in political parties and organizations, among them also the UFV. Former members of the UFV or of women's groups concentrated increasingly on different sociocultural and other projects.

Although accurate figures are not available, a huge number of sociocul-tural projects, self-help groups, law and other consultancy agencies, battered women and girls' shelters and women's libraries and cafés were snowballed into existence in East Germany by redundant and often academic women. This indicates that women, particularly in urban areas, are not prepared to sit back in idleness and wait for someone to redeem them. From the immediate *Wende*-days, women's groups and social, cultural, political and commercial projects emerged. These were designed to cater for the new needs, but also for the new chances brought about by the political changes. Similarly, a vast range of academic, economic, political and social initiatives have been undertaken by women in the course of the past five years. This has been their chief response to exclusion from equal opportunities and other forms of discrimina-tion. It has involved commitment, staying power, toughness, proficiency and adaptability.

On the whole, despite the loss of status and professional prospects and the lowering of living standards of many academics, these women refused to allow their skills, talents and commitment to go to waste. The work they are doing, for little and often no remuneration at all, is an indispensable contribution to many fields of research, cultural and art work and it involves them in a wide range of issues and practices. The bulk of the projects they engage in are of a generally acknowledged academic, social, educational or political relevance and reveal a high level of competence. But only a fraction of the staff are in permanent employment or have the chance of their work ever being rewarded by a permanent post. Most of the research projects are not funded by universities or other academic institutions but are part of the growing area of autonomous research. The projects may be attached to or sponsored by an official academic institution, but the academics often spend months writing applications and submitting research programmes to get them financed by some funding scheme. Hazardous as the future of these projects was from the start, they have been increasingly jeopardized because the government rigidly cut job-creation schemes at the end of December 1993 and also envisaged new cuts in the social services.[17]

Next to the academic, the sociocultural projects have also provided indispensable services to the community. In the course of the past five years, women's centres have been established in all major and many medium and small towns of the former GDR. They are generally given some financial and other material support by the local or regional equal-opportunities officers, who have thankfully survived the *velvet revolution* period. This support is sometimes used to pay the rising rent for premises. This means that some women's groups can offer children's leisure-time programmes and after-school childcare services. Other centres organize breakfasts for unemployed women, with or without children, and legal and health advice. Some offer amateur theatrical and art work, self-defence courses, educational features and retraining. There are self-help groups for girls, for pregnant and disabled women, but also groups catering for various activities such as rock music or painting on silk, puppetry or dancing sessions for elderly women, women's travel agencies, film and video clubs and so on. There are lesbian and mixed groups. Occasionally, projects involve the co-operation of East and West German women.

Most of the sociocultural projects are really unpaid services to the community, ones for which the State was previously responsible. The authorities have shifted the burden of this more and more on to women, who put up with underpayment and lack of decent prospects because it is the only way in which they can find the self-fulfilment their work had always provided them. The bulk of this work is paid under job-creation schemes financed by the Labour Ministry: that is, paid for by the tax payer.[18] Thus, more and more socially useful work is done by women in underpaid, insecure, short-term jobs, or under freelancing conditions, or by women on the dole or social security and on a completely voluntary basis with little prospect of ever being paid at all. There are academic projects investigating redundancy, teaching and consultancy ventures, research into women's history, women's involvement in the arts, theological, philological, sociological and economic studies. An archive was also initiated collecting evidence of feminist studies and organizations under the GDR regime. These projects manage to finance important publications, thereby proliferating information which, without these women's commitment, would not be available.

In the heyday of feminist ascendancy in West Germany and under tremendous pressure from women's organizations there, anti-discrimination legislation was adopted by many of the Federal State legislative bodies. Increasingly, as women's power waned, these laws have been disregarded, evaded and circumvented. A case in point is the Berlin Senate's ignoring of the anti-discrimination legislation passed by that city's legislative body as recently as January 1991. In Paragraph 6 it stipulates that 'in fields in which women are underrepresented, all women applicants or at least an equal number of men and women must be invited for interviews, provided they possess the formal qualification for the post advertised' (*Freitag*, 5 October 1991). This provision is not only ignored by most commercial enterprises, it is also taken little notice of in the civil service and in academic institutions. Thus the number of women professors and assistant professors at Humboldt University in Berlin dropped from 148 to 92 between December 1990 and August 1991. The situation at other East German universities was even worse (Petruschka, 1992, pp. 40–3). The bulk of the posts were filled by West German men. The number of East German women appointed to full professorships was insignificant, even that of West German women is by no means representative. Of the few eligible women most were appointed to lower grade professorships. East German academic women fought tooth and nail, in many instances successfully, to retain their middle-strata jobs. As they could not keep their permanent jobs, they tried to get at least temporary contracts for which they involved the equal-opportunity officers in negotiations with the university authorities. They even went to court. Though, to my knowledge, not a single East German woman was appointed to a professorship in the West German States, many of the younger women are building up reputations for themselves by accepting invitations to work as guest professors, contributing to conferences or publishing work in West German academic periodicals. Many have accepted temporary tutorships and other academic appointments abroad.

Many of the encroachments on women's rights were perfectly legal. But the frequent practice of depriving professional women of their seniority by disregarding, for the purpose of working out their salaries, their period of professional practice prior to unification was actually an infringement of civil rights. Some women thereupon moved to West Germany where their status was acknowledged, while others pressurized the union leadership to act on their behalf. One of the most blatant examples in the general campaign to push women back is the abortion law issue. On 27 June 1992, the Federal German Parliament passed a bill which had taken a group of women deputies of the established parties months to formulate. It gave women less self-determination in respect of the termination of an unwanted pregnancy than the West German women's movement had demanded in respect of their 1972 reform campaign and failed to get in 1974. It was also less satisfactory on the issue than the GDR ruling of 1972. While it was an advance on the legal situation prevailing in West Germany, it was light years behind the GDR

Central Round Table ruling of 1990: 'Women are entitled to a self-determined pregnancy. The State protects the unborn life by offering social assistance.'

Even this modest reform roused the wrath of the unborn life protection lobby inside and outside the Roman Catholic Church and the Bavarian establishment. Two hundred and forty-nine deputies of the conservative parties and the Bavarian State government applied to the German Constitutional Court for a ruling on whether the Bill was in keeping with the Constitution. The ruling given in summer 1993 was contradictory. Abortion is *unlawful* but under certain indications *legal*. After the required consultations, women could terminate their pregnancy unlawfully but legally at their own expense and afterwards claim a refund from social security. The ruling immediately came into force in the whole of Germany, repealing the much more emancipated GDR law (Behrend, 1993, pp. 71–8). Women's organizations, incidentally with the support of quite a number of prominent physicians, raised funds to be made available to women in need.

After the general elections in October 1994, new efforts have been made by women of the SPD to draft a bill based on the Constitutional Court ruling, but making financial relief available to women in the lower-income bracket desirous to terminate a pregnancy. Though the Constitutional Court ruling roused very little public outcry, even by East German women, opinion polls show that 72 per cent of East German interviewees were in favour of retaining the GDR model; only 4.5 per cent of the women interviewed favoured the West German legislation. Only 2 per cent are anti-abortionists, among these, incidentally, the Conservative Minister for Women and the Family, Frau Nolte, appointed in November 1994. Interestingly, there was hardly any difference in the response of women in different age groups. Even more striking was the fact that the difference in the response of men and women was small.[19]

Inevitably, with rising political backlash and criminal delinquency, public and private violence also rises. As always, it is, above all, directed against the physically weaker and less protected sections of the population. Violence against women and children, against refugees and foreign (looking) or disabled people has become very frequent. Many women have joined courses in self-defence and while elderly women prefer not to go out in the evenings, the bulk of younger women are, generally speaking, not intimidated.

A number of women's groups have opened international centres where refugees and redundant immigrant workers might meet and discuss their problems. There they are given assistance to overcome the bureaucratic obstacles placed in their way when they apply for residency, for a work permit or social benefits. They are also helped to find reasonably cheap accommodation and informed of available training facilities. Women have also been at the forefront of organizations promoting the integration of refugees and immigrants, protecting them from right-wing or police violence, accompanying them to police stations or courts and negotiating for their release from detention or saving them from deportation. A few women's projects have achieved commercial status and were eventually able to pay their way without public funding. They provided training facilities but also offered research data, along with other services.

Whither are East German Women Moving?

The majority of East German women have managed to cope with these totally new and unexpected conditions. They neither surrendered to the inevitable nor resigned their claim to a meaningful and self-determined life. Many have in fact enjoyed the chance of coming to grips with what seemed, at first, insurmountable difficulties. What political role are East German women playing? Only a minority of them are still or again involved in political parties and organizations. Many more, yet still a minority, are active in trade unions, shop stewards' councils, tenants' associations, parents' committees, sports clubs, women's centres and arts and crafts clubs. The political role played by women in East Germany is, therefore, part of a dynamically changing, partly still submerged, process. Thus, for example, most women textile workers in Saxony and Thuringia, who became redundant soon after unification when their workplaces died a quiet, almost unnoticed death, offered no appreciable resistance at the time. Yet, individually, most of them tried to find meaningful work of some kind. Two years later, the part played by the women at the potassium mine in Bischofferode, in East German Thuringia, was an example of a totally different scenario and highlighted the escalation of resistance to deindustrialization. There was always a contingent of women among the forty hunger strikers at Bischofferode. Other women, miners' wives but also employees of the mining company and supporters from outside, organized a temporary sit-in strike in the mine.

In recent years, many East German women have undergone a profound process of discovery about themselves and the world. As voters they have become more discriminating which, on the one hand, let to abstentions from voting on the part of a considerable number of young women but also, on the other hand, to the East German electorate's total rejection, so far, of neofascist parties and a remarkable move towards the left. An average of 20 per cent of the East German electorate voted for the PDS, which party they considered to be independent of the West German establishment. Among those advancing to new awareness, were women who were once enthusiastic about West German Chancellor Herr Kohl and others who bewailed, nostalgically, the passing of the GDR. They began to find their own identity, formulated their own questions and stopped accepting other people's answers.

What is already evident, however, is that they are determined to defy the tremendous pressure to become tame housewives and mere commodity consumers, dependent on a male or the State. They still want economic independence. They do not want to return to GDR paternalistic tutelage, but they no longer join in the chorus of those who merely abuse the past indiscriminately. While they reject the brutal competitiveness of the present system, with its deficits in human warmth and solidarity, they do appreciate their new options. Whether they will eventually combine with others in Europe and the world, irrespective of race, class, gender and age and gradually initiate the urgently needed global changes, will remain to be seen.

Notes

1 In May 1990, 48 per cent of the women had confidence that political freedom would benefit them; in May 1993 only 18 per cent had the same hopes (Schröter, 1994, p. 27).
2 In 1981, some 41 per cent of all industrial workers in the GDR were women and so were a quarter of all employees in typical men's jobs, in the iron and steel industry for instance. But 60 per cent of unskilled or semi-skilled jobs were held by women, also in agriculture. Thirty-eight per cent of all people working in agriculture and forestry were women in the GDR (IAB Kurzbericht 28 May 1991, Table 1).
3 In the period between 1982 and 1987, some 60 per cent of female school-leavers took up training in 30 different trades (which represented 10 per cent of the total range of trades and vocations offered). They filled some 85 per cent of the vacancies in these thirty categories of jobs (e.g. shop-assistant, secretary, jobs in the catering trade). In the processing industry, girl apprentices were concentrated in jobs in the textile and clothing industries, which have bleak prospects today. In the more attractive technical jobs, the proportion of girls was higher than in West Germany but still considerably lower than that of boys. Between 1980 and 1989, the figure for girl electronics specialists dropped from 50 to 20 per cent; for machinists, controlling and measuring jobs from 23 to 12 per cent; for machine tool operators from 28 to 15 per cent; for telecommunications from 25 to 18 per cent and for mechanics from 45 to 31 per cent (Winkler, 1990, p. 44).
4 The overall percentage of woman students was 48 per cent; in natural sciences and mathematics it was 46 per cent; in economics 67 per cent and in the technical branches 25 per cent (Winkler, 1990, p. 46ff).
5 In 1989–90 a third of all executives in enterprises and in the administration, as well as of mayors of towns and villages were women; they also made up 50 per cent of all judges and medical practitioners. This was well above the West German average at that time. However, the women mainly held the lower executive jobs at their workplaces. Of a hundred managing directors only two were women and out of a hundred deputy managing directors, twelve were women (DIW-Diskussionspapiere 1990, p. 5).

In October 1989 some 6.7 per cent of the women working in industry had a university degree; 18.5 per cent had attended a training college; 1.2 per cent had a craftsperson's certificate; 58.5 per cent were skilled workers; 2.9 per cent were semi-skilled and 12.3 per cent were without any training. An investigation on non-academic qualifications and employment of women in the GDR, commissioned by the Federal Minister of Education and Science, also confirmed that a professional qualification was a typical component in the working lives of women (Winkler, 1990, p. 38).

6 Spokespeople from all political parties, civil rights, women's, youth organizations and trade unions formed *Round Tables* chaired by officials of the two main churches. Until the General Elections in March 1990, they were a very influential advisory body both critical of and co-operating with the provisional GDR government. Similar bodies were established on regional and local levels as well as on specific issues, for example, women's needs. The *Round Tables* at national government level ended with the general elections; the other *Round Tables* gradually faded away with unification.

7 Time spent for rearing children is only recognized as such for the pension if East German women can prove that they gave up work for that time.

8 In some 40 per cent of the training facilities in East Germany only male applicants are welcome, whereas in West Germany the figure is 25 per cent. For only 30 per cent of the training facilities in the East and for 63 per cent in the West are applicants of either gender invited. This trend is increasing. Women are reduced, more often than men, to undergoing training at institutions unconnected with workplaces which, therefore, do not guarantee employment afterwards. Even though 47 per cent of the women take part in training courses, they make up more than 50 per cent of those who fail to get placed and become unemployed.

   In 1992 there were 53 per cent and in 1993 already 56 per cent of women among unemployed school-leavers or graduates (Schober, 9 March 1994). Only 18 per cent of the girls and 31 per cent of the boys undergoing training at East German firms expect to find employment with their company after completion of training (see Information der Bundesanstalt für Arbeit 1993, 3218).

9 Winkler, 1993, p. 131 cites average gross incomes for workers and employees in industry including building trades for October 1991 as 4.239.-DM (West) and 2.086.-DM (East Germany). The East–West relation of net incomes is given as 62 per cent for East German workers and employees; 50 per cent for average gainfully employed; and 47 per cent for non-waged households per member of household.

10 Increased expenditure for clothes and shoes was 5.7 per cent (as the price especially for children's wear more than doubled, this meant that new shoes were bought less frequently); rent rises were 402.7 per cent of the 1990 figure followed by household fuel price rises of 245.4 per cent of the 1990 figure (Winkler, 1993, p. 130).

11 Pensioners, children and young adults are registered gender-unspecifically. In that first post-*Wende* year, the number of pensioners on social assistance rose from 2022 to 2497; young people and children from 131 to 51,867 (Winkler, 1993, p. 158).

12 Eighteen per cent of families with children in the GDR were single parent

families; of these only a fraction were male parent families. The bulk of these single parent families are divorced or unmarried women (89 per cent); 78 per cent are under 44 years of age. Two-thirds have one, 25 per cent two and less than 10 per cent three or more children. Only 29 per cent of these single parent households have incomes of over 2000 DM as against 56 per cent of two-parent households. Their chances of staying in or re-entering gainful employment are very slim. It is therefore not surprising that these women, even if they have jobs, are the biggest faction of applicants for social benefits (Winkler, 1993, pp. 236–9).

13 This applies particularly to those who were ousted from gainful employment as early as 1990. Their early retirement pension or unemployment benefit is still based on the low GDR incomes.

14 The total income from interest on investments or banking accounts of West German pensioner households in 1987 amounted to 30,000 million Deutschmark (Winkler, 1993a, p. 255).

15 By October 1991, 25,000 teaching posts had been scrapped in four of the five new East German states.

16 By 1988 some 74 per cent had a skilled worker's and 7 per cent a master craftswoman's certificate; another 7 per cent had undergone college training and 3 per cent had a university degree (Panzig, 1992).

17 A 3 per cent reduction in unemployment benefits came into force in 1994, as did the freezing of public assistance for a whole year, notwithstanding the expected 8 per cent inflation rate which does not even include the expected rent rise. Further cuts are expected in the new 1995 budget for all official funds in support of social, educational, self-help and political projects. As private funding trusts and individual patrons are increasingly withdrawing from supporting the social sciences and arts in favour of the natural sciences, technology and engineering and as the financial means of the local authorities in East Germany are shrinking, the women involved in such projects are facing grim prospects.

18 Job-creation scheme rates in East Germany are 62 per cent of the West German rates.

19 Seventeen per cent of the women and 16 per cent of the men are for women deciding completely freely; 70 per cent of the women and 67 per cent of the men are in favour of the GDR model; 1 per cent of both the men and the women are against abortion under any circumstances ('sfz/Leben '92 nbl' in Winkler, 1993a, p. 55).

References

ARNDT, MARLIES, DETERS, MAGDALENE, HARTH, GABRIELE, JÄHNERT, GABRIELE, KOOTZ, JOHANNA, RIEGRAF, BIRGIT, RORSBACH, MANUELA and ZIMMERMAN, KARIN (Eds) (1993) *Ausgegrenzt und mittendrin: Frauen in der Wissenschaft*, Berlin, Ed. Sigma Bohn, Berlin.

BEHREND, HANNA (1993) '"Etwas ist faul im Staate Dänemark" (Hamlet 1/4). Der Paragraph 214 im neuesten Gewande' ["Something is rotten in the state of Denmark" (Hamlet 1/4), Paragraph 218 in new garb] in *ZiF Bulletin*, 7, Berlin, ZiF.

BERTRAM, BARBARA (1992) 'Frauen in den neuen Bundesländern: Wende wohin?' [Women in the new Federal states: Whither the Wende?] in *Einspruch, Leipziger Hefte*, no. 4, Leipzig, Leipziger Gesellschaft für Politik und Zeitgeschichte.

BERTRAM, BARBARA (1993) '"Nicht zurück an den Kochtopf" – Aus- und Weiterbildung in Ostdeutschland' ['No return to the kitchen sink – training and post-graduate training in East Germany'], in HELWIG, GISELA and NICKEL, HILDEGARD MARIA (Eds) *Frauen in Deutschland 1945–1992*, Berlin, Akademie Verlag.

BRAUN, ANNELIESE, JASPER, GERDA and SCHRÖTER, URSULA 'Rolling Back Gender Status of East German Women', in BEHREND, HANNA. *German Unification. The Destruction of an Economy*, London, Pluto.

DEUTSCHES INSTITUT FÜR WIRTSCHAFTSFORSCHUNG (DIW) (1990) *Erwerbsbeteiligung und Einkommen der Frauen in der DDR* [Proportion of women in gainful employment and incomes in the GDR], *DIW-Wochenbericht* No. 19/1990, Berlin, DIW.

DIW-DISKUSSIONSPAPIERE (1990) *Kindererziehung und Erwerbsarbeit – Marktwirtschaftliche Möglichkeiten einer erziehungsfreundlichen Erwerbsarbeit in Deutschland* [Childcare and gainful employment – ways of harmonizing childcare and gainful employment in the market economy of Germany], no. 7, Berlin, DIW.

ENGELBRECH, GERHARD (11/06/1993) 'Zwischen Wunsch und Wirklichkeit' [Between wishful thinking and reality] in IAB Werkstattbericht, Nuremberg, no. 8.

ENGELBRECH, GERHARD (1993) 'Beschäftigungssituation und Arbeitsmarktschancen von Frauen in Ostdeutschland und Möglichkeiten der Bekämpung von Arbeitslosigkeit' [Employment Situation and Job Opportunities for Women in East Germany and Possibilities of Fighting Unemployment] in Informationen für die Beratungs und Vermittlungsdienste der Bundesanstalt für Arbeit, ibv, Nuremberg, Bundesanstalt für Arbeit, issue 26/93.

FELBER, CHRISTINA (1993) 'Zur Situation von Wissenschaftlerinnen im Transformationsprozeß der Universitäten und Hochschulen in Ost-Berlin und im Land Brandenburg – Ein Vergleich mit dem männlichen Wissenschaftspersonal' [The situation of academic women in the transformation process at universities and colleges in East Berlin and in the Federal state of Brandenburg] in ARNDT, MARLIES, DETERS, MAGDALENE, HARTH, GABRIELE, JÄHNERT, GABRIELE, KOOTZ, JOHANNA, RIEGRAF, BIRGIT, RORSBACH, MANUELA and ZIMMERMAN, KARIN (Eds) *Ausgegrenzt und mittendrin: Frauen in der Wissenschaft*, Berlin, Ed. Sigma Bohn, Berlin.

GEIßLER, RAINER (1991) 'Soziale Ungerechtigkeit zwischen Männern und Frauen im geteilten Deutschland' [Social inequality between men and women in divided Germany] in *Aus Politik und Zeitgeschichte*, supplement to 'Das Parlament,' B 14–15/1991, Bonn.

GENSIOR, SABINE et al. (1990) 'Berufliche Weiterbildung für Frauen in den neuen Bundesländern' [Further training for women in East Germany], in *Bildung-Wissenschaft-Aktuell*, issue 11, Bundesminist für Bildung und Wissenschaft, Bonn.

HELWIG, GISELA and NICKEL, HILDEGARD MARIA (Eds) (1993) *Frauen in Deutschland 1945–1992*, [Women in Germany 1945–1992], Berlin, Akademie Verlag.

IAB KURZBERICHT (28/05/1991) 'Frauenbeschäftigung in der ehemaligen DDR in regionaler und wirtschaftlicher Gliederung. Ergebnisse aus der Beschäftigungserhebung 1989' [Employment of women in the former GDR, according to regional and economic structures].

INFORMATION DER BUNDESANSALT FÜR ARBEIT (1993) *Frauen: Ausbildung-Beschäftigung-Weiterbildung* [Women. Training-Employment-Further Training], Nuremberg, Bundesanstalt für Arbeit, no. 50/93.

INSTITUT FÜR SOZIOLOGIE UND SOZIALPOLITIK/EMPIRISCHE STUDIEN ZUR SOZIALEN LAGE IN DER DDR. BZW IN DEN NEUEN BUNDESLÄNDERN (ISS/Leben) (1990), in WINKLER, *Sozialreport 1992*, 85.

JASPER, GERDA (1992) *Veränderungen in der Erwerbstätigkeit von Frauen* [Changes in women's gainful employment], Berlin, unpubl.ms.

PANZIG, CHRISTEL (1992) 'Zur Arbeits- und Lebenssituation von Frauen in der Landwirtschaft unter besonderer Berücksichtigung des Landes Brandenburg' [On the living and working conditions of women in agriculture relating especially to the state of Brandenburg] in Dokumentation der DGB-Veranstaltung, 'Frauenarbeit und Frauenprojekte in Brandenburg,' 12 May 1992, Düsseldorf, DGB-Bundesvorstand Abt. Frauen, PF 101062.

PANZIG, CHRISTEL (1995) 'Changing the East German countryside', in BEHREND, HANNA (Ed.) *German Unification: The Destruction of an Economy*, London, Pluto.

PETRUSCHKA, GISELA (1992) 'Situation und Perspektiven der Frauen im Umstrukturierungsprozeß an der Humboldt-Universität zu Berlin' [Situation and prospects of women in the restructuring process at Humboldt University, Berlin] in *ZiF Bulletin*, 4, Frauen-Arbeitsmarkt-Wissenschaft, Berlin, ZiF.

SCHOBER, K. (09/03/1994), 'Duales System: Nur durch Arbeit trägt Ausbildung Früchte' [Dual System: Only work makes training profitable] in *IAB Kurzbericht*, Nuremberg, no. 5.

SCHRÖTER URSULA (February 1994) 'Ostdeutsche Frauen heute und gestern' [East German women today and yesterday], *Isda Studie* no. 15, Berlin.

STEFFEN, JOHANNES (1991) 'Familien auf dem Abstellgleis' [Families pushed aside], in *Sozialismus*, issue 5/1991, Hamburg.

Hanna Behrend

WINKLER, GUNNAR (Ed.) (1990) 'Frauenreport '90' [Report on women], Berlin, Die Wirtschaft.

WINKLER, GUNNAR (Ed.) (1993a) 'Sozialreport 1992: Daten und Fakten zur sozialen Lage in den neuen Bundesländern' [Social report. Data and facts on the social situation in the new Federal states], Berlin, Morgenbuch Verlag Volker Spiess.

WINKLER, GUNNAR (1993b) 'Die künftigen Alten' [The Future Elderly] in *Sozialreport* III/93, Neue Bundesländer, Sozialwissenschaftliches Forschungszentrum and Hans-Böckler-Stiftung.

Notes on Contributors

Magdalene Ang-Lygate obtained her M Litt in Women's Studies in 1993 and is currently completing her PhD in Sociology at the University of Strathclyde where she is a part-time tutor in Women's Studies and Computing. Before taking a career break to have her children, she worked as a computer programmer and systems analyst. Her research, which investigates women's experiences of diaspora and immigration, focuses on social, feminist and post-colonial theories of subjectivity. As a feminist activist, her personal interests also include drumming, surfing the internet and avoiding serious cooking. She is the co-editor (with Chris Corrin and Millsom Henry) of *Desperately Seeking Sisterhood: Still Challenging and Building*, Taylor & Francis, 1996.

Hanna Behrend taught English Literature and Women's Studies at Berlin's Humboldt University; published language textbooks and teaching aids to foreign students of English and on German and English history and literature and was a founding member of the East German Independent Women's Association (UVF). Recent publications: *German Unification. The Destruction of an Economy*, Pluto, 1995; editor of a series *Auf der Suche nach der verlorenen Zukunft* (*Searching for the Lost Future*), vol. 1, trafo-verlag dr. weist, 1995; 'Racist and anti-Semitic violence in Germany', *New Politics*, 5 (3), summer 1995.

Delia Davin is Reader in Chinese Social Studies at the Department of East Asian Studies at the University of Leeds. With W. J. F. Jenner she translated and edited *Chinese Lives: an Oral History of Contemporary China*, Penguin, 1989. She has written extensively on Chinese women and on population policy and labour migration in China.

Joanna de Groot lectures in History and Women's Studies at the University of York. Her interest in social and cultural history, in both a European and a Middle Eastern context, has led her to pursue the study of women and gender in relation to power relationships and social change generally. At present her particular concerns are the presence of women in political movements and processes and forms of cultural construction and representation of gender and ethnic identity, dominance and subordination. She has written articles on all these subjects and is co-editor (with Mary Maynard) of *Women's Studies in the 1990s. Doing Things Differently?* Macmillan, 1993.

Breda Gray left Ireland in 1984 to study in Canada and now lives in England. She is currently researching Irish national identity, gender and emigration for a PhD at Lancaster University.

Svetlana Kupryashkina has a doctorate degree in English from Kiev State University, translated feminist texts and attended a summer school 'Gender and Development' at the University of East Anglia in 1992. Fulbright Visiting Scholar at the Institute for Research on Women, Rutgers in 1994–5, Dr Kupryashkina has developed curricula for teaching Women's Studies courses in Ukraine.

Jitka Malečková is an Assistant Professor at the Institute of Middle Eastern and African Studies at the Charles University in Prague. In 1993–4, she was a research fellow at the Centre for the Study of Nationalism, Central European University in Prague and in 1994–5 a Jean Monnet Fellow at the European University Institute in Florence. She was co-author of *The Struggle for a Modern State in the Muslim World* (written in Czech), 1989, and has published articles on nineteenth century Ottoman-Turkish cultural and social history and on women's history.

Mary Maynard is Senior Lecturer in Sociology and Director of the Centre for Women's Studies at the University of York. Her publications include *Sexism, Racism and Oppression* (with Arthur Brittan), Blackwell, 1984; *Women, Violence and Social Control* (co-edited with Jalna Hanmer), Macmillan, 1987; *Sociological Theory*, Longman, 1989; *Women's Studies in the 1990s* (co-edited with Joanna de Groot), Macmillan, 1993; *Researching Women's Lives from a Feminist Perspective* (co-edited with June Purvis), Taylor & Francis, 1994; *The Dynamics of 'Race' and Gender* (co-edited with Haleh Afshar), Taylor & Francis, 1994; and *(Hetero)sexual Politics* (co-edited with June Purvis), Taylor & Francis, 1995. She is currently completing a book on feminists and social research practice and developing a research project on older widows.

Jan Jindy Pettman is Senior Lecturer in Feminist and International Politics at the Australian National University, Canberra, Australia. Her writings on gender, nationalism and political identities include *Living in the Margins: Sexism and Feminism in Australia*, Allen & Unwin, Sydney, 1992, and *Worlding Women: a Feminist International Politics*, Allen & Unwin, Sydney, 1996.

Jasbir Puar is a doctoral student in the Department of Ethnic Studies at the University of California at Berkeley. She works on South Asian critical theory, including transnational queer spaces, nationalisms and Bhangra music, as well as constructions of home and travel. Her publications include 'Writing my way "home": Travelling South Asian bodies and diasporic journeys', *Socialist Review*, 4, 1994, and 'Nicaraguan women, resistance and the politics of aid', in Haleh Afshar (Ed.) *From Margin to Centre: Women and Politics in the Third World*, Routledge, 1996.

June Purvis is Professor of Sociology at the University of Portsmouth and Founding Editor of *Women's History Review* and Editor of *Studies on Women Abstracts*. Recent publications include *Researching Women's Lives from a Feminist Perspective* (co-edited with Mary Manard), Taylor & Francis, 1994 and *(Hetero)sexual Politics* (co-edited with Mary Maynard), Taylor & Francis, 1995. She is currently researching the suffragette movement in Edwardian Britain and recent publications on this theme include ' "Deeds, not words": the daily lives of militant suffragettes in Edwardian Britain', *Women's Studies International Forum*, 18 (2) 1995 and 'A lost dimension? The political education of women in the suffragette movement in Edwardian Britain', *Gender and Education*, 6 (3) 1994.

Bunie M. Matlanyane Sexwale is an activist who also runs training workshops internationally on various aspects related to Women, Gender and Development and other social issues. Until recently (1995) she was the trainer at the Women and Development Training section of KIT, the Royal Tropical Institute, Amsterdam. She has been a research associate at the Institute of Social Studies, The Hague, where she also took part in teaching activities, mainly on the Women and Development MA programme.

Suruchi Thapar-Björkert is a research student at the Centre for the Study of Women and Gender, University of Warwick. She lectures part-time at the Centre and at the Department of Politics, University of Warwick. She has published earlier in *Manushi* and *Feminist Review*. She has also made entries to the *Concise Oxford Dictionary of Politics*, Oxford University Press.

Index